TALKS
TO
FARMERS

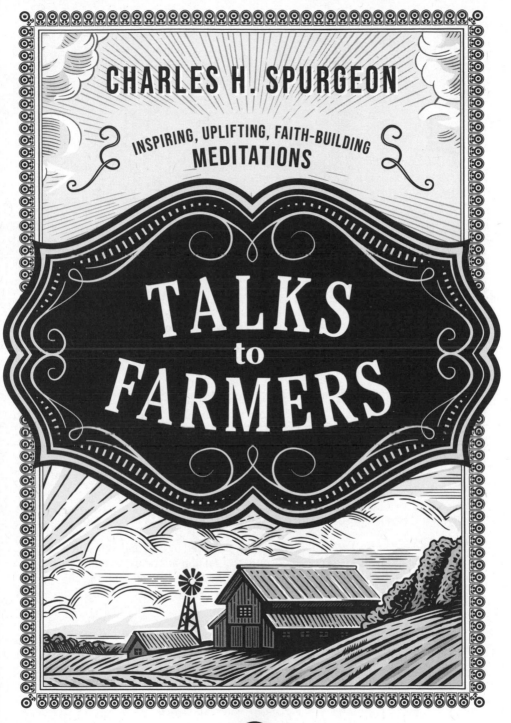

CHARLES H. SPURGEON

INSPIRING, UPLIFTING, FAITH-BUILDING
MEDITATIONS

TALKS to FARMERS

NELSON
BOOKS

An Imprint of Thomas Nelson

Talks to Farmers

© 2022 Nelson Books

All rights reserved. No portion of this book may be reproduced, stored in a retrieval system, or transmitted in any form or by any means—electronic, mechanical, photocopy, recording, scanning, or other—except for brief quotations in critical reviews or articles, without the prior written permission of the publisher.

Published in Nashville, Tennessee, by Nelson Books, an imprint of Thomas Nelson. Nelson Books and Thomas Nelson are registered trademarks of HarperCollins Christian Publishing, Inc.

Thomas Nelson titles may be purchased in bulk for educational, business, fundraising, or sales promotional use. For information, please email SpecialMarkets@ThomasNelson.com.

Scripture quotations are taken from the King James Version. Public domain.

Editor's note: *Talks to Farmers* was originally published in 1882 under the title *Farm Sermons* and is in the public domain. This edition has been modernized and edited for readability and clarity while also striving to maintain Spurgeon's original voice and intent.

ISBN 978-0-7852-9536-5 (softcover)
ISBN 978-0-7852-9537-2 (eBook)
ISBN 978-0-7852-9538-9 (audiobook

Library of Congress Cataloging-in-Publication Data on File

Printed in the United States of America

24 25 26 27 28 LBC 6 5 4 3 2

CONTENTS

FOREWORD

One of the hallmarks of Charles Spurgeon's preaching was his straightforward simplicity. He purposely spoke without pomposity or embellishment. He was so averse to flowery or high-flown language in his sermons that an 1870 article in *Vanity Fair* magazine characterized his pulpit vocabulary as "slang."[1]

That term, *slang*, has an unflattering connotation that doesn't do justice to the power and profundity of Spurgeon's preaching. He did purposely speak in ordinary, informal language. But he was never crude or tasteless. He wasn't attempting to sound streetwise or trendy. It was not an affectation. On the contrary Spurgeon despised the artificial, pretentious style of sermon delivery that was in vogue at the time in English pulpits. He told students in his pastors' college, "*Take care not to fall into the habitual and common affectations of the present day. Scarcely one man in a dozen in the pulpit talks like a man.*"[2]

Vanity Fair was not the only secular publication that remarked on this difference between Spurgeon and practically every other minister of the time. A cartoon published and widely circulated during Spurgeon's early years in London showed Spurgeon back-to-back against a vicar from the Church of England, both in their respective preaching postures. Spurgeon's profile cast a shadow on the wall in the shape of a young lion. The Anglican parson, bedecked in a billowing surplice, cast the shadow of an old woman.

Spurgeon firmly believed that the preaching of God's Word should always be robust, unembroidered, forthright, and natural. In his lecture to ministerial students "On the Voice," Spurgeon specifically lampooned two types of insincere intonation—one which he described as an unnaturally "dignified, doctorial, inflated, bombastic style," the other a delicate, dainty delivery. He referred to these styles of rhetoric as "sacred brogues, which I hope will soon be dead languages." His chief objection? He said, "I am persuaded that these tones and semitones and monotones are Babylonian, that they are not at all the Jerusalem dialect; for the Jerusalem dialect has this one distinguishing mark, that it is a man's own mode of speech, and is the same out of the pulpit as it is in it."[3]

In that same lecture he quoted from *The Clergy and the Pulpit in Their Relations to the People,* a book written in French by Isidore Mullois (a Catholic writer) and translated into English in 1867. Mullois wrote, "A man who has not a natural and true delivery should not be allowed to occupy the pulpit; from thence, at least, everything that is false should be summarily banished. . . . The instant you abandon the natural and the true, you forego the right to be believed, as well as the right of being listened to."

Victorian-era churches suffered from the same tendency that bedevils the evangelical movement today: too many preachers thought of themselves as *performers* rather than *ambassadors for Christ* (2 Corinthians 5:20). In Spurgeon's words, "You may go all round, to church and chapel alike, and you will find that by far the larger majority of our preachers have a holy tone for Sundays. They have one voice for the parlor and the bedroom, and quite another tone for the pulpit; so that, if not double-tongued sinfully, they certainly are so literally."[4]

Spurgeon preached to communicate, not to impress. His sermons on farm themes are quintessential examples of his ability to make the most sublime and transcendent truths clear using everyday words and imagery. He was a masterful illustrator. He saw analogies pointing to eternal truths everywhere he looked in the temporal world. Once while lecturing to ministerial students on the proper use of illustrations, he told his students, "If your minds were thoroughly aroused, and yet you could see nothing else in the world but a single tallow candle, you might find enough illustrations in that luminary to last you for six months."

The students gave "a groan of unbelief," so Spurgeon replied, "I will prove my words." Then for his next lecture series, he gave a two-part discourse titled "Sermons in Candles." (Those two lectures were preserved for posterity in a superb little volume, decorated with woodcut images.) He proceeded to give more than three dozen clever ways a simple candle can be used as a rich illustration of some vital biblical truth.[5]

In a similar way, over the whole course of his ministry, Spurgeon commonly employed ideas and word pictures borrowed from farm life to illustrate biblical truths. He was uniquely drawn to topics or passages of Scripture where allusions to agriculture were prominent on the face of the biblical text. Victorian society, even in the cities, was more agrarian than suburban Christians today would be accustomed to. Spurgeon's wife owned a dozen dairy cows and a wagon festooned with a sign: "Charles H. Spurgeon, Milk Dealer." But Spurgeon himself was never really a farmer.

He was, however, a keen observer of the world around him, and during his early childhood (owing to his mother's ill health) young Charles had lived for several years with his grandfather, who served as pastor of a rural church in north Essex. So the Prince of Preachers was comfortably familiar with farm life, and he had an extraordinary gift for weaving farm themes and rich doctrinal instruction seamlessly together.

In 1882 Spurgeon published a generous collection of slightly abridged, somewhat simplified versions of his best-known farm-themed messages. The book, an attractive volume originally titled *Farm Sermons,* featured nineteen chapters chosen from four decades of Spurgeon's preaching. The version of that book you hold in your hands has been further adapted to make it more accessible to twenty-first–century readers. Of course, Spurgeon's trademark candor and clarity still shine through—and whether you're personally familiar with farm life or not, I'm confident you will be edified and encouraged as you read these heartwarming sermons.

As Spurgeon himself said, "Cains and Noahs will plow furrows and reap harvests until the end come. Hence there will always be need of farm sermons. . . . So long as the soul is fed, it is small matter whether the subjects were suggested by the palace or the barn."[6]

JOHN MACARTHUR

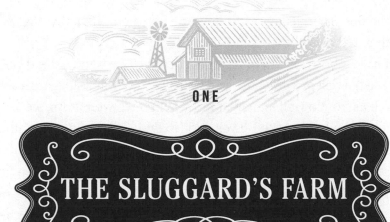

ONE

THE SLUGGARD'S FARM

I went by the field of the slothful, and by the vineyard of the man void of understanding; and, lo, it was all grown over with thorns, and nettles had covered the face thereof, and the stone wall thereof was broken down. Then I saw, and considered it well: I looked upon it, and received instruction.

(PROVERBS 24:30–32)

No doubt Solomon was sometimes glad to lay aside the robes of state, escape from the forms of court, and travel through the country unknown. On one occasion when he was doing so, he looked over the broken wall of a little estate which belonged to a farmer of his country. This estate consisted of a piece of plowed land and a vineyard. One glance showed him that it was owned by a sluggard who had neglected it, for the weeds had grown plentifully and covered all the face of the ground. From this Solomon gathered instruction. Men generally learn wisdom if they have wisdom. The artist's eye sees the beauty of the landscape because she has beauty in her mind. "To him that has shall be given," and he shall have abundance, for he shall reap a harvest even from the field that is covered with thorns and nettles. There is a great difference between one individual and another in the use of the mind's eye.

I have a book titled *The Harvest of a Quiet Eye*, and a good book it is: the harvest of a quiet eye can be gathered from a sluggard's land as well as from a well-managed farm. When we were boys, we were taught a little poem called "Eyes and No Eyes." This poem contained much truth, for some people have eyes and see not (which is much the same as having no eyes), while others have quick eyes for spying out instruction. Some look only at the surface, while others see not only the outside shell but also the living kernel of truth, which is hidden in all outward things.

WE MAY FIND INSTRUCTION EVERYWHERE

To a spiritual mind, nettles have their use, and weeds have their doctrine. Are not all thorns and thistles meant to be teachers to sinful people? Are they not brought forth of the earth on purpose so they can show us what sin has done, as well as the kind of produce that will come when we sow the seed of rebellion against God? "I went by the field of the slothful, and by the vineyard of the man void of understanding," says Solomon; "I saw, and considered it well: I looked upon it, and received instruction." Whatever you see, take care to consider it well, and you will not see it in vain. You can find books and sermons everywhere—on the land and in the sea, on the earth and in the skies—and you can learn from every living beast and bird and fish and insect, as well as from every useful (or even useless) plant that springs out of the ground.

WE MAY ALSO GATHER RARE LESSONS FROM THINGS WE DO NOT LIKE

I am sure that Solomon did not admire the thorns and the nettles that covered the face of the vineyard, but he nevertheless found instruction in them. Many are stung by nettles, but few are taught by them. Some are hurt by briers, but here is one who was improved by them. Wisdom has a way of gathering grapes of thorns and figs of nettles, and she distills good from herbs, which in themselves are harmful and evil. So do not fret over thorns, but instead get something good out of them. Do not begin stinging yourself with nettles. Instead, grip them firmly, and then use them for your soul's health. Trials and troubles, worries and turmoils, little concerns and disappointments, may all help you if you let them. Like Solomon, see and consider them well—look upon them and receive instruction.

Let us now consider *Solomon's description of a sluggard*: He is a "man void of understanding." Second, we shall notice *his description of the sluggard's land*: "It was all grown over with thorns, and nettles had covered the face thereof." When we have attended to these two matters, we will close by *endeavoring to gather the instruction which this piece of wasteland may yield us*.

Solomon's Description of a Slothful Man

Solomon was a man whom none of us would contradict, for he knew as much as all of us put together. Besides that, he was under divine inspiration when he wrote the book of Proverbs. Solomon says that a sluggard is "a man void of understanding." The slothful does not think so; he puts his hands in his pockets, and you would think from his important air that he had all the Bank of England at his disposal. You can see that he is a very wise man in his own esteem, for he gives himself airs which are meant to impress you with a sense of his superior abilities. How he has come by his wisdom, it would be hard to say. He has never taken the trouble to think, and yet I dare not say that he jumps at his conclusions, because he never does such a thing as jump—he lies down and rolls into a conclusion. Yet he knows everything and has settled all points: meditation is too hard work for him, and learning he never could endure; but to be clever by nature is his delight. He does not want to know more than he knows, for he knows enough already, and yet he knows nothing.

The proverb is not complimentary to him, but I am certain that Solomon was right when he called him "a man void of understanding." Solomon was rather rude according to the good manners of the present times, because this gentleman had a field and a vineyard, and as Poor Richard said, "When I have a horse and a cow every man bids me good morrow." How can a man be void of understanding who has a field and a vineyard? Is it not generally understood that you must measure a man's understanding by the amount of his ready cash? Regardless, a person should be admired for his achievements if he has achieved wealth. Such is the way of the world, but such is not the way of Scripture. Whether he has a field and a vineyard or not, says Solomon, if he is a sluggard, he is a fool—or, if you would like to see his character spelled out a little more clearly, he is a man empty of understanding. Not only does he not understand anything, but he has no understanding to understand with. He is empty-headed if he is a sluggard. He may be called a gentleman, he may be a wealthy landowner, he may have a vineyard and a field; but he is none the better for what he has. Actually, he is much the worse, because he is a man void of understanding and is therefore unable to make use of his property.

I am glad to be told by Solomon so plainly that a slothful man is void of understanding, for it is useful information. I have met with people who thought they perfectly understood the doctrines of grace, who could speak about the election of the saints, the predestination of God, the firmness of the divine decree, the necessity of the Spirit's work, and all the glorious doctrines of grace which build up the fabric of our faith; but these individuals have inferred from these doctrines that they have to do nothing, and they have become sluggards. *Do-nothingism* is their creed. They will not even urge other people to labor for the Lord because, as they say, "God will do his own work. Salvation is all of grace!" The notion of these sluggards is that individuals are to wait and do nothing; they are to sit still and let the grass grow up to their ankles in the hope of heavenly help. To take action would be an interference with the eternal purpose, which they regard as altogether unwarrantable. I have known them to look sour, shake their aged head, and say hard things against earnest people who were trying to win souls. I have known them to run down young people and, like a great steam ram, sink them to the bottom by calling them foolish and ignorant.

How shall we survive the criticisms of these dogmatic people? How shall we escape from these very knowing and very critical sluggards? Solomon hastens to the rescue and extinguishes these people by informing us that they are void of understanding. Why, they are the standard of orthodoxy, and they judge everybody! Yet Solomon applies another standard to them and says they are void of understanding. They may know the doctrine, but they do not understand it, or else they would know that the doctrines of grace lead us to seek the grace of the doctrines. And that when we see God at work, we learn that he works in us—not to make us go to sleep, but to will and to do of his own good pleasure. God's predestination of a people is his ordaining them to do good works so that they may show forth his praise. So if you or I shall infer from any doctrines—however true— that we are justified in being idle and indifferent about the things of God, we are void of understanding. We are acting like fools. We are misusing the gospel. We are taking what was meant for meat and turning it into poison. The sluggard, whether he is sluggish about his business or about his soul, is a person void of understanding.

As a rule, we may measure a person's understanding by their useful activities; this is what the wise man very plainly tells us. Certain people call themselves "cultured," and yet they cultivate nothing. Modern thought, as far as I have seen anything of its actual working, is a bottle of smoke out of which comes nothing solid. Yet we know individuals who can distinguish and divide, debate and discuss, refine and refute, and all the while the hemlock is growing in the furrow and the plow is rusting. Friend, if your knowledge, if your culture, if your education, does not lead you practically to serve God in your day and generation, you have not learned what Solomon calls wisdom and you are not like the Blessed One, who was incarnate wisdom, of whom we read that he "went about doing good" (Acts 10:38). A lazy man is not like our Savior, who said, "My Father worketh hitherto, and I work" (John 5:17). True wisdom is practical; boastful culture brags and theorizes. Wisdom plows its field, wisdom hoes its vineyard, wisdom looks to its crops, wisdom tries to make the best of everything, and he who does not do so—whatever may be his knowledge of this, that, or the other—is a man void of understanding.

Why is the sluggard void of understanding? Is it not *because he has opportunities which he does not use*? His day has come, his day is going, and he lets the hours glide by to no purpose. Let me not press too hard on anyone, but let me ask you all to press as hard as you can on yourselves, asking, *Am I making good use of my time as it flies by?* The sluggard had a vineyard, but he did not cultivate it; he had a field, but he did not till it. Do you, friends, use all your opportunities? I know we each have some power to serve God, but do we use it? If we are his children, he has not put one of us where we will be useless. Somewhere we may shine by the light he has given us, though that light be only a tiny candle. Are we still shining? Do we sow beside all waters? Do we in the morning sow our seed, and in the evening still stretch out our hand? If not, we are rebuked by the sweeping censure of Solomon, who said that the slothful is a "man void of understanding."

Having opportunities, he did not use them; and next, *being bound to the performance of certain duties, he did not fulfill them.* When God appointed that every Israelite should have a piece of land, under that admirable system which made every Israelite a landowner, he meant that each individual should possess their plot, not let it go to waste but instead to cultivate it. When God put Adam in the garden of Eden, it was not so Adam should walk through the glades and watch the spontaneous luxuriance of the unfallen earth, but that he might dress it and keep it. He had the same end in view when he allotted each Jew his piece of land. He meant for the holy soil to reach the utmost point of fertility through the labor of those who owned it.

The possession of a field and a vineyard involved responsibilities upon the sluggard which he never fulfilled, and therefore he was void of understanding. What is your position, dear friend? A father? A mother? A master? A servant? A minister? A teacher? Well, you have your farms and your vineyards in those particular spheres, but if you do not use those positions rightly, you will be void of understanding because you neglect the end of your existence. You miss the high calling which your Maker has set before you.

The slothful farmer was unwise in these two respects, and also in another, *for he had capacities which he did not employ.* He could have tilled the field and cultivated the vineyard if he had chosen to do so. He was not a sickly man who was forced to keep to his bed, but he was a lazybones who was there because of his own choice.

You are not asked to do in the service of God that which is utterly beyond you, for God expects actions of us according to what we have, not according to what we have not. The woman of two talents is not required to bring in the interest of five, but she is expected to bring in the interest of two. Solomon's slothful man was too idle to attempt tasks which were quite within his power. Many have a number of dormant faculties of which they are scarcely aware, and many more have abilities which they are using for themselves yet not for Him who created them. Dear friends, if God has given us any power to do good, pray let us do it, for this is a wicked, weary world. We should not even cover a glowworm's light in such a darkness as this. We should not keep back a syllable of divine truth in a world that is so full of falsehood and error. However feeble our voices, let us lift them up for the cause of truth and righteousness. Do not let us be void of understanding because we have opportunities that we do not use, obligations that we do not fulfill, and capacities which we do not exercise.

As far as soul matters, the sluggard is indeed void of understanding, for *he trifles with matters which demand his most earnest heed.* Friend, have you never cultivated your heart? Has the plowshare never broken up the clods of your soul? Has the seed of the Word never been sown in you, or has it taken no root? Have you never watered the young plants of desire? Have you never sought to pull up the weeds of sin that grow in your heart? Are you still a piece of the open spaces or wild land? Poor soul! You can care for your body and spend time looking in the mirror, but do you not care for your soul? How long you take to clothe yourself, which would not matter if God took away your breath! And yet all the while your soul is uncombed, unwashed, undressed, a poor neglected thing. Oh, it should not be so. You take care of the worse part and leave the better to perish through neglect. This is the height of folly! He who is a sluggard in the vineyard of his heart is a person void of understanding. If I must be idle, let it be seen in my field and my garden, but not in my soul.

Or are you a Christian? Are you really saved, and are you negligent in the Lord's work? Then, indeed, whatever you may be, I cannot help saying you have too little understanding; for surely, when someone is saved by God, and understands the danger their friends' souls are in, they must be in earnest in trying to pluck the firebrands from the flame. A Christian sluggard! Is there such a being? A *Christian* on half time? A Christian working not at all for the Lord? How shall I speak of such a person? *Time* does not tarry, DEATH does not tarry, HELL does not tarry; Satan is not lazy, all the powers of darkness are busy. How is it that you and I can be sluggish, if the Master has put us into his vineyard? Surely we must be void of understanding if, after being saved by the infinite love of God, we do not spend and be spent in his service. The eternal fitness of things demands that a saved individual should be an earnest individual.

Christians who are slothful in their Master's service *have no idea what they are losing,* for the very heart of religion lies in holy consecration to God. Some people have just enough religion to make it questionable whether they have any or none. They have enough godliness to make them uneasy in their ungodliness. They have washed enough of their face to show the dirt upon the rest of it. "I am glad," said a servant, "that my mistress takes the sacrament, for otherwise I should not know she had any religion at all." You smile, and well you may. It is ridiculous that some people should have no goods in their shop, and yet advertise their business in all the papers. In the same way some people make a show of religion and yet have none of the Spirit of God. I wish some professors would do Christ the justice to say, "No, I am *not* one of his disciples; do not think so badly of him as to imagine that I can be one of them."

We ought to be reflections *of* Christ; but I fear many are reflections *upon* Christ. When we see a lot of lazy servants, we are apt to think that their master must also be a very idle person, or they would never put up with them. Those who employ sluggards and are satisfied with their snail-like pace, cannot be very active people themselves. We should never let the world think that Christ is indifferent to human woe, that Christ has lost his zeal, that Christ has lost his energy. Yet I fear some will say it or think it if they see those who profess to be laborers in the vineyard of Christ as nothing better than mere sluggards. The slothful, then, are those void of understanding; they lose the honor and pleasure they would find in serving their Master. They are a dishonor to the God they profess to worship. Let that stand as settled—the slothful, whether they be a minister, deacon, or private Christian, is a person void of understanding.

SOLOMON'S DESCRIPTION OF A SLUGGARD'S LAND

"I went by the field of the slothful, and by the vineyard of the man void of understanding; and, lo, it was all grown over with thorns, and nettles had covered the face thereof" (vv. 30–31).

The Land Will Produce Something

Soil which is good enough to be made into a field and a vineyard must and will yield some fruit or other, so you and I—in our hearts and in the sphere God gives us to occupy—will be sure to produce something. We cannot live in this world as entire blanks; we shall either do good or do evil, as sure as we are alive. If you are idle in Christ's work, you are active in the devil's work. By sleeping, the sluggard was doing more for the cultivation of thorns and nettles than he could have done by any other means. As a garden will either yield flowers or weeds, fruits or thistles, so something either good or evil will come out of our household, our class, or our congregation. If we do not produce a harvest of good wheat, by laboring for Christ, we shall grow weeds to be bound up in bundles for the last harvest burning.

If Not Farmed for God, the Soul Will Yield Its Natural Produce

What is the natural produce of land left to itself? It is thorns and nettles, or some other useless weeds. What is the natural produce of your heart and mine? It is sin and misery. What is the natural produce of your children if you leave them untrained for God? It is unholiness and vice. What is the natural produce of this great city if we leave its streets, and lanes, and alleys without the gospel? It is crime and infamy. Some harvest there will be, and the sheaves will be the natural produce of the soil, which is sin, death, and corruption.

If We Are Slothful, the Natural Produce of Our Heart
Will Be Inconvenient and Unpleasant

Nobody can sleep on thorns or make a pillow of nettles. No rest can come out of idleness which does not by God's Spirit strive to uproot evil. While you are sleeping, Satan will be sowing. If you withhold the seed of good, Satan will be lavish with the seed of evil, and from that evil will come anguish and regret for some time—and maybe even for eternity. Oh, friend, the garden has been put in your charge, and if you waste your time in slumber, you will be rewarded with all that is unpleasant and painful: "Thorns also and thistles shall it bring forth to thee" (Genesis 3:18).

In Many Instances There Will Be a Great Deal of This Evil Produce

A field and a vineyard will yield more thistles and nettles than a piece of ground that has never been reclaimed. If the land is good enough for a garden, it will present its owner with a fine crop of weeds if only she does nothing. A choice bit of land fit for a vineyard of red wine will render such a profusion of nettles to the slothful that he shall rub his eyes with surprise. The person who might do the most for God, if they were renewed, will bring forth the most for Satan if they be let alone. The very region which would have glorified God the most if the grace of God were there to convert its inhabitants, will be the region out of which the vilest enemies of the gospel will arise. Rest assured of that—the best will become the worst if we neglect it. Neglect is all that is needed to produce evil. If you want to know the way of salvation, I must take some pains to tell you; but if you want to know the way to be lost, my reply is easy, for it is only a matter of negligence: "How shall we escape if we neglect so great salvation?" If you desire to bring forth a harvest to give to God, I may need to spend a lot of time instructing you in plowing, sowing, and watering. But if you wish your mind to be covered with Satan's hemlock, you have only to leave the furrows of your nature to themselves. The slothful asks for "A little sleep, a little slumber, a little folding of the hands to sleep," and the thorns and this-tles multiply beyond all numbering and prepare for him many a sting.

Let Us Peep Into the Sluggard's Heart

While we look upon the lazy man's vineyard, let us also peep into the ungodly sluggard's heart. He does not care about repentance and faith. To think about his soul, to be in earnest about eternity, is too much for him. He wants to take things easy, to fold his arms to sleep. What is growing in his mind and character? In some of these spiri-tual sluggards you can see drunkenness, uncleanness, covetousness, anger, and pride, and all sorts of thistles and nettles. Where these more vigorous weeds do not appear, you find other sorts of sin. The heart cannot be altogether empty—either Christ or the devil will possess it. My dear friend, if you are not decided for God, you cannot be neutral. In this war every man is for God or for the Enemy. You cannot remain like a sheet of blank paper. The legible handwriting of Satan is upon you—can you not see the ink? Unless Christ has written across the page his own sweet name, the autograph of Satan is visible. You may say, "I do not sin; I am a good person," and so forth. But if you would but look and consider and search your heart, you would see that enmity to God and to his ways, and hatred of purity, are there. You do not love God's law, nor love his Son, nor love his gospel; you are alienated in your heart, and there is in you all manner of evil desires and vain thoughts. These will flourish and increase so long as you are a spiritual sluggard, and they will leave your heart uncultivated. May the Spirit of God arouse you, may you be stirred to anxious, earnest thought. Then you will see that these weeds must be uprooted, and that your heart must be turned up by the plow of conviction, and sown with the good seed of the gospel, until a harvest rewards the great Gardener.

Friend, if you believe in Christ, I want to peep over the hedge into *your heart*. If you are a lazy Christian, I fear that nettles and thistles are threatening you also. Did I not hear you sing the other day—"'Tis a point I long to know"? That point will often be raised, for doubt is a seed which is sure to grow in a lazy person's mind. I do not remember reading in Mr. Wesley's diary a question about his own salvation. He was so busy laboring in the harvest of the Master that it did not occur to him to distrust his God. Some Christians have little faith because they have never sown the grain of mustard seed which they have received. If you do not sow your faith by using it, how can it grow? When a man lives by faith in Christ Jesus, and his faith exercises itself actively in the service of his Lord, it takes root, grows upward, and become strong, until it chokes his doubts.

Some people live their lives unhappy, fretful, and selfish, all because they are idle and only weeds grow in their gardens. I have known the slothful to become so irritable that nothing could please them. The most earnest Christian can do no right by them, the most loving Christian cannot be affectionate enough, and the most active church cannot be energetic enough. These people detect all sorts of wrong where God himself saw much of the fruit of his Spirit. This tendency to criticize, to be contentious, to perpetually complain, is one of the nettles that is quite sure to grow in the gardens of those who fold their arms in sinful ease. If your heart does not yield fruit to God, it will certainly bring forth that which is mischievous in itself, painful to you, and injurious to others. Often the thorns choke the good seed, but it is a very blessed thing when the good seed comes up so thick and fast that it chokes the thorns. God enables certain Christians to become so fruitful in Christ that their graces and works grow strong together, and when Satan throws in the weeds, they cannot grow because there is no room for them. The Holy Spirit by his power makes evil become weak in the heart, so that it no longer keeps the upper hand. If you are slothful, friend, look over the field of your heart, and weep at the sight.

Let Us Look Into the Sluggard's Own House and Home

May I next ask you to look into *your own house* and home? It is a dreadful thing when a man does not cultivate the field of his own family. I recollect in my early days a man who used to walk out with me into the villages when I was preaching. I was glad of his company until I found out certain facts about him, and then I shook him off. After that, I believe he started following somebody else, for he was one of those people who needed to be gadding about every evening of the week. He had many children, and they grew up to be wicked young men and women because their father, while spending time at this meeting and that, never tried to bring his own children to the Savior. What is the use of zeal abroad if there is neglect at home? How sad to say, "My own vineyard have I not kept." Have you never heard of one who said he did not teach his children the ways of God because he thought they were too young to influence, and he preferred to allow them to choose their own religion when they grew older? One of his boys broke his arm, and while the surgeon was setting it, the boy was swearing the entire time. "Ah," said the good doctor, "I told you what would happen. You were afraid to influence your boy in the right way, but the devil had no such qualms; he has influenced him the other way, and pretty strongly too." It is our duty to influence our field in favor of corn, or it will soon be covered with thistles. Cultivate a child's heart for good, or it will go wrong of itself, for it is already depraved by nature. We must be wise enough to think of this, and leave no little one to become prey to the destroyer.

As It Is with Homes, so It Is with Schools

A gentleman who joined this church some time ago had been an atheist for years, and in conversing with him I found that he had been educated at one of our great public schools, and to that fact he traced his infidelity. He said that the boys were stowed away on Sunday in a lofty gallery at the far end of a church, where they could scarcely hear a word that the clergyman said, sitting imprisoned in a place where it was dreadfully hot in summer and cold in winter. On Sundays there were prayers, and prayers, and prayers—but nothing that ever touched his heart—until he became so sick of prayers that he vowed once he got out of school, he would be done with religion. This is a sad result, but a frequent one. You Sunday school teachers can make your classes so tiresome to the children that they will hate Sunday. You can fritter away the time in school without bringing the boys and girls to Christ, and so you may do more harm than good. I have known Christian fathers who, by their severity and want of tenderness, have sown their family field with the thorns and thistles of hatred of religion instead of scattering the good seed of love of faith. We should make it our priority to live among our children that they may not only love us, but also love our Father who is in heaven. May fathers and mothers set such an example of cheerful piety that sons and daughters shall say, "Let us tread in our father's footsteps, for he was a happy and a holy man. Let us follow our mother's ways, for she was sweetness itself." If godliness is not a priority in your house, when we pass by your home we will see disorder, disobedience, pride, foolishness, and the beginnings of wickedness. Do not allow your home to become a sluggard's field, or you will regret it for years to come.

Let every deacon, every leader, and also every minister inquire diligently into the state of the field he has to cultivate. You see, brothers and sisters, if you and I are in charge of any department of our Lord's work, and we are not diligent in it, we will become like barren trees planted in an orchard, which are a loss altogether because they occupy the places of other trees, which might have brought forth good fruit. We shall be a burden on the earth, and do damage to our Lord's work, unless we give him our actual service. Will you think of this? If you live your life as a person who has no influence in Christ's work in the world, that would be very sad. But even that isn't true, as you will cause a loss unless you create a gain. May you be profitable to our Lord and Master through the grace of God! Who among us can look upon his life work without some sorrow? If anything has been done right, we credit it all to the grace of God—but how much there is to weep over! How much that we would wish to amend! Let us not spend time in idle regrets but pray for the Spirit of God, that in the future we may not be void of understanding, but instead may know what we ought to do, find the strength with which to do it, and then give ourselves up to the doing of it.

Look at the Great Field of the World

I beg you once more to look at the great field of *the world*. Do you see how it is overgrown with thorns and nettles? If an angel could take a survey of the whole world, what tears he would shed, if angels could weep! What a tangled mass of weeds the whole earth is! Vast regions are smothered with the thistles of faithlessness and idolatry. The world is full of cruelty, oppression, drunkenness, rebellion, filthiness, misery. What the moon sees! What God's sun sees! What scenes of horror! How far is all this to be attributed to a neglectful church? Nearly nineteen hundred years are gone, and the sluggard's vineyard is but little improved! England has been touched with the spade, but I cannot say that it has been thoroughly weeded or plowed yet. Across the ocean another field equally favored knows well the plowman, and yet the weeds are rank. Here and there a little good work has been done, but in the vast mass of the world still lies a moorland never broken up, a waste, a howling wilderness.

What has the church been doing all these years? She ceased after a few centuries to be a missionary church, and from that hour she almost ceased to be a living church. Whenever a church does not labor for the reclaiming of the desert, it becomes itself a waste. You shall not find on the roll of history that for a length of time any Christian community has flourished after it has become negligent of the outside world. I believe that if we are put into the Master's vineyard and choose not to take away the weeds, the vine will not flourish, and the corn will not yield its increase. However, instead of asking what the church has been doing for these nineteen hundred years, let us ask ourselves, *What are we going to do now?* Are the missions of the churches of the world always to be such poor, feeble things? Are the best of our Christian young people always going to stay at home? We go on plowing the home field a hundred times over, while millions of acres abroad are left to the thorn and nettle. Will it always be so? We must ask God to send us more spiritual life and wake us up from our sluggishness, or else when the holy watcher gives his report, he will say, "I went by the field of the sluggish church, and it was all grown over with thorns and nettles, and the stone wall was broken down so that one could scarcely tell which was the church and which was the world. Yet still she slept, and slept, and slept, and nothing could awaken her."

That There Must Be Some Lesson in All This

I cannot teach it as I would, but I want to learn it myself. I will speak it as though I were talking to myself.

Unaided Nature Will Always Produce Thorns and Nettles and Nothing Else

If it were not for grace, this is all that my soul would have produced. Beloved, are you producing anything else? It is not nature, but the grace of God, that makes you produce it. Your lips that now most charmingly sing the praises of God would have been delighted with an idle ballad if the grace of God had not sanctified them. Your heart that now cleaves to Christ would have continued to cling to your idols—you know what they were—if it had not been for grace divine. And why should grace have visited you or me—why? What answer can we give? "Even so, Father: for so it seemed good in thy sight" (Matthew 11:26). Let the recollection of what grace has done move us to manifest the result of that grace in our lives. Come, brothers and sisters, as previously we were rich enough in the soil of our own nature to produce so much of nettle and thistle—and God only knows how much we did produce—let us now pray that our lives may yield as many good crops for the great Gardener. Will you serve Christ less than you served your own wants? Will you make less sacrifice for Christ than you did for your sins? If you were wholehearted in the service of the Evil One, will you be halfhearted in the service of God? Will the Holy Spirit produce less fruit in you than that which you yielded under the spirit of evil?

God grant that we may not be left to prove what nature will produce if left to itself.

The Little Value of Natural Good Intentions

This man, who left his field and vineyard to be overgrown, always meant to work hard one of these fine days. To do him justice, we must admit that he did not mean to sleep much longer, for he said—"Yet a little sleep, a little slumber, a little folding of the hands to sleep" (Proverbs 24:33). Only a little doze, and then he would roll up his sleeves and get back to work. Probably the worst people in the world are those who have the best intentions but never carry them out. This is the way Satan lulls many to sleep. They hear an earnest sermon, but they do not arise and go to their Father. They only get as far as saying, "Yes, yes, the far country is not a fit place for me; I will not stay here long. I mean to go home by-and-by." They said that forty years ago, but nothing came of it. When they were quite young, they were almost persuaded to become Christians, and yet they are not Christians even now. They have been slumbering for forty years! Surely that is a very long nap! They never intended to dream for so long, and now they do not mean to lie in bed much longer. They will not turn to Christ at once, but they are resolved to do so one day.

When are you going to do it, friend? "Before I die." Going to put it off to the last hour or two, are you? When unconscious and drugged to relieve pain, is that when you will begin to think of your soul? Is this wise? Surely you are void of understanding. Perhaps you will die in an hour. Did you not hear the other day of the alderman who died in his carriage? Little must he have dreamed of that. How would it have fared with you had you also been taken from this earth while riding at your ease? Have you not heard of people who fall dead at their work? What is to stop you from dying with a spade in your hand? I am often startled when I am told that one whom I saw just the pre-vious Sunday is dead—gone from the shop to the judgment seat. It is not a very long time ago since one went out at the doorway of the tabernacle and fell dead on the threshold. We have had deaths in the house of God, unexpected deaths; and sometimes people are hur-ried away unprepared—people who never meant to die unconverted, who always had from their youth up some kind of desire to be ready, only still they wanted a little more sleep. Friends, pay attention to those little delays and procrastinations. You have wasted time enough already; come to the point at once before the clock strikes again. May God the Holy Spirit bring you to decision.

"Surely you do not object to my having a little more sleep?" says the sluggard. "You have waked me so soon. I only ask another little nap." "My dear man, it is far into the morning." He answers, "It is rather late, I know; but it will not be much later if I take just another doze." You wake him again, and tell him it is noon. He says, "It is the hottest part of the day. I daresay if I had been up, I should have gone to the sofa and taken a little rest from the hot sun." You knock at his door when it is almost evening, and he replies, "It is of no use to get up now, for the day is almost over." You remind him of his overgrown field and weedy vineyard, and he answers, "Yes, I must get up, I know." He shakes himself and says, "I do not think it will matter much if I wait till the clock strikes. I will rest another minute or two." He is glued to his bed, dead while he lives, buried in his laziness. If he could sleep forever he would, but he cannot, for the judgment day will rouse him. It is written, "And in hell he lift up his eyes, being in torments" (Luke 16:23). God grant that you spiritual sluggards may wake before that, but you will not unless you awaken yourselves early, for "now is the accepted time" (2 Corinthians 6:2); and it may be now or never. Tomorrow is only to be found in the calendar of fools; today is the time of the wise man, the chosen season of our gracious God. May the Holy Spirit lead you to seize the present hour, that you may at once give yourselves to the Lord by faith in Christ Jesus, and then from his vineyard—

> Quick uproot
> The noisome weeds, that without profit suck
> The soil's fertility from wholesome plants.[7]

TWO

THE BROKEN FENCE

I went by the field of the slothful, and by the vineyard of the man void of understanding; and lo, it was all grown over with thorns, and nettles had covered the face thereof, and the stone wall thereof was broken down. Then I saw, and considered it well: I looked upon it and received instruction.

(Proverbs 24:30-32)

This slothful man did no harm to his fellow humans: he was not a thief, nor a ruffian, nor a meddler in anybody else's business. He did not trouble himself about other people's concerns, for he did not even attend to his own—it required too much exertion. He was not overly vicious; he had not energy enough to be that way. He was one who liked to take things easily. He always let well alone, and, for the matter of that, he let ill alone, too, as the nettles and the thistles in his garden plainly proved. What was the use of disturbing himself? It would be all the same a hundred years from now, and so he took things just as they came. He was not a bad man, so some said of him; and yet perhaps there is no worse man in the world than the man who is not good, for in some respects he is not good enough to be bad. He has not enough force of character about him to serve either God or Baal. He simply serves himself, worshiping his own ease and adoring his own comfort. Yet he always meant to be right. Dear me! He was not going to sleep much longer; he would only have forty winks more, and then he would be at his work and show what he could do. One of these days he meant to work hard and make up for lost time. The time never actually came for him to begin, but it was always coming. He always meant to repent, but he went on in his sin. He meant to believe, but he died an unbeliever. He meant to be a Christian, but he lived without Christ. He remained undecided between two choices because he could not trouble himself to make up his mind, and so he perished of delay.

This picture of the slothful man and his garden and field overgrown with nettles and weeds represents many who have professed to be Christians, but who have become slothful in the things of God. Spiritual life has withered in them. They have backslidden and fallen from the condition of healthy spiritual energy into one of listlessness and indifference to the things of God. While things have gone wrong within their hearts, all sorts of troubles have come into them and grown in their lives, with trouble also taking place externally in their daily conduct. The stone wall which guarded their character has been broken down, and they lie open to all evil. Upon this point we will now meditate: "The stone wall thereof was broken down."

Come, then, let us take a walk with Solomon, and stand with him and consider and learn while we *look at this broken-down fence.* When we have examined it, let *us consider the consequences of broken-down walls*; and then, finally, let us try to *rouse up this sluggard that his wall may yet be repaired.* If this slothful person should be one of ourselves, may God's infinite mercy rouse us up before this ruined wall has let in a herd of prowling vices.

Look at This Broken Fence

You will see that in the beginning it was a very good fence, for it was a stone wall. Fields are often surrounded with wooden palings which soon decay or with hedges which may very easily have gaps made in them, but this was a stone wall. Such walls are very common in regions where stone is plentiful. It was a substantial protection to begin with, and well shut in the pretty little estate which had fallen into such bad hands. The man had a field for agricultural purposes, and another strip of land for a vineyard or a garden. It was fertile soil, for it produced thorns and nettles in abundance, and where these flourish better things can be produced; yet the idler took no care of his property, but instead allowed the wall to get into bad repair and in many places to become quite broken down.

Let me mention some of the stone walls that men permit to be broken down when they backslide.

In Many Cases Sound Principles Instilled in Youth Have Been Forgotten

What a blessing is Christian education! Our parents, both by persuasion and example, taught many of us the things that are pure and honest and of good repute. We saw in their lives how to live. They also opened the Word of God before us, and they taught us the ways of righteousness both toward God and toward men. They prayed for us, and they prayed with us, until the things of God were placed round about us and shut us in as with a stone wall. We are never entirely able to get rid of our early impressions. Even in times of wandering, before we knew the Lord saved us, these things had a healthy power over us; we were checked when we would have done evil, we were assisted when we were struggling to get to know Christ. It is very sad when people permit these first principles to be shaken and removed like stones which fall from a boundary wall.

Young people talk lightly of the old-fashioned ways of their parents. As time goes on, it becomes not merely the old-fashionedness of the ways but the ways themselves that they despise. They seek other company, and from that other company they learn nothing but evil. They seek pleasure in places which it horrifies their parents to think of. This leads to worse, and if they do not bring their fathers' gray hairs with sorrow to the grave, it is no virtue of theirs. I have known young men, who really were Christians, sadly backslide through being induced to modify, conceal, or alter those holy principles in which they were trained from their mothers' knees. It is a great calamity when those who profess to follow Christ become unpredictable, unstable, and carried about with every wind of doctrine. It shows great faultiness of mind, and unsoundness of heart, when we can trifle with those grave and solemn truths which have been sanctified by a mother's tears and by a father's earnest life. "I am thy servant," said David, "and the son of thine handmaid" (Psalm 116:16). David felt it to be a high honor and, at the same time, a sacred bond which bound him to God, that he was the son of one who could be called God's handmaid. Take care, those of you who have had Christian training, that you do not trifle with it. "My son, keep thy father's commandment, and forsake not the law of thy mother: bind them continually upon thine heart, and tie them about thy neck" (Proverbs 6:20–21).

Our Character Is Also Protected When Solid Doctrines Have Been Learned

This is a fine stone wall. Many of us have been taught the gospel of the grace of God, and we have learned it well, so that we are able to contend earnestly for the faith once delivered to the saints. Happy are those of us who have a religion grounded upon a clear knowledge of eternal truths. A religion which is all excitement, and has little instruction in it, may serve for transient use, but for permanent life purposes there must be a knowledge of those great doctrines which are fundamental to the gospel. I tremble when I hear of a man's giving up, one by one, the vital principles of the gospel and boasting of his liberality. I hear him say, "These are my views, but others have a right to their views also." That is a very proper expression in reference to mere "views," but we may not speak this way of *truth* itself as revealed by God. That truth is one and unalterable, and all are bound to receive it. It is not your own view of truth, for that is an imperfect thing, but the very truth itself which will save you if your faith embraces it. I will readily yield my way of stating a doctrine, but not the doctrine itself. One man may put it in this way, and one in another; but the truth itself must never be given up. The spirit of the "Anything Goes" way of believing robs us of rightness and certainty. I should like to ask some great individuals of that order whether they believe that anything is taught in the Scriptures which would be worthwhile for a person to die for, and whether the martyrs were not great fools for laying down their lives for mere opinions which might be right or might be wrong. This too-broad way of thinking is a breaking down of stone walls, and it will let in the devil and all his crew, and do infinite harm to the church of God, if it is not stopped. A loose state of belief does great damage to anyone's mind.

We are not fanatics, but we should be none the worse if lived so that others called us so. I met a man the other day who was accused of fanaticism, and I said, "Give me your hand, old fellow. I like to meet with fanatics now and then, for the fine old creatures are getting scarce, and the stuff they are made of is so good that if there were more of it, we might see a few men among us again and fewer mollusks." Lately we have seen few people with backbone—most have been of the jellyfish order. I have lived in times in which I should have said, "Be open-minded and shake off all narrowness," but now I am obliged to alter my tone and cry, "Be steadfast in the truth." The faith once delivered to the saints is now all the more attractive to me because it is called narrow, for I am weary of that distance which comes of broken hedges. There are fixed points of truth, and definite certainties of creed, and woe to those who allow these stone walls to crumble. I fear that the slothful are a numerous band, and that generations to come may have to lament the carelessness which has been embraced by the current negligent generation.

Another Fence Too Often Neglected Is That of Godly Habits

The sluggard allows this wall to be broken down. This wall is made up of some valuable guards of life and character.

Secret Prayer

One is the habit of *secret prayer*. Private prayer should be regularly offered, at least in the morning and in the evening. We cannot do without set seasons for drawing near to God. To look into the face of man without having first seen the face of God is very dangerous, and to go out into the world without locking up the heart and giving God the key is to leave it open to all sorts of spiritual vagrants. At night, to go to your rest as the swine roll into their sty, without thanking God for the mercies of the day, is shameful. The evening sacrifice should be devoutly offered as surely as we have enjoyed the evening fireside, as we put ourselves under the wings of our Preserver. It may be said, "We can pray at all times." I know we can, but I fear that those who do not pray at certain hours seldom pray at all. Those who pray in season are the most likely people to pray at all seasons. Spiritual life does not care for a cast-iron regulation, but since life casts itself into some mold or other, be careful of its external habit as well as its internal power. Never allow great gaps in the wall of your habitual private prayer.

Family Prayer

I will go a step farther; I believe that there is great power in *family prayer*. Gather your children together, read a passage of Scripture, pray, and sing the praises of God together as a family. This is how the saints kept the faith from generation to generation. Household devotion and the pulpit are, under God, the stone walls of the faith, and my prayer is that these may not be broken down.

Weeknight Services

Another fence to protect piety is found in *weeknight services*. I notice that when people forsake weeknight meetings, the power of their religion evaporates. I do not speak of those lawfully detained to watch the sick and attend to farm work and other business, or those employed as domestic servants and the like, as there are exceptions to all rules. But I mean those who could attend if they had a mind to do so. When people say, "It is quite enough for me to be wearied with the Sunday sermons; I do not want to go out to prayer meetings, and lectures, and so forth," it is clear that they have no appetite for the Word, and surely this is a bad sign. If you have a bit of wall built to protect Sunday and then six times the distance left without a fence, I believe that Satan's cattle will get in and do no end of mischief.

Bible Reading

Take care, also, of the stone wall of *Bible reading,* and of speaking often to each other concerning the things of God. Associate with the godly and commune with God, and you will, by the blessing of God's Spirit, keep up a good fence against temptations, which otherwise will get into the fields of your soul and devour all good fruits.

Much Protection for the Field of Daily Life Comes with a Public Profession of Faith

I am speaking to those of you who are real believers, and I know you have often found it a great safeguard to be known and recognized as a follower of Jesus. I have never regretted—and I never shall regret—the day on which I walked to the little River Lark, in Cambridgeshire, and was there baptized in Christ. In this I acted contrary to the opinions of all my friends whom I respected and esteemed, but as I had read the Greek Testament for myself, I felt bound to be immersed upon the profession of my faith, and I was so. By that act I said to the world, "I am dead to you, and buried to you in Christ, and I hope henceforth to live in newness of life." That day, by God's grace, I imitated the tactics of the general who meant to fight the enemy until he conquered them, burning his own boats so that there might be no way of retreat. I believe that a solemn confession of Christ before others is as a hedge of thorns that keeps one within bounds and holds off those who hope to draw you aside. Of course, it is nothing but a hedge, and it is of no use to fence in a field of weeds, but when wheat is growing, a hedge is of great consequence. You who imagine that you can be the Lord's, and yet lie open like public land, are making a great mistake; you ought to be set apart from the world and obey the voice which says, "Come out from among them, and be ye separate" (2 Corinthians 6:17). The promise of salvation is to the man who with his heart believes and with his mouth confesses. Boldly say, "Let others do as they will; as for me and my house, we will serve the Lord." By this act you come out into the King's highway and put yourself under the protection of the Lord, and he will take care of you. When otherwise you might have hesitated, you will say, "The vows of the Lord are upon me; how can I draw back?" I pray that you set up the stone wall and keep it up, and if it has at any corner been tumbled over, set it up again. Let your conduct and conversation show that you are a follower of Jesus, and do not be ashamed to have that known.

Hold fast to your religious principles, and do not turn aside for the sake of gain or respectability. Do not let wealth break down your wall, for I have known some who have made a great gap to let their carriage go through, letting in the wealth of the world for the sake of their society. Those who compromise their principles to please men will in the end be lightly esteemed, but those who are faithful will have the honor which comes from God. Keep up this hedge; look after your faith, and you will find a great blessing in it.

Another Stone Wall—Firmness of Character

Our holy faith teaches a person to be decided in the cause of Christ and determined in getting rid of evil habits. Does the ninth chapter of Mark ask us, "If thine eye offend thee"—protect your eyes? No, "pluck it out." "If thine arm offend thee"—hang it in a sling? No, "cut it off and cast it from thee." True religion is very thorough in what it recommends. It says to us, "Touch not the unclean thing" (2 Corinthians 6:17). But many individuals are so idle in the ways of God that they have no mind of their own. Evil companions tempt them, and they cannot say, "No." They need to construct a stone wall made up of nos. Here are the stones: "no, *no*, NO." Dare to stand firm. Resolve to keep close to Christ. Determine to permit nothing in your life, however gainful or pleasurable, if it would dishonor the name of Jesus. Be dogmatically true, obstinately holy, immovably honest, desperately kind, fixedly upright. If God's grace sets up this hedge around you, even Satan will feel that he cannot get in and will complain to God, "Hast not thou made an hedge about him?" (Job 1:10).

THE CONSEQUENCES OF A BROKEN-DOWN FENCE

I have kept you looking over the wall long enough. Let me invite you in, and for a few minutes let us consider the consequences of a broken-down fence.

First, the Boundary Has Gone

Those lines of separation, kept up by the good principles which were instilled in the believer by religious habits, a bold profession, and a firm resolve, have vanished and now the question is, "Are they a Christian, or are they not?" The fence is so far gone that they do not know which is the Lord's property and which remains an open common. In fact, they do not know whether they themselves are included in the Royal domain or left to become mere waste of the world's manor. This is what happens when we do not keep up the fences. If someone has lived near to God, if they have walked in his integrity, if the Spirit of God has richly rested on them in all holy living and waiting upon God, they would know where the boundary was, and they would see whether their land lay in the parish of All-Saints, or in the region called No-Man's-Land, or in the district where Satan is the lord of the manor.

The other day, I heard of a dear old saint who, when she was near death, was attacked by Satan. Waving her finger at the Enemy, in her gentle way, she routed him by saying, "Chosen! Chosen! Chosen!" She knew that she was chosen, and she remembered the verse, "The LORD that hath chosen Jerusalem rebuke thee" (Zechariah 3:2). When the wall stands in its integrity all around the field, we can resist the devil by bidding him leave the Lord's property alone: "Be gone! Look somewhere else. I belong to Christ, not to you." To do this, you must mend the hedges well so that there will be a clear boundary, and you can say, "Trespassers, beware!" Do not yield an inch to the Enemy, but the more he seeks to enter, the higher you make the wall. Do not allow this adversary to ever find a gap to enter by!

Next, When the Wall Has Fallen, the Protection Is Gone

When a person's heart has its wall broken, all their thoughts will go astray and wander upon the mountains of vanity. Like sheep, thoughts need careful tending, or they will wander off in no time. "I hate vain thoughts," said David (Psalm 119:113), but slothful individuals are sure to have plenty of them, for there is no keeping your thoughts out of vanity unless you stop at every gap and shut every gate. Holy thoughts, comfortable meditations, devout longings, and gracious contemplations will vanish if we sluggishly allow the stone wall to get out of repair.

This is not all, for as good things go out, bad things come in. When the wall is gone, every passerby sees, as it were, an invitation to enter. You have set before others an open door, and in they come. Are there fruits? They pluck them, of course. They walk about as if it were a public place, and they pry everywhere. Is there any secret corner of your heart which you will keep for Jesus? Satan or the world will walk in, and do you wonder? Every passing goat or roaming ox or stray donkey visits the growing crops and spoils more than he eats, and who can blame the creature when the gaps are so wide? All manner of evil lust and desires and imaginations prey upon an unfenced soul. It is of no use for you to say, "Lead us not into temptation" (Matthew 6:13; Luke 11:4). God will hear your prayer and he will not lead you there, but you are leading yourself into it. You are tempting the devil to tempt you. If you leave yourself open to evil influences, the Spirit of God will be grieved, and he may leave you to deal with the consequences of your mistake. What do you think, friend? Had you not better attend to your fences at once?

Then There Is Another Evil—The Land Itself Will Go Away

"No," you say, "how can that be?" If a stone wall is broken down around a farm on level ground, a man does not necessarily lose his land, but in many parts of the world, the land is all ups and downs on the sides of the hills, and every bit of ground is terraced and kept up by walls. When the walls fall, the soil slips over them, terrace upon terrace, and the vines and trees go down with it. Then the rain comes and washes the soil away, and nothing is left but barren crags which would starve a lark. In the same manner, a person may so neglect themself, and so neglect the things of God, and become so careless and indifferent about doctrine and holy living, that their power to do good ceases and their mind, heart, and energy all seem to be gone.

The prophet said, "Ephraim also is like a silly dove without heart" (Hosea 7:11). There exist flocks of such silly doves. Those who trifle with religion play with their own soul, and will soon deteriorate into so much of a trifler that they will be averse to solemn thought and incapable of real usefulness. I charge you, dear friends, to be sternly true to yourselves and to your God. Stand for your principles in this evil and wicked day. Now, when everything seems to be turned into marsh and mire and mud, and religious thought appears to be silently sliding and slipping along, descending like a stream of slime into the Dead Sea of Unbelief—get solid walls built around your life, around your faith, and around your character. Stand fast, and having done all, still stand. May God the Holy Spirit cause you to be rooted and grounded, built up and established, fixed and confirmed, and "Cast not away . . . your confidence, which hath great recompence of reward" (Hebrews 10:35).

I Want to Wake Up the Sluggard

I would like to throw a handful of gravel up to his window. It is time to get up, for the sun has drunk up all the dew. He craves "a little more sleep." My dear fellow, if you take a little more sleep, you will never wake at all until you lift up your eyes in another world. Wake at once. Leap from your bed before you are smothered in it. Wake up! Do you not see where you are? You have let things alone until your heart is covered with sins like weeds. You have neglected God and Christ until you have grown worldly, sinful, careless, indifferent, ungodly. I am speaking to some of you who were once named with the sacred name. You have become like someone who is only concerned with this present world, and you are almost as far from being what you ought to be as others who make no profession of faith at all.

Look at yourselves and see what has come of your neglected walls. Then look at some of your fellow Christians, and mark how diligent they are. Look at many among them who are poor and uneducated, and yet they are doing far more than you are doing for the Lord Jesus. In spite of your talents and opportunities, you are an unprofitable servant, letting all things run to waste. Is it not time that you awakened yourself? Look again at others who, like yourself, went to sleep and meant to wake up in a little while. What has become of them? They have fallen into sin and dishonored their character. They have fallen away from the church of God, yet they have only gone a little farther than you have gone. Your state of heart is much the same as theirs, and if you should be tempted as they have been, you will probably make shipwreck as they have done. Remember, you that slumber, that an idle person is ready for anything. A slothful heart is tinder for the devil's tinderbox; does your own heart invite the sparks of temptation?

Remember, lastly, the coming of the Lord Jesus Christ. Shall he come and find you sleeping? Remember the judgment. What will you say to excuse yourself, for opportunities lost, time wasted, and talents wrapped up in a napkin, when the Lord shall come?

As for you, my unconverted friend, if you go dreaming through this world, without any sort of trouble, and never look to the state of your heart at all, you will be lost beyond all question. The slothful can have no hope, for "if the righteous scarcely [are] saved" (1 Peter 4:18), who strive to serve their Lord, where will those appear who sleep on in defiance of the calls of God? Salvation is wholly and alone of grace, as you well know, but God's grace never results in slumbering and indifference. Rather, it tends toward energy, activity, fervor, persistence, and self-sacrifice. May God grant us the indwelling of his Holy Spirit, that all things may be set in order, the sins of our heart destroyed at their roots. May our hearts be protected by sanctifying grace from the destroyers which lurk around, hoping to enter where the wall is low. Lord, please remember us in mercy, fence us in with your power, and keep us from the sloth which would expose us to evil, for Jesus' sake. Amen.

THREE

FROST AND THAW

He giveth snow like wool: he scattereth the hoarfrost
like ashes. He casteth forth his ice like morsels: who
can stand before his cold? He sendeth out his word,
and melteth them: he causeth his wind to blow, and
the waters flow.

(PSALM 147:16–18)

Looking out of our window one morning, we saw the earth robed in a white mantle. In a few short hours the earth had been covered to a considerable depth with snow. We looked out again a few hours later and saw the fields as green as ever, and the plowed fields as bare as if no single flake had fallen. It is no uncommon thing for a heavy fall of snow to be followed by a rapid thaw.

These interesting changes are wrought by God, not only with a purpose toward the outward world but with some design toward the spiritual realm. God is always a teacher. In every action that he performs, he is instructing his own children and opening up to them the road to inner mysteries. Happy are those who find food for their heaven-born spirits, as well as for their mental powers, in the works of the Lord's hand.

I shall ask your attention, first, *to the operations of nature spoken of in the text*; and, secondly, *to those operations of grace of which they are the most fitting symbols.*

CONSIDER FIRST THE OPERATIONS OF NATURE

We shall not consider a few minutes wasted if we call your attention to the hand of God in frost and thaw, even upon natural grounds.

1. Observe the Directness of the Lord's Work

I rejoice, as I read these words, to find how present our God is in the world. It is not written, "the laws of nature produce snow," but "HE *giveth snow*," as if every flake came directly from the palm of his hand. We are not told that certain natural regulations form moisture into hoarfrost, but as Moses took ashes from the furnace and scattered them upon Egypt, so it is said of the Lord, "HE *scattereth the hoarfrost like ashes*." We are not told that the Eternal has set the world in motion and by the operation of its machinery, ice is produced. Instead, we are told that every single granule of ice descending in the hail is from God: "HE *casteth forth his ice like morsels*." Even as the slinger distinctly sends the stone out of his sling, so the path of every hailstone is marked by the Divine power. The ice is called, you observe, *his* ice—and in the next sentence we read of *his* cold. These words make nature strangely magnificent. When we look upon every hailstone as God's hail, and upon every fragment of ice as his ice, how precious the watery diamonds become! When we feel the cold nipping our limbs and penetrating through our clothes, it consoles us to remember that it is *his* cold. When the thaw comes, see how the text speaks of it: "*he sendeth out his word*." He does not leave it to certain forces of nature, but like a king, "*He sendeth out his word and melteth them: he causeth* HIS *wind to blow*." He has a special property in every wind; whether it comes from the north to freeze, or from the south to melt, it is *his* wind. In God's temple, everything speaks of his glory.

Learn to see the Lord in all scenes of the visible universe, for truly he has created all things.

This thought of the directness of the Divine operations must be carried into our lives. It will greatly comfort you if you can see God's hand in your losses and crosses; surely you will not murmur against the direct agency of your God. This manner of thinking will put an extraordinary sweetness into daily mercies and make the comforts of life more comfortable still, because they are from your Father's hand. If your table is meagerly furnished, your heart should still be content, for you know that your Father spread it for you in wisdom and love. He blesses your bread and your water, makes the bare walls of an ill-furnished room as resplendent as a palace, and turns a hard bed into a couch of down. Our Father does it all. We see his smile of love even when others see nothing but the black hand of Death taking away our most beloved. We see a Father's hand when pestilence leaves our cattle dead upon the plain. We see God at work in mercy when we ourselves are stretched upon the bed of languishing. It is ever our Father's act and deed. Do not let us get beyond this, but rather let us expand our view of this truth and remember that it is true of the little as well as of the great. Let the lines of a true poet strike you:

> If pestilence stalk through the land, ye say the Lord hath
> 　　done it—
> Hath he not done it when an aphis creepeth upon the
> 　　rosebud?
> If an avalanche tumbles from its Alp, ye tremble at the
> 　　will of Providence—
> Is not that will as much concerned when the sere leaves
> 　　fall from the poplar?[8]

Let your hearts sing of everything, Jehovah-Shammah, the Lord is there.

2. Observe, with Thanksgiving, the Ease of Divine Working

These verses read as if the making of frost and snow were the simplest matter in all the world. A man puts his hand into a wool-pack and tosses out the wool; God gives snow as easily as that: "He giveth snow like wool." A man takes up a handful of ashes, and throws them into the air, so that they fall around: "He scattereth the hoarfrost like ashes." Frost and snow are marvels of nature. Those who have observed the extraordinary beauty of ice crystals have been enraptured, and yet these crystals are easily formed by the Lord: "He casteth forth his ice like morsels." The Lord scatters the ice crystals just as easily as we, on a wintry day, cast crumbs of bread outside the window to the robins.

When the rivers are frozen solid and the earth is held in iron chains, how does the thaw happen? Not by kindling innumerable fires, nor by sending electric shocks from huge batteries through the interior of the earth. No, instead: "He sendeth out his word, and melteth them; he causeth his wind to blow, and the waters flow." The whole matter is accomplished with a word and a breath. If you and I had any great thing to do, what puffing and panting, what straining and tugging, there would be! Even the great engineers, who perform marvels by machinery, make much noise and stir about it. It is not so with the Almighty One. Our globe spins round in four-and-twenty hours, and yet it does not make so much noise as a humming top; and yonder ponderous worlds rolling in space track their way in silence. If I enter a factory I hear a deafening din, or if I stand near the village mill, which is turned by water dropping over a wheel, there is a never-ceasing click-clack or an undying hum. But God's great wheels revolve without noise or friction; divine machinery works smoothly. This ease is seen in providence as well as in nature. Your heavenly Father is as able to deliver you as he is to melt the snow, and he will deliver you in as simple a manner if you rest in him. He opens his hand and supplies the needs of every living thing as readily as he works in nature. Mark the ease of God's working—all he does is open his hand.

3. Notice the Variety of the Divine Operations in Nature

When the Lord is at work with frost as his tool, he creates snow, a wonderful production with every crystal being a marvel of art. But then he is not content with just snow—from the same water he makes another form of beauty, which we call frost, and yet a third lustrous, sparkling substance in the form of glittering ice. All these he creates by the one agency of cold. What a marvelous variety the educated eye can detect in the various forms of frozen water! The same God who solidified the flood with cold soon melts it with warmth, but even in thaw there is no monotony of manner. The joyous streams rush with such suddenness from their imprisonment that rivers are swollen, and floods cover the plain; at another time, by slow degrees and in scanty droplets, the water regains its freedom. The same variety can be seen in every part of nature. In this world the Lord has a thousand forms of frosty trials with which to try his people, and he has ten thousand beams of mercy with which to cheer and comfort them. He can afflict you with the snow trial, or with the frost trial, or with the ice trial, if he will; and he can also with his word relax the bonds of adversity, doing that in countless ways. Whereas we are tied to two or three methods in accomplishing our will, God is infinite in understanding and works as he wills by ways our mortal minds could never imagine.

4. Consider the Works of God in Nature in Their Swiftness

It was thought a wonderful thing in the days of Ahasuerus that letters were sent by post upon swift dromedaries. In our country we thought we had arrived at the age of miracles when the axles of our cars glowed with speed, and now that the telegraph is at work we stretch out our hands into infinity, but what is our rapidity compared with that of God's operations? As Psalm 147:15 says, "He sendeth forth his commandment upon earth: his word runneth very swiftly." Forth went the word, "Open the treasures of snow," and the flakes descended in innumerable multitudes; and then it was said, "Let them be closed," and not another snowflake was seen. Then the Master spoke: "Let the south wind blow and the snow be melted," and it disappeared at the sound of his voice.

Friend, you cannot tell how soon God may come to your help. "He rode upon a cherub, and did fly:" says David, "Yea, he did fly upon the wings of the wind" (Psalm 18:10). The Lord will come from above to rescue his beloved. He will separate the heavens and come down; he will descend with such speed that he will not linger to draw the curtains of heaven, but he will divide them in his haste. He will make the mountains to flow down at his feet, so he may deliver those who cry out to him in their hour of trouble. That mighty God who can melt the ice so speedily can take to himself the same eagle wings and hurry to your deliverance. Arise, O God! and let your children be helped, from the very break of day.

5. Consider the Goodness of God in All the Operations of Nature and Providence

Think of that goodness negatively: "Who can stand before his cold?" You cannot help thinking of the poor in a hard winter—only a hard heart can forget them when you see the snow lying deep. But suppose that snow continued to fall! What is there to hinder it? The same God who sends us snow for one day could do the like for fifty days if he pleased. Why not? And when the frost pinches us so severely, why should it not be continued month after month? We can only thank the goodness which does not send "His cold" to such an extent that our spirits give up. Travelers to the North Pole tremble at this question: "Who can stand before his cold?" For cold has a degree of omnipotence in it when God is pleased to let it loose. Let us thank God for the restraining mercy by which he holds the cold in check.

Positively, there is mercy in the snow. Isn't that a wonderful metaphor? "He giveth snow *like wool*." The snow is said to warm the earth; it protects those little plants which have just begun to peep above the ground and might otherwise be frostbitten. As with a garment of down, the snow protects new growth from the extreme severity of cold. Hence Watts sings, in his version of the hundred and forty-seventh Psalm—

> His flakes of snow like wool he sends,
> And thus, the springing corn defends.[9]

It was an idea of the ancients that snow warmed the heart of the soil and gave it fertility, and therefore they praised God for it. Certainly, there is much mercy in the frost, for pestilence might run a far longer race if it were not for the frost that cries to it, "Hitherto shalt thou come, but no farther." Destructive insects would multiply until they devoured the precious fruits of the earth, if sharp nights did not destroy millions of them so that these pests were swept off the earth. Though we may hate the cold, we must love the One who ordains the winter. The quaint saying of one of the old writers that "snow is wool, and frost is fire, and ice is bread, and rain is drink," is true, though it sounds like a paradox. There is no doubt that in breaking up the soil, the frost promotes fruitfulness, and so the ice becomes bread. Those agencies that for the moment deprive our workers of their means of sustenance, are the means by which God supplies every living thing. Mark, then, God's goodness as clearly in the snow and frost as in the thaw that clears the winter's work away.

Christian, remember the goodness of God in the frost of adversity. Rest assured that when God is pleased to send out the biting winds of affliction, he is in them—and he is always love, as much love in sorrow as when he breathes upon you the soft south wind of joy. See the lovingkindness of God in every work of his hand! Praise him—he makes summer and winter—let your song go round the year! Praise him—he gives day and sends night—thank him at all hours! Cast not away your confidence, for it has great recompense of reward. As David wove the snow and rain and stormy wind into a song, even so combine your trials, your tribulations, your difficulties and adversities into a sweet psalm of praise and say perpetually—

Let us, with a gladsome mind,
Praise the Lord, for he is kind.[10]

That is all I will say about the operations of nature. It is a very tempting theme, but other fields invite me.

Frost and Thaw Are the Outward Symbols of the Operations of Grace

I would address you very earnestly and solemnly on the operations of grace, of which frost and thaw are the outward symbols. There is a period with God's own people when he comes to deal with them by *the frost of the law*. The law is to the soul as the cutting north wind. Faith can see love in it, but the carnal eye of sense cannot. It is a cold, terrible, comfortless blast. To be exposed to the full force of the law of God is likened to being frostbitten with everlasting destruction, and even to feel it for a season would congeal the marrow of one's bones and make one's whole being stiff with fright. "Who can stand before his cold?" When the law comes forth thundering from its treasury, who can stand before it? The effect of the law upon the soul is to bind up the rivers of human delight. No man can rejoice when the terrors of conscience are upon him. When the law of God is sweeping through the soul, music and dancing lose their joy, the bowl forgets its power to cheer, and the enchantments of earth are broken. The rivers of pleasure freeze to icy despondency. The buds of hope are suddenly nipped, and the soul finds no comfort. It was once satisfied to grow rich, but rust and canker are now upon all gold and silver. Every promising hope is frostbitten, and the spirit is winter-bound in despair. This cold makes the sinner feel how ragged his garments are. In summer he could strut about and imagine his rags as royal robes, but now the cold frost finds every opening in his garment, and in the hands of the terrible law he shivers like the leaves upon the aspen. The north wind of judgment searches him through and through. He did not know what was in him, but now he sees that his inward parts are filled with corruption and rottenness. These are some of the terrors of the wintry breath of the law.

This frost of law and terror only tends to harden. Nothing splits the rock or makes the cliff tumble like frost when followed by thaw, but frost alone makes the earth like a mass of iron, breaking the plowshare which would seek to pierce it. A sinner under the influence of the law of God, apart from the gospel, is hardened by despair and cries, "There is no hope, and therefore I will go after my desires. There is no heaven for me after this life, so I will make a heaven out of this earth; and since hell awaits me, I will at least enjoy such sweets as sin may afford me here." This is not the fault of the law. The blame lies with the corrupt heart which is hardened by it; yet, nevertheless, such is its effect.

When the Lord has worked by the frost of the law, he sends *the thaw of the gospel*. When the south wind blows from the land of promise, bringing precious remembrances of God's loving mercy and tender lovingkindness, the heart begins to soften, and a sense of blood-bought pardon speedily dissolves it. The eyes fill with tears, the heart melts in tenderness, rivers of pleasure flow freely, and buds of hope open in the cheerful air. A heavenly spring whispers to the flowers that were sleeping in the cold earth; they hear its voice and lift up their heads, for "the rain is over and gone; the flowers appear on the earth; the time of the singing of birds is come, and the voice of the turtle is heard in our land" (Song of Solomon 2:11–12). God sends his Word, saying, "Her warfare is accomplished . . . her iniquity is pardoned" (Isaiah 40:2). When that blessedly cheering word comes with power to the soul, and the sweet breath of the Holy Spirit acts like the warm south wind upon the heart, then the waters flow and the mind is filled with holy joy, and light, and liberty.

> The Jewish wintry state is gone,
> The mists are fled, the spring comes on,

The sacred turtle-dove we hear
Proclaim the new, the joyful year.[11]

Having shown you that there is a parallel between frost and thaw in nature and law and gospel in grace, I would utter the same thoughts concerning grace which I gave you concerning nature.

1. We Began with the Directness of God's Works in Nature

Now, beloved friends, we will talk about the *directness of God's works in grace*. When the heart is truly affected by the law of God, when sin is made to appear exceeding sinful, when earthly hopes are frozen to death by the law, when the soul is made to feel its barrenness and utter death and ruin—this is the finger of God. It does not come from the minister. He may have preached earnestly, and God may have used him as an instrument, but it all comes from God. When the thaw of grace comes, I pray that you discern the distinct hand of God in every beam of comfort which gladdens the troubled conscience, for it is the Lord alone who binds up the brokenhearted and heals all their wounds. We are far too apt to stop in instrumentalities. Folly makes men look to sacraments for heart-breaking or heart-healing, but sacraments all say, "It is not in us." Some of you look to the preaching of the Word, and look no higher; but all true preachers will tell you, "It is not in us." Eloquence and earnestness at their highest pitch can neither break nor heal a heart. This is God's work—and not God's secondary work, in the sense in which the philosopher admits that God is in the laws of nature, but rather it is God's personal and immediate work. He puts forth his own hand when the conscience is humbled, and it is by his own right hand that the conscience is eased and cleansed.

I pray that this thought may abide upon your minds, for otherwise you will not praise God, nor will you be sound in doctrine. All departures from sound doctrine on the point of conversion arise from forgetfulness that it is a divine work from first to last; that the faintest desire after Christ is as much the work of God as the gift of his dear

Son; and that through our whole spiritual history—from the Alpha to the Omega—the Holy Spirit works in us to will and to do his own good pleasure. As you have evidently seen the finger of God in casting forth his ice and in sending thaw, so I pray you recognize the handiwork of God in giving you a sense of sin and in bringing you to the Savior's feet. Join together in heartily praising the wonderworking God, who does all things according to the counsel of his will.

> Our seeking thy face
> was the fruit of thy grace;
> Thy goodness deserves and shall have all the praise:
> No sinner can be
> beforehand with Thee;
> Thy grace is preventing, almighty and free.[12]

2. The Ease with Which the Lord Works on Our Souls

There was no effort or disturbance. Transfer that to the work of grace. How easy it is for God to work on our souls! You stubborn sinner, *you* cannot touch him, and even providence has failed to awaken him. He is dead—altogether dead in trespasses and sins. But if the glorious Lord will graciously send forth the wind of his Spirit, that will melt him. The swearing reprobate, whose mouth is blackened with profanity, if the Lord looks upon him with his irresistible grace, he will yet praise God and bless his name and live to his honor. Do not limit the Holy One of Israel. Persecuting Saul became loving Paul, and why should not that person be saved of whose case you almost despair? Your husband may have many points which make his case difficult, but no case is desperate with God. Your son may have offended both against heaven and against you, but God can save the most hardened. The sharpest frost of obstinate sin must yield to the thaw of grace. Even huge icebergs of crime must melt in the Gulf Stream of infinite love.

Friend, I cannot leave this point without a word to you. Perhaps the Master has sent the frost to you, and you think it will never end. Let me encourage you to hope, and yet more, to pray for gracious visitations. Miss Steele's verses will just suit your mournful yet hopeful state.

Stern winter throws his icy chains,
　　Encircling nature round:
How bleak, how comfortless the plains,
　　Late with gay verdure crown'd!

The sun withdraws his vital beams,
　　And light and warmth depart:
And, drooping lifeless, nature seems
　　An emblem of my heart—

My heart, where mental winter reigns
　　In night's dark mantle clad,
Confined in cold, inactive chains;
　　How desolate and sad!

Return, O blissful sun, and bring
　　Thy soul-reviving ray;
This mental winter shall be spring,
　　This darkness cheerful day.[13]

It is easy for God to deliver you. He says, "I have blotted out, as a thick cloud, thy transgressions." (Isaiah 44:22). I stood the other evening looking up at a black cloud which was covering all the heavens, and I thought it would surely rain. I entered the house, and when I came out again the sky was all blue—the wind had driven the cloud away. So may it be with your soul. It is an easy thing for the Lord to put away the sin of repenting sinners. All obstacles which hindered our pardon were removed by Jesus when he died upon the tree, and if you believe in him, you will find that he has cast your sins into the depths of the sea. If you can believe, all things are possible.

3. The Variety of the Lord's Work in Nature

Frost produces a sort of trinity in unity—snow, hoarfrost, ice; and when the thaw comes, its ways are many. So it is with God's work in the heart. Conviction does not come alike to all. Some convictions fall as the snow from heaven: you never hear the flakes descend, they alight so gently one upon the other. There are soft-coming convictions; they are felt, but we can scarcely tell when we began to feel them. A true work of repentance may be of the gentlest kind. On the other hand, the Lord casts forth his ice like morsels, the hailstones rattle against the window, and you think they will surely force their way into the room. And so, to many, convictions come beating down until they remind us of hailstones. There is variety. It is as true a frost which produces the noiseless snow as that which brings forth the terrible hail. Why should you want hailstones of terror? Be thankful that God has visited you, but do not dictate to him the way of his working.

With regard to the gospel thaw—if you have been pardoned by Jesus, do not question the manner of his grace. Thaw is universal and gradual, but its commencement is not always discernible. The chains of winter are unloosed by degrees: the surface ice and snow melt, and by and by the warmth permeates the entire mass until every rock of ice gives way. But while thaw is universal and visible in its effects, you cannot see the mighty power which is doing all this. Even so you must not expect to discern the Spirit of God. You will find him gradually operating upon the entire man, enlightening the understanding, freeing the will, delivering the heart from fear, inspiring hope, waking up the whole spirit, gradually and universally working upon the mind and producing the manifest effects of comfort, and hope, and peace; but you can no more see the Spirit of God than you can see the south wind. The effect of his power is to be felt, and when you feel it, do not marvel if it is somewhat different from what others have experienced. After all, there is a singular likeness in snow and frost and ice, and so there is a remarkable sameness in the experience of all God's children; but still there is a great variety in the inward operations of divine grace.

4. The Rapidity of God's Works

"His word runneth very swiftly" (Psalm 147:15). It did not take many days to get rid of the last snow. A contractor would take many days to cart it away, but God sends forth his word, and the snow and ice disappear at once. So is it with the soul: the Lord often works rapidly when he cheers the heart. You may have spent a long time under the operation of his frosty law, but there is no reason why you should be under it for even another hour. If the Spirit enables you to trust in the finished work of Christ, you may go out of this house rejoicing that every sin is forgiven. Poor soul, do not think that the way from the horrible pit is to climb, step by step, to the top. Oh, no; Jesus can set your feet upon a rock before even an hour has passed. He can in an instant bring you from death to life, from condemnation to justification. "Today shalt thou be with me in paradise," Jesus said to a dying thief, wicked and defiled with sin (Luke 23:43). If we believe in the atoning sacrifice of Jesus Christ, we will be saved.

5. The Goodness of God's Operation in It All

What a blessing that God did not send us more law than he did! "Who can stand before his cold?" When God has taken away from us natural comfort, and made us feel divine wrath in our soul, it is an awful thing. Imagine a haunted individual—nobody needs to be haunted with a worse ghost than the remembrance of their old sins. The childish tale of the sailor with the old man of the mountain on his back, who pressed him more and more heavily, is more than realized in the history of the troubled conscience. If one sin leaps on a person's back, it will sink the sinner through every place he can possibly stand upon; he will go down, down, under its weight, until he sinks to the lowest depths of hell. There is no place where sin can be borne until you stand upon the Rock of Ages, and even there the joy is not that *you* bear it but that Jesus has borne it all for you. The spirit would utterly fail before the law, if it had full sway. Thank God, "he stayeth his rough wind in the day of his east wind" (Isaiah 27:8). At the same time, how thankful we may be, that we ever felt the frost of the law in our soul. The folly of self-righteousness is killed by the winter of conviction. We should have been a thousand times more proud and foolish and worldly than we are, if it had not been for the sharp frost with which the Lord nipped our sin in the bud.

But how will we thank him sufficiently for the thaw of his loving-kindness? How great the change which his mercy made in us as soon as its beams reached our soul! Hardness vanished, cold departed, warmth and love abounded, and the life-floods leaped in their channels. The Lord visited us, and we rose from our grave of despair, even as the seeds arise from the earth. As the bulb of the crocus holds up its golden cup to be filled with sunshine, so did our newborn faith open itself to the glory of the Lord. As the primrose peeps up from the sod to gaze upon the sun, so did our hope look forth for the promise, and delight itself in the Lord. Thank God that springtime has with many of us matured into summer, and winter has gone never to return. We praise the Lord for this every day of our lives, and we will praise him when time shall be no more in that sunny land—

> There everlasting spring abides,
>   and never-withering flowers;
> death, like a narrow sea, divides
>   that heavenly land from ours.[14]

Believe in the Lord, those of you who shiver in the frost of the law, and the thaw of love shall soon bring you warm days of joy and peace. So be it. Amen.

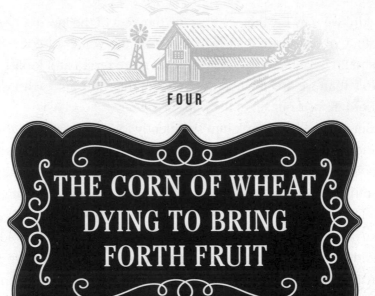

FOUR

THE CORN OF WHEAT DYING TO BRING FORTH FRUIT

And Jesus answered them, saying, The hour is come, that the Son of man should be glorified. Verily, verily, I say unto you, Except a corn of wheat fall into the ground and die, it abideth alone: but if it die, it bringeth forth much fruit. He that loveth his life shall lose it; and he that hateth his life in this world shall keep it unto life eternal.

(John 12:23–25)

Certain Greeks desired to see Jesus. These were Gentiles, and it was remarkable that they should, just at this time, have sought an interview with our Lord. I suppose that the words "We would see Jesus" (John 12:21) did not merely mean that they would like to look at him, for that they could have done in the public streets; but they would "see" him as we speak of seeing a person with whom we wish to hold a conversation. They desired to be introduced to him, and to have a few words of instruction from him.

These Greeks were the advanced guard of that great multitude that no man can number, of all nations, and people, and tongues, who are yet to come to Christ. The Savior would naturally feel a measure of joy at the sight of them, but he did not say much about it, for his mind was absorbed just then with thoughts of his great sacrifice and its results. Yet he took so much notice of the coming of these Gentiles to him that it gave a distinctive depth to the words which are here recorded by his servant John.

I notice that the Savior here *displays his broad humanity*, announcing himself as the "Son of man." He had done so before, but here he does so with new intent. He says, "The hour is come, that the Son of man should be glorified." Not as "the Son of David" does he here speak of himself, but as "the Son of man." No longer does he make prominent the Jewish side of his mission, though as a preacher he was not sent to save the lost sheep of the house of Israel; but as the dying Savior he speaks of himself as one of humankind— not the Son of Abraham or of David, but rather "the Son of man," as much a brother to the Gentile as to the Jew. Let us never forget the broad humanity of the Lord Jesus. In him all people of the earth are joined as one, for he is not ashamed to bear the nature of our universal personhood—black and white, prince and pauper, sage and savage, all see in his veins the one blood by which all people are constituted one family. As the Son of man, Jesus is related by blood to every person everywhere.

Now that the Greeks were included, too, our Lord *speaks of his glory* as approaching. "The hour is come," says he, "that the Son of man should be glorified." He does not say "that the Son of man should be crucified," though that was true, and the crucifixion must come before the glorification; but the sight of those firstfruits from among the Gentiles makes him dwell upon his glory. Though he remembers his death, he speaks rather of the glory which would grow out of his great sacrifice. Remember, friends, that Christ is glorified in the souls he saves. As a physician wins honor by those he heals, so the

Physician of souls gets glory from those who come to him. When these devout Greeks came saying, "Sir, we would see Jesus," though a mere desire to see him is only as the green blade, yet he rejoiced in it as the pledge of the harvest, and he saw in it the dawn of the glory of his cross.

I think, too, that the coming of these Greeks *led the Savior to use the metaphor of the buried corn.* We are informed that wheat was largely mixed up with Grecian mysteries, but that is of small importance. It is more to the point that our Savior was then undergoing the process which would burst the Jewish husk in which, if I may use such terms, his human life had been enveloped. I mean this: in times now past, our Lord said that he was not sent save to the lost sheep of the house of Israel, and when the Syrophoenician woman pleaded for her daughter (Mark 7:25–29), he reminded her of the restricted nature of his commission as a prophet among men. When he sent out the seventy, he bade them not to go into the cities of the Samaritans, but to seek after the house of Israel only. Now, however, that blessed corn of wheat is breaking through its protective outer layer. Even before it is put into the ground to die, the divine corn of wheat begins to show its living power, and the true Christ is being manifested. The Christ of God—though assuredly the Son of David—was, on the Father's side, neither Jew nor Gentile but simply man, and the great sympathies of his heart were with all humankind. He regarded all whom he had chosen as his own brothers and sisters without distinction of sex, or nation, or the period of the world's history in which they should live; and, at the sight of these Greeks, the true Christ came forth and manifested himself to the world as he had not done before. This, perhaps, is the meaning behind the peculiar metaphor which we have now to explain.

In the Scripture passage that began this chapter, dear friends, we have two things upon which I will speak briefly, as I am helped by the Spirit. First, we *have profound doctrinal teaching*, and, secondly, we have *practical moral principle.*

PROFOUND DOCTRINAL TEACHING

Our Savior suggested to his thoughtful disciples a number of what might be called doctrinal paradoxes.

First Paradox—Glorious As He Was, He Was Yet to Be Glorified

"The hour is come, that the Son of man should be glorified." Jesus was always glorious. It was a glorious thing for the human person of the Son of man to be personally one with the Godhead. Our Lord Jesus had also great glory all the while he was on earth, in the perfection of his moral character. The gracious end for which he came here was real glory to him: his condescending to be the Savior of all of us was a great glorification of his loving character. His way of going about his work—the way in which he consecrated himself to his Father and was always about his Father's business, the way in which he put aside Satan's flattery and would not be bribed by all the kingdoms of the world—all this was his glory.

I should not speak incorrectly if I were to say that Christ was never more glorious than when throughout his life on earth he was obscure, despised, rejected, and yet remained the faithful servant of God and the ardent lover of humankind. John 1:14 says, "The Word was made flesh, and dwelt among us, (and we beheld his glory, the glory as of the only begotten of the Father,) full of grace and truth," in which he refers not only to the transfiguration, in which there were special glimpses of the divine glory, but to our Lord's dwelling among men and women in the common walks of life. Saintly, spiritual minds beheld the glory of his life, the glory of grace and truth such as never before had been seen in anyone living on Earth. But though he was, for all intents and purposes, already glorious, Jesus had yet to be glorified. Something more was to be added to his personal honor. Remember, then, that when you think you have the clearest conceptions of your Lord, there is still a glory to be added to all that you can see even with the Word of God in your hands. Glorious as the living

Son of man had been, there was a further glory to come upon him through his death, his resurrection, and his entrance within the veil. He was a glorious Christ, and yet he had to be glorified.

Second Paradox—His Glory Was to Come to Him Through Shame

He says, "The hour is come, that the Son of man should be glorified," and then he speaks of his death. The greatest fullness of our Lord's glory arises out of his emptying himself and becoming obedient to death, even the death on the cross. It is his highest reputation that he made himself of no reputation. His crown derives new luster from his cross; his living is rendered more honorable by the fact of his dying unto sin. Those blessed cheeks would never have been so fair as they are in the eyes of his chosen if they had not once been spat upon. Those dear eyes had never had so overpowering a glance if they had not once been dimmed in the agonies of death for sinners. His hands are as gold rings set with the beryl, but their brightest adornments are the prints of the cruel nails. As the Son of God his glory was all his own by nature, but as Son of man his present splendor is due to the cross, and to the public shame which surrounded it when he bore our sins in his own body. We must never forget this, and if ever we are tempted to merge the crucified Savior in the coming King, we should feel rebuked by the fact that by doing so we would rob our Lord of his highest honor. Whenever you hear men speak lightly of the atonement, stand up for it at once, for out of this comes the main glory of your Lord and Master. They say, "Let him now come down from the cross, and we will believe him" (Matthew 27:42). If he did so, what would remain to be believed? It is on the cross, it is from the cross, it is through the cross that Jesus mounts to his throne, and the Son of man has a special honor in heaven today because he was slain and has redeemed us to God by his blood.

Third Paradox—Jesus Must Be Alone or Abide Alone

Notice the text as I read it: "Except a corn of wheat fall into the ground and die," and so gets alone, "it abideth alone." The Son of man must be alone in the grave, or he will be alone in heaven. He must fall into the ground like the corn of wheat, and be there in the loneliness of death, or else he will abide alone. This is a paradox readily enough explained. Our Lord Jesus Christ as the Son of man—unless he had trodden the winepress alone, unless beneath the olives of Gethsemane he had wrestled on the ground, and as it were sunk into the ground until he died, if he had not been there alone, and if on the cross he had not cried, "My God, my God, why hast thou forsaken me?" (Matthew 27:46) so that he felt quite deserted and alone, like the buried corn of wheat—could not have saved us. If he had not actually died, he would as man have been alone forever: not without the eternal Father and the divine Spirit, not without the company of angels, but there had not been anyone else to keep him company. Our Lord Jesus cannot bear to be alone. A head without a body is a ghastly sight, crown it as you may. Do you not know that the church is his body, the fullness of him that fills all in all? Without his people Jesus would have been a shepherd without sheep; surely it is not a very honorable profession to be a shepherd without a flock.

He would have been a husband without his spouse, but he loves his bride so well that for this purpose he left his Father and become one flesh with her whom he had chosen. He cleaved to her, and died for her; and had he not done so he would have been a bridegroom without a bride. This could never be. His heart is not of the kind that can enjoy a selfish happiness which is shared by none. If you have read Solomon's Song, where the heart of the Bridegroom is revealed, you have seen that he desires the company of his love, his dove, his undefiled. His delights were with the sons of men. Simon Stylites on the top of a pillar is not Jesus Christ. The hermit in his cave may mean well, but he finds no warrant for his solitude in him whose cross he professes to venerate. Jesus was the friend of men and women, not avoiding them but seeking the lost. It was truly said of him, "This man receiveth sinners, and eateth with them" (Luke 15:2). He draws all people to him, and for this cause, he was lifted up from the earth. Yet this great man must have been alone in heaven if he had not been alone in Gethsemane, alone before Pilate, alone when mocked by soldiers, and alone upon the cross. If this precious grain of wheat had not descended into the dread loneliness of death, it had remained alone, but since he died he "bringeth forth much fruit."

Fourth Paradox—Christ Must Die to Give Life

"Except a corn of wheat fall into the ground and die, it abideth alone: but if it die, it bringeth forth much fruit." Jesus must die to give life to others. People who do not think confuse dying with nonexistence and living with existence—very, very different things. Ezekiel 18:4 says, "The soul that sinneth, it shall die." The soul will never go out of existence, but it will die by being severed from God who is its life. There are many individuals who exist and yet do not have true life, and will not see life, but "the wrath of God abideth" on them (John 3:36). The grain of wheat dies when it is put into the ground; do we mean that it ceases to be? Not at all. What is death? It is the resolution of anything possessing life into its primary elements. With us, it is the body parting from the soul; with a grain of wheat, it is the dissolving of the elements which made up the corn. Our divine Lord, when put into the earth, did not see corruption, but his soul was parted from his body for a while, and thus he died; and unless he had literally and actually died, he could not have given life to any of us.

Beloved friends, this teaches us where the vital point of Christianity lies: *Christ's death is the life of his teaching.* If Christ's preaching had been the essential point, or if his example had been the vital point, he could have brought forth fruit and multiplied Christians by his preaching and by his example. But he declares that unless he dies, he will not bring forth fruit. Am I told that this was because his death would be the completion of his example, and the seal of his preaching? I admit that it was so, but I can conceive that if our Lord had rather continued to live on—if he had been here constantly all over the world preaching and living as he did, and if he had wrought miracles as he did, and put forth that mysterious, attracting power, which was always with him, he might have produced a marvelous number of disciples. If his teaching and living had been the way in which spiritual life could have been bestowed, without an atonement, why did not the Savior prolong his life on earth? But the fact is that no one among us can know anything about spiritual life except through the atonement.

There is no way by which we can come to a knowledge of God except through the precious blood of Jesus Christ, by which we have access to the Father. If, as some tell us, the ethical part of Christianity deserves much more of our thought than its particular doctrines, then why did Jesus die at all? The ethical might have been brought out better by a long life of holiness. He might have lived on until now if he had chosen, and still have preached and set an example among us, but he assures us that only by death could he have brought forth fruit. Not with all that holy living? No. Not by that matchless teaching? No. Not one among us could have been saved from eternal death except through an atonement wrought by Jesus' sacrifice. Not one of us could have been quickened into spiritual life except through Christ himself dying and being risen from the dead.

Friends, all the spiritual life there is in the world is the result of Christ's death. We live under a dispensation which shadows forth this truth to us. Life first came into the world by creation: that was lost in the garden. Since then, the father of humanity is Noah, and life by Noah came to us by a typical death, burial, and resurrection. Noah went into the ark, and was shut in, and so buried. In that ark Noah went among the dead, himself enveloped in the rain and in the ark, and he came out into a new world, rising again, as it were, when the waters were assuaged. That is the way of life today. We are dead with Christ, we are buried with Christ, we are risen with Christ, and there is no real spiritual life in this world except that which has come to us by the process of death, burial, and resurrection with Christ.

Do you know anything about this, dear friends? If you do not, you do not know the life of God. You know the theory, but do you know the experimental power of this within your own spirit? Whenever we hear the doctrine of the atonement attacked, let us stand up for it. Let us tell the world that while we value the life of Christ even more than they do, we know that it is not the example of Christ that saves anybody, but instead his death for our sakes. If the blessed Christ had lived here all these many years, without sin, teaching all his marvelous precepts with his own sublime and simple eloquence, he would have not produced one single atom of spiritual life among all of human-kind. Without dying he brings forth no fruit. If you want life, my dear friend, you will not get it as an unrepentant individual by attempting to imitate the example of Christ. You may get good of a certain sort that way, but you will never obtain spiritual life and eternal salvation by that method. You must believe that Jesus died for you. You have to understand that the blood of Jesus Christ, God's dear Son, cleanses us from all sin. When you have learned that truth, you will be able to study his life with advantage, but unless you recognize that the grain of wheat is cast into the ground and made to die, you will never real-ize any fruit from it in your own soul, or see fruit in the souls of others.

One other blessed lesson of deep divinity we can learn from the Scripture passage: *since Jesus Christ did really fall into the ground and die, we may expect much as the result of it.* "If it die, it bringeth forth much fruit." Some have a little Christ, and they expect to see little things come of him. I have met with good people who appear to think that Jesus Christ died for the sound people who worship at Zoar Chapel and, perhaps, for a few more who go to Ebenezer in a neighboring town, and they hope that one day a chosen few—a scanty company indeed they are, and they do their best by mutual quarreling to make them fewer—will glorify God for the salvation of a very small remnant. I will not blame these dear friends, but I do wish that their hearts were more generous. We do not yet know all the fruit that is to come out of our Lord Jesus. May there not come a day when the millions of London shall worship God with one consent?

I look for a day when the knowledge of the glory of God shall cover the earth as the waters cover the sea, when kings shall fall down before the Son of God, and all nations shall call him blessed. "It is too much to expect," says one. "Missions make very slow progress." I know all that, but missions are not the seed. All that we look for is to come out of that corn of wheat which fell into the ground and died— this will bring forth much fruit. When I think of my Master's blessed person as perfect Son of God and Son of man, when I think of the infinite glory which he laid aside and of the indescribable pangs he bore, I ask whether angels can understand the value of the sacrifice he offered. God only knows the love of God that was manifested in the death of his Son, and do you think there will be all this planning and working and sacrifice of infinite love, and then an insignificant result? It is not like God that it should be so. The trials of the Son of God will not bring forth only a little bit of good. The result will be equivalent with the means, and the effect will be parallel with the cause. The Lord shall reign forever and ever. Hallelujah! As the groan- ings of the cross must have astounded angels, so will the results of the cross amaze the seraphim and make them admire the excess of glory which has arisen from the shameful death of their Lord. Oh beloved, great things are yet to come from the work of Jesus. Be courageous, you that are disheartened. Be brave, you soldiers of the cross. Victory awaits your banner. Wait patiently, work hopefully, suffer joyfully, for the kingdom is the Lord's, and he is the governor among the nations.

PRACTICAL MORAL PRINCIPLE

Now that I have spoken about profound divinity, I will close with a few words about PRACTICAL INSTRUCTION. Know that what is true of Christ is in measure true of every child of God: "Except a corn of wheat fall into the ground and die, it abideth alone: but if it die, it bringeth forth much fruit." This is applicable to our own lives, as the next verse indi- cates: "He that loveth his life shall lose it; and he that hateth his life in this world shall keep it unto life eternal."

1. We Must Die If We Are to Live

There is no spiritual life for you, for me, for any man, except by dying into it. Do you have a finespun righteousness of your own? It must die. Do you have any faith in yourself? It must die. Only then can you enter into life. The withering power of the Spirit of God must be experienced before his quickening influence can be known: "The grass withereth, the flower fadeth: because the spirit of the Lord bloweth upon it" (Isaiah 40:7). You must be slain by the sword of the Spirit before you can be made alive by the breath of the Spirit.

2. We Must Surrender Everything to Keep It

"He that loveth his life shall lose it." Friend, you can never have spiritual life, hope, joy, peace, or heaven, except by giving everything up into God's hands. You shall have everything in Christ when you are willing to have nothing of your own. You must ground your weapons of rebellion, you must drop the plumes of your pride, you must give up into God's hand all that you are and all that you have; and if you do not lose everything in will, you will lose everything in fact—indeed, you have lost it already. A full surrender of everything to God is the only way to keep it. Some of God's people find this literally true. Wealthy people have worshipped their wealth, and as they were God's people, he has broken their idols into pieces. You must lose your all if you would keep it, and renounce your most precious thing if you would have it preserved to you.

3. We Must Lose Self in Order to Find Self

"He that hateth his life shall keep it unto life eternal." You must entirely give up living for yourself, and then you yourself shall live. Those who live for themselves do not live; they lose the essence, the pleasure, the crown of existence. But if you live for others and for God, you will find the life of life. "But seek ye first the kingdom of God, and his righteousness; and all these things shall be added unto you" (Matthew 6:33). There is no way of finding yourself in personal joy like losing yourself in the joy of others.

Once more, if you *wish to be the means of life to others, you must in your measure die yourself.* "Oh," you say, "will it actually come to death?" Well, it may not, but you should be prepared for it if it should. Who are those who have most largely blessed the present age? I will tell you. I believe we owe our gospel liberties mainly to the poor men and women who died at the stake for the faith. Call them Lollards, Anabaptists, or what you will, the people who died for their faith gave life to the holy cause. Some of all ranks did this, from bishops downward to poor boys. Many of them could not preach from the pulpit, but they preached grander sermons as they were being persecuted than all the reformers could thunder from their rostrums. They fell into the ground and died, and their fruit abides to this day. The self-sacrificing death of her saints was the life and increase of the church. If we wish to achieve a great purpose, establish a great truth, and raise up a great agency for good, it must be by the surrender of ourselves— indeed, of our very lives—to the one all-absorbing purpose. In no other way can we succeed. You cannot give to others without taking much out of yourself. Those who serve God and find that it is easy work will find it hard work to give their account to God one day. A sermon that costs nothing is worth nothing; if it did not come from the heart, it will not go to the heart. Take it as a rule that wear and tear must go on, even to exhaustion, if we are to be largely useful. Death precedes growth. The Savior of others cannot save himself. We must not, therefore, grudge the lives of those who die under evil climates, if they die for Christ. Nor must we murmur if here and there God's best servants are cut down by exhaustion, for it is the law of divine agriculture that by death comes increase.

And you, dear friend, must not say, "Oh, I cannot longer teach in the Sunday school. I work so hard all the week that I—I—I . . ." Shall I finish the sentence for you? You work so hard for yourself all the week that you cannot work for God one day in the week. Is that it? "No, not quite so, but I am so exhausted." Very true, but think of your Lord. He knew what weariness was for you, and yet he wearied not in well-doing. You will never sweat blood as he did. Come, dear friend, will you be a corn of wheat laid up on the shelf alone? Will you be like that wheat in the mummy's hand, unfruitful and forgotten, or would you grow? I hear you say, "Sow me somewhere." I will try to do so. Let me drop you into the Sunday school field, or into the tract-handing-out acre, or into the street-preaching parcel of land. "But if I make any great exertion, it will half kill me." Yes, and if it shall quite kill, you will then prove the verse, "If it die, it bringeth forth much fruit." Those who have killed themselves of late in our Lord's service are not so numerous that we need be distressed by the fear that an enormous sacrifice of life is likely to occur. Little cause is there just now to repress fanaticism, but far more reason to denounce self-seeking. My friends, let us rise to a condition of consecration more worthy of our Lord and of his glorious cause, and henceforth may we be eager to be as the buried, hidden, dying, yet fruit-bearing wheat for the glory of our Lord. Here have I merely glanced at the passage; another day may it be our privilege to dive into its depths.

FIVE

THE PLOWMAN

Doth the plowman plow all day to sow?

[Isaiah 28:24]

Unless they are cultivated, fields yield us nothing but briers and thistles. In this we may see ourselves. Unless the great Gardener shall till us by his grace, we will produce nothing that is good, but everything that is evil. If one of these days I hear that a country has been discovered where wheat grows without the work of the farmer, I may then, perhaps, hope to find one of our kind who will bring forth holiness without the grace of God. Up until this very time, all land on which the foot of humankind has trodden has needed labor and care; and even so among us the need of gracious tillage is universal. Jesus says to all of us, "Ye must be born again" (John 3:7). Unless God the Holy Spirit breaks up the heart with the plow of the law and sows it with the seed of the gospel, not a single ear of holiness will any of us produce, even though we may be children of godly parents and regarded as excellent moral people by those with whom we live.

The plow is needed not only to produce that which is good but to destroy that which is evil. There are diseases which, in the course of ages, wear themselves out and do not appear again among us, and there may be forms of vice, which under changed circumstances do not so much abound as they used to. But human nature will always remain the same, and therefore there will always be plentiful crops of the weeds of sin in our fields, which nothing can control but spiritual gardening, carried on by the Spirit of God. You cannot destroy weeds by exhortations, nor can you tear out the roots of sin from the soul by moral persuasion; something sharper and more effective must be used on them. God must put his own right hand to the plow, or the hemlock of sin will never be replaced by the corn of holiness. Good is never spontaneous in unrenewed humanity, and evil is never cut up until the plowshare of almighty grace is driven through it.

The passage leads our thoughts in this direction and gives us practical guidance through asking the simple question, "Doth the plowman plow all day to sow?" *This question may be answered in the affirmative*, "Yes, in the proper season he does plow all day to sow"; and secondly, *this passage may more properly be answered in the negative*, "No, the plowman does not plow every day to sow; he has other work to do according to the season."

Our Passage May Be Answered in the Affirmative

"Yes, the plowman does plow all day to sow." When it is plowing time, he keeps at it until his work is done. If it requires one day, or two days, or twenty days to finish his fields, he continues at his task while the weather permits. The perseverance of the plowman is instructive, and it teaches us a double lesson. First, when the Lord comes to plow our hearts, he plows all day, and herein is his patience. Secondly, so ought the Lord's servants to labor all day with our hearts, and herein is our perseverance.

"Doth the plowman plow all day?" *So does God plow the heart of man, and herein is his patience.* The team was in the field—in the case of some of us, very early in the morning, for our first recollections have to do with conscience and the furrows of pain which it made in our youthful mind. When we were little children we woke in the night under a sense of sin; our fathers' teaching and our mothers' prayers made strong impressions on us, and though we did not then yield our hearts to God, we were greatly stirred and all indifference to religion was made impossible. When we were children, the reading of a chapter in the Word of God, or a speaker at a Bible class, or a solemn sermon, so affected us that we felt uneasy for weeks. The strivings of the Spirit of God within urged us to think of higher and better things. Though we quenched the Spirit, though we stifled conviction, we still bore the marks of the plowshare; furrows were made in the soul, and certain foul weeds of evil were cut up by the roots, although no seed of grace had been yet sown in our hearts. Some have continued in this state for many years, plowed but not sown; but, blessed be God, it was not so with others of us, for we had not left childhood before the good seed of the gospel fell upon our heart.

There are many who do not yield to God's grace, and with them the plowman plows all day to sow. I have seen the young man coming to London in his youth, yielding to its temptations, drinking in its poisoned sweets, violating his conscience, and yet continuing unhappy in it all, fearful, unrestful, stirred about even as the soil is agitated by the plow. In how many cases has this kind of work gone on for years, and all to no avail? I have also known the man come to middle life, and still he has not received the good seed, neither has the ground of his hard heart been thoroughly broken up. He has gone on in business without God; day after day he has risen and gone to bed again with no more religion than his horses, and yet all this while there has been ringing in his ears warnings of judgment to come, and chidings of conscience, so that he has not been at peace. After a powerful sermon he has not enjoyed his meals, or been able to sleep, for he has asked himself, "What shall I do in the end?" The plowman has plowed all day, until the evening shadows have lengthened, and the day has faded to a close. What a mercy it is when the furrows are at last made ready and the good seed is cast in, to be received, nurtured, and multiplied a hundredfold.

It is sobering to remember that we have seen this plowing continue until the sun has touched the horizon and the night dews have begun to fall. Even then the long-suffering God has followed up his work—plowing, plowing, plowing, plowing, until darkness ended all. Do I address any aged ones whose lease must soon run out? I would affectionately beg them to consider their position. What! Sixty years old and yet unsaved? Forty years did God allow the Israelites to wander in the wilderness, but he has borne with you for sixty years. Seventy years old, and yet not converted? Ah, my friend, you will have but little time in which to serve your Savior before you go to heaven. But will you go there at all? Is it not growing dreadfully likely that you will die in your sins and perish forever? How happy are those who are brought to Christ in early life; but still remember—

> While the lamp holds out to burn,
> The vilest sinner may return.[15]

It is late, it is very late, but it is not too late. The plowman plows all day; and the Lord waits that he may be gracious unto you. I have seen many aged persons converted, and therefore I would encourage other old folks to believe in Jesus. I once read a sermon in which a minister asserted that he had seldom known any converted who were over forty years of age if they had been hearers of the gospel all their lives. There is certainly much need to caution those who are guilty of delay, but there must be no manufacturing of facts. Whatever that minister might think, or even observe, my own observation leads me to believe that about as many people are converted to God at one age as at another, taking into consideration the fact that the young are much more numerous than the old. It is a dreadful thing to have remained an unbeliever all these years, but the grace of God does not stop short at a certain age. Those who enter the vineyard at the eleventh hour shall have their penny, and grace shall be glorified in the old as well as in the young. Come along, old friend, Jesus Christ invites you to come to him even now, though you have waited so long. You have been a sadly tough piece of ground, and the plowman has plowed all day; but if at last the sods are turned, and the heart is lying in ridges, there is hope of you yet.

"Doth the plowman plow all day?" I answer—Yes, however long the day may be, God in mercy plows still; he is long-suffering and full of tenderness and mercy and grace. Do not spurn such patience, but yield to the Lord who has acted toward you with so much gentle love.

The verse, however, not only sets forth patience on God's part, but it teaches *perseverance on our part.* "Doth the plowman plow all day?" Yes, he does; then if I am seeking Christ, ought I to be discouraged because I do not immediately find him? The promise is, "for every one that asketh receiveth; and he that seeketh findeth; and to him that knocketh it shall be opened" (Matthew 7:8). There may be reasons why the door is not opened at our first knock. What then? "Doth the plowman plow all day?" Then will I knock all day. It may be that at the first seeking, I do not find it; what then? "Doth the plowman plow all day?" Then I will seek all day. It may happen that at my first asking, I shall not receive; what then? "Doth the plowman plow all day?" Then I will ask all day. Friends, if you have begun to seek the Lord, the short way is, "Believe on the Lord Jesus Christ, and thou shalt be saved." (Acts 16:31). Do that at once. In the name of God, do it at once, and you are saved at once. May the Spirit of God bring you to faith in Jesus, and may you be at once in the kingdom of Christ. But if perhaps in seeking the Lord, you are ignorant of this or do not see your way, never give up seeking. Get to the foot of the cross, lay hold of it, and cry, "If I perish, I will perish here. Lord, I come to you in Jesus Christ for mercy, and if you are not pleased to look at me immediately and forgive my sins, I will cry to you until you do." When God's Holy Spirit brings us to downright earnest prayer which will not take a denial, we are not far from peace. Careless indifference and shilly-shallying with God hold us in bondage. We find peace when our hearts are roused to strong resolve to seek until they find. I like to see people search the

Scriptures until they learn the way of salvation, and hear the gospel until their souls live by it. If they are resolved to drive the plow through doubts and fears and difficulties, until they come to salvation, they will soon come to it by the grace of God.

The same is true in seeking the salvation of others. "Doth the plowman plow all day?" Yes, when it is plowing time. Then, I will work on, and on, and on. I will pray and preach, or pray and teach, however long the day may be that God shall appoint me, for—

> 'Tis all my business here below
> The precious gospel seed to sow.[16]

Brother or sister worker, are you getting a little weary? Never mind, rouse yourself, and plow on for the love of Jesus and dying men. Our day of work has in it only the appointed hours, and while they last let us fulfill our task. Plowing is hard work, but as there will be no harvest without it, let us put forth all our strength and never flag until we have performed our Lord's will, and by his Holy Spirit wrought conviction in the souls of others. Some soils are very hard, and cling together, and the labor is heartbreaking. Others are like the untilled waste, full of roots and tangled bramble; they need a steam plow, and we must pray the Lord to make us such, for we cannot leave them untilled and therefore must put forth more strength that the labor may be done.

I heard some time ago of a minister who called to see a poor man who was dying, but he was not able to gain admittance. He called the next morning, and some idle excuse was made so that he could not see him. He called again the next morning, but he was still refused. He went on until he had called twenty times in vain, but on the twenty-first occasion he was permitted to see the sufferer, and by God's grace he saved a soul from death. "Why do you tell your child a thing twenty times?" someone asked a mother. "Because," said she, "I find nineteen times is not enough." Now, when a soul is to be plowed, it may so happen that hundreds of furrows will not do it. What then?

Why, plow all day until the work is done. Whether you are ministers, missionaries, teachers, or private soulwinners, never grow weary, for your work is noble and the reward of it is infinite. The grace of God is seen in our being permitted to engage in such holy service; it is greatly magnified in sustaining us in it, and it will be preeminently conspicuous in enabling us to hold out until we can say, "I have finished the work which you gave me to do."

We prize that which costs us labor and service, and we will set a higher value upon the saved ones when the Lord grants them to our efforts. It is good for us to learn the value of our sheaves by going forth weeping to the sowing. When you think of the plowman's plowing all day, be moved to plod on in earnest efforts to win souls. Seek—

> With cries, entreaties, tears, to save,
> To snatch them from the gaping grave.[17]

Does the plowman plow all day for a little bit of oats or barley, and will you not plow all day for souls that will live forever, if saved, to adore the grace of God, or will live forever, if unsaved, in outer darkness and woe? By the terrors of the wrath to come and the glory that is to be revealed, prepare yourself for hard work, and plow all day.

I would beg all the members of our churches to keep their hands on the gospel plow with their eyes set straight before them. "Doth the plowman plow all day?" Let Christians do the same. Start close to the hedge, and go right down to the bottom of the field. Plow as close to the ditch as you can, and leave small headlands. If though there are fallen women, thieves, and drunkards in the slums around you, do not neglect any of them; for if you leave a stretch of land to the weeds, they will soon spread among the wheat.

When you have gone right to the end of the field once, what should you do next? Why, just turn around and go back to the place you started from. And when you have already been up and down, what next? Why, up and down again. And what next? Why, up and down again. You have visited that district with tracts; do it again, fifty-two times in the year—multiply your furrows. We must learn how to continue in well doing. Your eternal destiny is to go on doing good for ever and ever, and it is well to go through a rehearsal here. So just plow on, plow on, and look for results as the reward of continued perseverance. Plowing is not done with a skip and jump; the plowman plows all day. Dash and flash are all very fine in some things, but not in plowing; there the work must be steady, persistent, regular. Certain people soon give it up; it wears out their gloves, blisters their soft hands, tires their bones, and makes them physically more exhausted than they care for. Those whom the Lord fills with his grace will keep to their plowing year after year, and they shall have their reward. "Doth the plowman plow all day?" Then let us do the same, being assured that one day every hill and valley will be tilled and sown, and every desert and wilderness will yield a harvest for our Lord, and the angel reapers shall descend, and the shouts of the harvest home will fill both earth and heaven.

Our Passage May Be Answered in the Negative

"Doth the plowman plow all day to sow?" No, he does not always plow. After he has plowed, he breaks the clods, sows, reaps, and threshes. In the chapter before us you will see that other works of farming are mentioned. The plowman has many other things to do beside plowing. There is an advance in what he does; this teaches us that there is the like on God's part, and should be the like on ours.

First, *on God's part, there is an advance in what he does.* "Doth the plowman plow all day?" No, he goes forward with other matters. It may be that in the case of some of you, the Lord has been using certain painful actions to plow you. You are feeling the terrors of the law, the bitterness of sin, the holiness of God, the weakness of the flesh, and the shadow of the wrath to come. Is this going to last forever? Will it continue until the spirit fails and the soul expires? Listen: "Doth the plowman plow all day?" No, he is preparing for something else—he plows to sow. This is how the Lord deals with you; therefore, be of good courage, as there is an ending to the wounding and slaying, and better things are in store for you. You are poor and needy—and you seek water, and there is none and you are thirsty—but the Lord will hear you and deliver you. He will not contend forever, neither will he always be angry. He will turn again, and he will have compassion upon us. He will not always make furrows by his chiding; he will come and cast in the precious corn of consolation, and water it with the dews of heaven and smile upon it with the sunlight of his grace. And there will soon be in you, first the blade, then the ear, after that the full corn in the ear, and in due season you shall joy as with the joy of harvest.

Those of you who are painfully wounded in the place of dragons, I hear you cry, "Does God always send terror and conviction of sin?" Listen to this: "If ye be willing and obedient, ye shall eat the good of the land" (Isaiah 1:19), and what is the call of God to the willing and obedient but this: "Believe on the Lord Jesus Christ, and thou shalt be saved" (Acts 16:31). You will be saved now, find peace now, if you will stop looking to your own good works to save you, and will turn to him who paid the ransom for you upon the tree. The Lord is gentle and tender and full of compassion; he will not always chide, neither will he keep his anger forever. Many of your doubts and fears come of unbelief, or of Satan, or of the flesh, and are not of God at all. Blame him not for what he does not send and does not wish you to suffer. His mind is for your peace, not for your distress; for so he speaks: "Comfort ye, comfort ye my people, saith your God. Speak ye comfortably to Jerusalem, and cry unto her, that her warfare is accomplished, that her iniquity is pardoned" (Isaiah 40:1–2); and, "I have blotted out, as a thick cloud, thy transgressions, and, as a cloud, thy sins: return unto me; for I have redeemed thee" (Isaiah 44:22). He has smitten, but he will smile; he has wounded, but he will heal; he has slain, but he will make alive; we should turn to him at once and receive comfort at his hands. The plowman does not plow forever, or else he would reap no harvest; and God is not always heart-breaking—he also draws near on heart-healing errands.

You see, then, that the great Gardener advances from painful actions, and I want you to note that he goes on to *productive work* in the hearts of his people. He will take away the furrows; you shall not see them, for the corn will cover them with beauty. As she that was in agony remembers no more her sorrow for joy that a man is born into the world, so shall you, who are under the legal rod, remember no more the misery of conviction, for God will sow you with grace and make your soul—even your poor, barren soul—bring forth fruit for his praise and glory. "Oh!" says one, "I wish that would come true to me." It will. "Doth the plowman plow all day to sow?" You expect by-and-by to see plowed fields clothed with springing corn; and you may look to see repentant hearts gladdened with forgiveness. And so be of good courage.

You shall advance, also, to a *joyful experience*. See that plowman; he whistles as he plows, he does not own much of this world's goods, but still he is merry. He looks forward to the day when he will be on the top of the big wagon, joining in the shout of the harvest home, and so he plows in hope, expecting a crop. And, dear soul, God will yet joy and rejoice over you when you believe in Jesus Christ, and you, too, shall be brimful of joy. Be of good cheer—the better portion is yet to come, press forward to it. Gospel sorrowing leads on to gospel hoping, believing, rejoicing, and the rejoicing knows no end. God will not chasten all day, but he will lead you on from strength to strength, from glory unto glory, until you will be like him. This, then, is the advance that there is in God's work among men, from painful actions to productive work and joyful experience.

But what if the plowing should never lead to sowing? What if you should be not responsive to him, and should go on to resist it all? Then God will try again, but it will be to put up the plow, and to command the clouds that they rain no rain upon the land, and then its end is to be burned. Friend, there is nothing more awful than for your soul to be left uncultivated, with God himself giving you up. Surely that is hell. He that is unholy will be unholy still. The law of fixed character will operate eternally, and no hand of the merciful One shall come near to till the soul again. What worse than this can happen?

We conclude by saying that *this advance is a lesson to us*, for we, too, are to go forward. "Doth the plowman plow all day?" No, he plows to sow, and in due time he sows. Some churches seem to think that all they have to do is to plow; at least, all they attempt is a kind of scratching of the soil, and talking of what they are going to do. It is fine talk, certainly; but does the plowman plow all day? You may write up a large program and promise great things, but pray do not stop there. Don't be making furrows all day; do get to your sowing. I fancy that those who promise most, perform the least. Men who do much in the world have no plan at first. Their course works itself out by its own inner force by the grace of God; they do not propose but instead perform. They do not plow all day to sow, but they are like our Lord's servant in the parable of whom he said, "A sower went out to sow his seed" (Luke 8:5).

Let the ministers of Christ also follow the rule of progress. *Let us go from preaching the law to preaching the gospel.* "Doth the plowman plow all day?" He does plow; he would not sow in hope if he had not first prepared the ground. Robbie Flockhart, who preached for years in the Edinburgh streets, says, "It is in vain to sew with the silk thread of the gospel, unless you use the sharp needle of the law." Some of my fellow believers do not care to preach eternal wrath and its terrors. This is a cruel mercy, for they ruin souls by hiding from them their ruin. If they must attempt to sew without a needle, I cannot help it; but I do not mean to be so foolish myself. My needle may be old-fashioned, but it is sharp, and when it carries with it the silken thread of the gospel, I am sure good work is done by it. You cannot get a harvest if you are afraid of disturbing the soil, nor can you save souls if you never warn them of hellfire. We must tell the sinner what

God has revealed about sin, righteousness, and judgment to come. Still, friends, we must not plow all day. No, no, the preaching of the law is only preparatory to the preaching of the gospel. The stress of our business lies in proclaiming glad tidings. We are not followers of John the Baptist but of Jesus Christ; we are not rugged prophets of woe but joyful heralds of grace. Be not satisfied with revival services, and stirring appeals, but preach the doctrines of grace so as to bring out the full compass of covenant truth. Plowing has had its turn, now it is time for planting and watering. Reproof may now give place to consolation. We are first to make disciples of men, and then to teach them to observe the things Jesus has commanded us. We must pass on from the rudiments to the higher truths, from laying foundations to further upbuilding.

And now, another lesson to those of you who are as yet hearers and nothing more. I want you to go from plowing to something better, namely, *from hearing and fearing to believing*. How many years some of you have been hearing the gospel! Do you mean to continue in that state forever? Will you never believe in him of whom you hear so much? You have been stirred up a good deal; the other night you went home almost brokenhearted. I should think you are plowed enough by this time, and yet you have not received the seed of eternal life, for you have not believed in the Lord Jesus. It is dreadful to be always on the brink of everlasting life, and yet never to be alive. It will be an awful thing to be almost in heaven, and yet forever shut out. It is a wretched thing to rush into a railway station just in time to see the train steaming out; I had much rather be half an hour behind time. To lose a train by half a second is most annoying. If you go on as you have done for years, you will have your hand on the latch of heaven, and yet be shut out. You will be within a hair's breadth of glory, and yet be covered with eternal shame. Beware of being so near to the kingdom, and yet lost; almost, but not altogether saved.

God grant that you may not be among those who are plowed, and plowed, and plowed, and yet never sown. It will be of no avail at the last to cry, "Lord, we have eaten and drunk in your presence, and you have taught in our streets. We had a seat at the chapel, we attended the services on week-nights as well as on Sundays, we went to prayer meetings, we joined a Bible class, we distributed tracts, we gave our offering, we renounced every open sin, we prayed, and read a chapter of the Bible every day." All these things may be done, and yet there may be no saving faith in the Lord Jesus. Take heed lest your Lord should answer, "With all this, your heart never came to me; therefore, depart from me, I never knew you." If Jesus once knows a person, he always knows them. He can never say to *me*, "I never knew you," for he has known me, as his poor dependent, a beggar for years at his door. Some of you have been all that is good except that you never came into contact with Christ, never trusted him, never knew him. How sad your state! Will it be always so?

Lastly, I would say to you who are being plowed and are agitated about your souls, go at once to the next stage of believing. If people knew how simple a thing believing is, surely they would believe. Yet they do not know it, and it becomes all the more difficult for them because in itself it is so easy. The difficulty of believing lies in there being no difficulty in it. "If the prophet had bid thee do some great thing, wouldest thou not have done it?" (2 Kings 5:13). Oh, yes, you would have done it, and you would have thought it easy too; but when he simply says, "Wash, and be clean," there is a difficulty with pride and self. If you can truly say that you are willing to humble your pride, and do anything which the Lord bids you, then I pray you understand that there is no further preparation required, and believe in Jesus at once. May the Holy Spirit make you sick of self and ready to accept the gospel. The Word is near to you; let it be believed. It is in your mouth; let it be swallowed down. It is in your heart; let it be trusted. With your heart believe in Jesus, and with your mouth confess of him, and you shall be saved. A main part of faith lies in the giving up of all other confidences. Give up at once every false hope. I tried once to show what faith was by quoting Dr. Watts's lines:

A guilty, weak, and helpless worm,
  On thy kind arms I fall.
Be thou my strength, and righteousness,
  My Jesus and my all.[18]

I tried to represent faith as falling into Christ's arms, and I thought I made it so plain that the wayfaring man could make no mistake. When I had finished preaching, a young man came to me and said, "But, sir, I cannot fall into Christ's arms." I replied at once, "Tumble into them anyhow; faint away into Christ's arms, or die into Christ's arms, so long as you get there." Many talk of what they can do and what they cannot do, and I fear they miss the vital point. Faith is leaving off *can*-ing and *cannot*-ing, and leaving it all to Christ, for *he* can do all things, though you can do nothing. "Doth the plowman plow all day to sow?" No, he makes progress, and goes from plowing to sowing. Go, and do thou likewise; sow unto the Spirit the precious seed of faith in Christ, and the Lord will give you a joyous harvest.

SIX

PLOWING THE ROCK

*Shall horses run upon the rock? will one plow there
with oxen?*

(Amos 6:12)

These expressions are proverbs, taken from the familiar sayings of
the east country. A proverb is generally a sword with two edges,
or, if I may so say, it has many edges, or is all edge, and hence it may
be turned this way and that way, and every part of it will have force
and point. A proverb has often many bearings, and you cannot always
tell what the precise meaning of the person was who uttered it. An
ancient commentator asserts that it has seven meanings, and that any
one of them would be consistent with the context. I cannot deny the
assertion, and if it is correct, it is only one among many instances of
the manifold wisdom of the Word of God. Like those curiously carved
Chinese balls in which there is one ball within another, so in many a
holy text there is sense within sense, teaching within teaching, and
each one worthy of the Spirit of God.

The first meaning of the verse, about which I will say just a word
or two, is this: The prophet is discussing with the ungodly their *pursuit of happiness where it never can be found.* These ungodly people

were endeavoring to grow rich and great and strong by oppression. The prophet says, "Ye have turned judgment into gall, and the fruit of righteousness into hemlock" (Amos 6:12). Justice was bought and sold among them, and the book of the law was made the instrument of fraud. "Yet," says the prophet, "there is no gain to be gotten in this way—no real profit, no true happiness. As well may horses run upon a rock, and oxen plow the sand, it is labor in vain."

If any of you try to content yourselves with this world, if any of you hope to find a heaven in the midst of your business and your family without looking upward for it, you labor in vain. If you hope to find pleasure in sin, and think that it will go well with you if you despise the law of God, you will make a great mistake. You might as well seek for roses in the grottoes of the sea, or look for pearls on the pavements of the city. You will find what your soul requires nowhere but in God. To seek after happiness in evil deeds is to plow a rock of granite. To labor after true prosperity by dishonest means is as useless as to till the sandy shore. "Wherefore do ye spend money for that which is not bread? and your labour for that which satisfieth not?" (Isaiah 55:2). Young people, you are killing yourself with ambition; you seek your own honor and payment, and this is a poor, poor object for an immortal soul. Others of you are wearing out your life with care; your mind and body both fail you in endeavoring to amass riches, as if a person's life consisted in the abundance of things possessed. You are plowing a rock; your cares will not bring you joy of heart or contentment of spirit; your toil will end in failure. And you, too, who labor to weave a righteousness by your works apart from Christ and fancy that with the diligent use of outward ceremonies, you may be able to do the work of the Holy Spirit upon your own heart—you, too, are plowing thankless rock. The strength of fallen nature exerted at its utmost can never save a soul. Why, then, plow the rock any longer? Give over the foolish task.

So far, I believe, we have not misread the passage, but have mentioned a very probable meaning of the words. Still another strikes me, which I think equally suitable, and upon it I shall dwell, by God's help.

It is this: *God will not always send his ministers to call others to repentance.* When people's hearts remain stubborn, and they do not and will not repent, then God will not always deal with them in mercy. "My Spirit shall not always strive with man" (Genesis 6:3). There is a time of plowing, but when it is evident that the heart is willfully hardened, then wisdom itself suggests to mercy that she should give over her efforts. "Shall horses run upon the rock? will one plow there with oxen?" No, there is a limit to the efforts of kindness, and in fullness of time the labor ceases, and the rock remains unplowed henceforth and forever.

MINISTERS LABOR TO BREAK UP PEOPLE'S HEARTS

The wise preacher tries by the power of the Holy Ghost to break up the hard clods of the heart, so that it may receive the heavenly seed.

Many truths are used like sharp plowshares to break up the heart. Individuals must be made to feel that they have sinned, and they must be led to repent of sin. They must receive Christ, not with the head only but also with the heart, for with the heart we believe unto righteousness. There must be emotion; we must cut into the heart with the plowshare of the law. A farmer who is too tenderhearted to break up the land will never see a harvest. Here is the failing of certain theologians: they are afraid of hurting anyone's feelings, and so they keep clear of all truths which are likely to excite fear or grief. They have not a sharp plowshare on their premises, and are never likely to have a stack in their rickyard. They angle without hooks for fear of hurting the fish, and fire without bullets out of respect to the feelings of the birds. This kind of love is real cruelty to our souls. It is much the same as if a surgeon should permit a patient to die because he would not pain him with the lancet, or by the necessary removal of a limb. It is a terrible tenderness which leaves people to sink into hell rather than distress their minds.

It is pleasant to prophesy smooth things, but woe to those who thus degrade themselves. Is this the spirit of Christ? Did he conceal the sinner's peril? Did he cast doubt upon the unquenchable fire and the undying worm? Did he lull souls into slumber by smooth strains of flattery? No, but with honest love and anxious concern, he warned us of the wrath to come, and bade us to repent or perish. Let the servant of the Lord Jesus follow his Master, and plow deep with a sharp plowshare, which will not be resisted by the hardest clods. This we must teach ourselves to do. If we really love the souls of others, let us prove it by honest speech. The hard heart must be broken, or it will still refuse the Savior who was sent to bind up the brokenhearted. There are some things which we may or may not have, and yet may be saved; but those things which go with the plowing of the heart are indispensable. There must be a holy fear and a humble trembling before God; there must be an acknowledgment of guilt and a penitent petition for mercy; there must, in a word, be a thorough plowing of the soul before we can expect the seed to bring forth fruit.

AT TIMES MINISTERS LABOR IN VAIN

"Shall horses run upon the rock? will one plow there with oxen?" In a short time a plowman feels whether the plow will go or not, and so does the minister. He may use the very same words in one place which he has used in another, but he feels in the one place great joy and hopefulness in preaching, while with another audience he has heavy work and little hope. The plow in the last case seems to jump out of the furrow; and a bit of the share is broken off now and then. He says to himself, "I do not know how it is, but I do not get on at this," and he finds that his Master has sent him to work upon a particularly heavy soil. All laborers for Christ know that this is occasionally the case. You must have found it so in a Sunday-school class, or in a cottage meeting, or in any other gathering where you have tried to teach and preach Jesus. You have said to yourself every now and then, "Now I am plowing a rock. Before, I turned up rich soil which a yoke of oxen might plow with ease, and a horse might even run at the work; but now the horse may tug, and the oxen may wearily toil until they irritate their shoulders, but they cannot cut a furrow; the rock is stubborn to the last degree."

There are such hearers in all congregations. They are as iron, and yet they are side by side with a fine plot of ground. Their sister, their brother, their son, their daughter, all these have readily felt the power of the gospel; but *they* do not feel it. They hear it respectfully; and they so far allow it free course that they permit it to go in at one ear and out at the other, but they will have nothing more to do with it. They would not like to be Sabbath breakers and avoid worship; they there- fore do the gospel the questionable compliment of coming where it is preached and then refusing to regard it. They are hard, hard, hard bits of rock; the plow does not touch them.

Many, on the other hand, are equally hard, but it is in another way. The impression made by the word is not deep or permanent. They receive it with joy, but they do not retain it. They listen with attention, but it never comes to practice with them. They hear about repentance, but they never repent. They hear about faith, but they never believe. They are good judges of what the gospel is, and yet they have never accepted it for themselves. They will not eat, but still they insist that good bread must be put on the table. They are great sticklers for the very things which they personally reject. They are moved to feeling; they shed tears occasionally; but still their hearts are not really bro- ken up by the word. They go their way and forget what manner of men they are. They are rocky hearted through and through; all our attempts to plow them are failures.

Now this is all the worse, because certain of these rocky-hearted people have been plowed for years, and have become harder instead of softer. Once or twice plowing, and a broken share or two, and a disappointed plowman or two, we might not mind if they would yield at last; but these have since their childhood known the gospel and never given way before its power. For some of them it has been a good while since their childhood. Their hair is turning gray, and they themselves are getting feeble with years. They have been entreated and persuaded times beyond number, but labor has been lost upon them. In fact, they used to feel the word, in a certain fashion, far more years ago than they do now. The sun, which softens wax, hardens clay, and the same gospel which has brought others to tenderness and repentance has exercised a contrary effect upon them, and made them more careless about divine things than they were in their youth. This is a mournful state of things, is it not?

Why are certain individuals so extremely rocky? Some are so from a *particularly unemotional nature.* There are many people in the world whom you cannot very well move; they have a great deal of granite in their constitution and are more nearly related to Mr. Obstinate than to Mr. Pliable. Now, I do not think badly of these people, because one knows what it is to preach to excitable people, and to get them all stirred, and to know that in the end they are none the better; whereas some of the more unemotional and immovable people are moved indeed when they are moved. When they do feel, they feel intensely, and they retain any impression that is made. A little chip made in granite by very hard blows will abide there, while the lashing of water, which is easy enough, will leave no trace even for a moment. It is a grand thing to get hold of a fine piece of rock and to exercise faith about it. The Lord's own hammer has mighty power to break, and in the breaking great glory comes to the Most High.

Worse still, certain individuals are hard because of their *infidelity*— not heart-infidelity all of it, but an infidelity which springs out of a desire not to believe, which has helped them to discover difficulties. These difficulties exist, and were meant to exist, for there would be no room for faith if everything were as plain as the nose on one's face. These people have gradually come to doubt, or to think that they doubt, essential truths, and this renders them impervious to the gospel of Christ.

Many others are orthodox enough, but hard-hearted for all that. *Worldliness* hardens an individual in every way. It often eliminates all charity to the poor, because the person must make money, and they think that their property taxes are sufficient enough to provide for the poor, thus shirking their own responsibility. The worldly individual has no time to think of the next world; they must spend all his thoughts upon the present one. Money is tight, and therefore they must hold it tight; and when money brings in little interest, they find therein a reason for being all the more stingy. They have no time for prayer, they *must* get down to the counting house. They have no time for reading their Bible, their ledger wants them. You may knock at their door, but their heart is not at home; it is in the counting house, wherein they live and move and have their being. Their god is their gold, their bliss is their business, their all in all is themself. What is the use of preaching to them? As well may horses run upon a rock, or oxen drag a plow across a field sheeted with iron a mile thick.

With some, too, there is a hardness, produced by what I might almost call the opposite of stern worldliness, namely, a *general levity*. They are naturally butterflies flitting about and doing nothing. They never think, or want to think. Half a thought exhausts them, and they must be diverted, or their feeble minds will utterly weary. They live in a round of amusement. To them the world is a stage, and all the men and women only players. It is of little use to preach to them. There is no depth of earth in their superficial nature; beneath a sprinkling of shifting worthless sand lies an impenetrable rock of utter stupidity and senselessness. I might thus multiply reasons why some are harder than others, but it is a well-assured fact that they are so, and there I leave the matter.

It Is Unreasonable to Expect That God's Servants Should Always Continue to Labor in Vain

I shall now ask everybody to judge whether the running of horses upon a rock and the plowing there with oxen shall always be continued. These people have been preached to, taught, instructed, admonished, reasoned earnestly with, and advised; shall this unrecompensed work be always performed? We have given them a fair trial; what do reason and prudence say? Are we bound to persevere until we are worn out by this unsuccessful work? We will ask it of men who plow their own farms; do they recommend perseverance when failure is certain? Shall horses run upon the rock? Shall one plow there with oxen? Surely not forever.

I think we will all agree that labor in vain cannot be continued forever if we consider *the plowman*. He does not want to be much considered, but still his Master does not overlook him. See how weary he grows when the work discourages him. He goes to his Master and says, "Who hath believed our report? and to whom is the arm of the LORD revealed?" (Isaiah 53:1). "Why have you sent me," says he, "to a people that have ears but hear not? They sit as your people sit, and they hear as your people hear, and then they go their way, and they forget every word that is spoken, and they obey not the voice of the Lord." See how disappointed the preacher becomes. It is always hard work when you appear to get no further, although you do your utmost. No one, whoever they may be, likes to be set upon work which appears to be altogether a waste of time and effort. To their own mind it seems to have a touch of the ridiculous about it, and they fear that they will be despised for aiming at the impossible. Will it always be the lot of God's ministers to be trifled with? Will the great Gardener bid his plowmen spill their lives for nothing? Must his preachers continue to cast pearls before swine? If the consecrated workers are so bidden by their Lord, they will persevere in their painful task; but their Master is considerate of them, and I ask *you* also to consider whether it is reasonable to expect a zealous heart to be forever occupied with the salvation of those who never respond to its anxiety. Shall the horses always plow upon the rock? Shall the oxen always labor there?

Again, there is *the Master* to be considered. The Lord—is he always to be resisted and provoked? Many of you have had eternal life set before you as the result of believing in Jesus, and you have refused to believe. It is a wonder that my Lord has not said to me, "You have done your duty with them; never set Christ before them again; my Son shall not be insulted." If you offer a beggar in the street a shilling and he will not have it, you cheerfully put it into your purse and go your way; you do not entreat him to have his wants relieved. But behold, our God in mercy begs sinners to come to him, and implores them to accept his Son. In his condescension he even stands like a salesman in the market, crying, "Ho, every one that thirsteth, come ye to the waters, and he that hath no money; come ye . . . buy wine and milk without money and without price" (Isaiah 55:1). In another place he says of himself, "All day long have I stretched forth my hands unto a disobedient and gainsaying people" (Romans 10:21). If the Lord of mercy has been refused so long in the sight of you who reverence him, does not some indignation mingle with your pity? And while you love sinners and would have them saved, do you not feel in your heart that there must be an end to such insulting behavior? I ask even the careless to think of the matter in this light, and if they do not respect the plowman, yet let them have regard to his Master.

And then, again, there are so many *other people* who are needing the gospel, and who would receive it if they had it, that it would seem to be wise to leave off wearying oneself about those who despise it. What did our Lord say? He said that if the mighty things which had been done in Bethsaida and Chorazin had been done in Tyre and Sidon, they would have repented. What is more wonderful still, he says that if he had wrought the same miracles in Sodom and Gomorrah which were wrought in Capernaum, they would have repented in sackcloth and ashes. Does it not occur to us at once to give the Word to those who will have it, and leave the despisers to perish in their own will-fulness? Does not reason say, "Let us send this medicine where there are sick people who will value it?" Thousands of people are willing to hear the gospel. See how they crowd wherever the preacher goes— how they tread upon one another in their anxiety to listen to him; and if these people who hear him every day will not receive his message,

"In God's name," says he, "let me go where there is a probability of finding soil that can be plowed." "Shall horses run upon the rock? Will one plow there with oxen?" Must I work always where nothing comes of it? Does not reason say, let the Word go to China, to India, or to the utmost parts of the earth, where they will receive it? For those who have it preached in the corners of their streets, despise it.

I will not lengthen this argument but shall solemnly ask the question again. Would any of you continue to pursue an object when it has proved to be hopeless? Do you wonder that when the Lord has sent his servants to speak kind, gracious, tender words, and people have not heard, he says to them, "They are joined to their idols; leave them alone"? There is a boundary to the patience of humankind, and we soon arrive at it; and assuredly there is a limit, though it is long before we outrun it, to the patience of God. "At length," he says, "it is enough. My Spirit shall no longer strive with them." If the Lord says this, can any of us complain? Is not this the way of wisdom? Does not prudence itself dictate it? Any thoughtful mind will say, "True, a rock cannot be plowed forever."

THERE MUST BE AN ALTERATION, THEN, AND A SPEEDY ONE

The oxen shall be removed from such toil. It can be easily done, and done soon. This can happen in three ways.

First, the unprofitable hearer can be removed so that they will no longer hear the gospel from the lips of their favorite minister. There is a preacher who has some sort of power over them; but as they reject his testimony and remain impenitent, they will be removed to another town, where they will hear monotonous discourses which will not touch their conscience. They will go where they will no longer be persuaded and entreated, and there they will sleep themself into hell. That may be readily enough done; perhaps some of you are making arrangements even now for your own removal from the field of hope.

Another way is to take away the plowman. He has done his work as best he could, and he shall be released from his hopeless task. He is weary. Let him go home. The soil would not break up, but he could not help that; let him have his wage. He has broken his plow at the work; let him go home and hear his Lord say, "Well done." He was willing to keep on at the disheartening labor as long as his Master bade him, but it is evidently useless; therefore, let him go home, for his work is done. He has been worn out; let him die and enter into his rest. This is by no means improbable.

Or there may happen something else. The Lord may say, "That piece of work will never trouble the plowman anymore. I will take it away." And he may take it away in this fashion: the individual who has heard the gospel, but rejected it, will die. I pray my Master that he will not suffer any one of you to die in your sins, for then we cannot reach you anymore or indulge the faintest hope for you. No prayer of ours can follow you into eternity. There is one name by which you may be saved, and that name is sounded in your ears—the name of Jesus; but if you reject him now, even that name will not save you. If you do not take Jesus to be your Savior, he will appear as your judge. I pray you, do not destroy your own souls by continuing to be obstinate against almighty love.

God grant that some better thing may happen. Can nothing else be done? This soil is rock; can we not sow it without breaking it? No. Without repentance there is no remission of sin. But is there not a way of saving men and women without the grace of God? The Lord Jesus did not say so, but he said, "He that believeth and is baptized shall be saved; but he that believeth not shall be damned" (Mark 16:16). He did not hint at a middle course or hold out a "larger hope," but he declared, "He that believeth not shall be damned," *and so he must be*. Dream not of a back door to heaven, for the Lord has provided none.

What then? Shall the preacher continue his fruitless toil? If there is only half a hope left him, he is willing to go on and say, "Hear, you deaf, and see, you blind, and live, you dead." He will even speak so this day, for his Master bids him preach the gospel to every creature;

but it will be hard work to repeat the word of exhortation for years to those who will not hear it.

Happily, there is one other turn which affairs may take. There is a God in heaven; let us pray to him to put forth his power. Jesus is at his side; let us invoke his intervention. The Holy Ghost is almighty; let us call for his aid. Brothers who plow and sisters who pray cry to the Master for help. The horse and the ox evidently fail, but there remains One above who is able to work great marvels. Did he not once speak to the rock and turn the flint into a stream of water? Let us pray him to do the same now.

And if there is one who feels and mourns that his heart is like a piece of rock, I am glad he feels it, for he who feels that his heart is a rock gives some evidence that the flint is being transformed. Oh, rock, instead of smiting you, as Moses smote the rock in the wilderness and erred by doing so, I would speak to you. Oh, rock, would you become like wax? Oh, rock, would you dissolve into rivers of repentance? Listen to God's voice! Oh, rock, break with good desire! Oh, rock, dissolve with longing after Christ, for God is working upon you now. Perhaps at this very moment you shall begin to crumble down. Do you feel the power of the Word? Does the sharp plowshare touch you just now? Break and break again, until by contrition you are dissolved, for then will the good seed of the gospel come to you, and you will receive it in your bosom, and we will all behold the fruit of that. And so I will fling one more handful of good corn, and be finished. If you desire eternal life, trust Jesus Christ, and you will be saved at once. "Look unto me, and be ye saved, all the ends of the earth," says Christ, "for I am God, and there is none else" (Isaiah 45:22). Anyone who believes in him has everlasting life. "And as Moses lifted up the serpent in the wilderness, even so must the Son of man be lifted up: that whosoever believeth in him should not perish, but have eternal life" (John 3:14–15).

Lord, break up the rock, and let the seed drop in among its broken substance, and receive a harvest from the dissolved granite, at this time, for Jesus Christ's sake. Amen.

SEVEN

THE PARABLE OF THE SOWER

And when much people were gathered together, and were come to him out of every city, he spake by a parable: A sower went out to sow his seed: and as he sowed, some fell by the way side; and it was trodden down, and the fowls of the air devoured it. And some fell upon a rock; and as soon as it was sprung up, it withered away, because it lacked moisture. And some fell among thorns; and the thorns sprang up with it, and choked it. And other fell on good ground, and sprang up, and bare fruit an hundredfold. And when he had said these things, he cried, He that hath ears to hear, let him hear.

(LUKE 8:4-8)

In our country, when a sower goes forth to his work, he generally enters into an enclosed field and scatters the seed from his basket along every ridge and furrow; but the East—the corn-growing country, close to a small town—it is usually scattered in an open area. It is divided into different properties, but there are no visible divisions, except the ancient landmarks, or perhaps ridges of stones. Through these open lands there are footpaths, the most frequented being called the highways. You must not imagine these highways to be like our mac-adamized roads; they are merely paths, trodden tolerably hard. Here and there you notice byways, along which travelers who wish to avoid the public road may journey with a little more safety when the main road is infested with robbers. Hasty travelers also strike out shortcuts for themselves, and so open fresh tracks for others.

When the sower goes forth to sow, he finds a plot of ground scratched over with the primitive Eastern plow. He aims at scattering his seed there most plentifully; but a path runs through the center of his field, and unless he is willing to leave a broad headland, he must throw a handful upon it. Yonder, a rock crops out in the midst of the plowed land, and the seed falls on its shallow soil. Here is a corner full of the roots of nettles and thistles, and he flings a little here; the corn and the nettles come up together, and the thorns being the stronger soon choke the seed, so that it brings forth no fruit to perfection. The recollection that the Bible was written in the East, and that its meta-phors and allusions must be explained to us by Eastern travelers, will often help us to understand a passage far better than if we think of English customs.

The preacher of the gospel is like the sower. He does not make his seed; it is given him by his divine Master. No man could create the smallest grain that ever grew upon the earth, much less the celestial seed of eternal life. The minister goes to his Master in secret and asks him to teach him his gospel, and this is how he fills his basket with the good seed of the kingdom. He then goes forth in his Master's name and scatters precious truth. If he knew where the best soil was to be found, perhaps he might limit himself to that which had been prepared by the plow of conviction. But not knowing people's hearts, it is his business to preach the gospel to every creature—to throw a handful on the hardened heart, and another on the mind which is overgrown with the cares and pleasures of the world. He has to leave the seed in the care of the Lord who gave it to him, for he is not responsible for the harvest; he is only accountable for the care and industry with which he does his work. If no single ear should ever make glad the reaper, the sower will be rewarded by his Master if he had planted the right seed with careful hand. If it were not for this fact, with what despairing agony should we utter the cry of Esaias, "Who hath believed our report? and to whom is the arm of the LORD revealed?" (Isaiah 53:1).

Our duty is not measured by the character of our hearers but by the command of our God. We are bound to preach the gospel, whether others will hear, or whether they will not listen. It is ours to sow beside all waters. Let people's hearts be what they may; the minister must preach the gospel to them. He must sow the seed on the rock as well as in the furrow, on the highway as well as in the plowed field.

I will now address myself to the four classes of hearers mentioned in our Lord's parable. We have, first of all, those who are represented by the *wayside*, those who are "hearers only"; then those represented by the *stony ground*; these are temporarily impressed, but the word produces no lasting fruit; then, those *among thorns*, on whom a good impression is produced, but the cares of this life, and the deceitfulness of riches, and the pleasures of the world choke the seed; and lastly, that small class—God be pleased to multiply it exceedingly—that small class of *good ground* hearers, in whom the Word brings forth abundant fruit.

THE FIRST HEARERS—THOSE REPRESENTED BY THE WAYSIDE

"Some fell by the way side; and it was trodden down, and the fowls of the air devoured it." Many of you do not go to the place of worship desiring a blessing. You do not intend to worship God, or to be affected by anything that you hear. You are like the highway, which was never intended to be a cornfield. If a single grain of truth should fall into your heart and grow, it would be as great a wonder as for corn to grow up in the street. If the seed shall be dexterously scattered, some of it will fall upon you and rest for a while upon your thoughts. It is true that you will not understand it; but, nevertheless, if it is placed before you in an interesting style, you will talk about it until some more congenial entertainment will attract you. Even this slender benefit is brief, for in a little while you will forget all that you have heard. Would to God we could hope that our words would linger with you, but we cannot hope it, for the soil of your heart is so hard beaten by continual traffic that there is no hope of the seed finding a living roothold.

Satan is constantly passing over your heart with his company of blasphemies, lusts, lies, and vanities. The chariots of pride roll along it, and the feet of greedy mammon tread it until it is hard as adamant. The good seed finds not a moment's respite; crowds pass and repass. In fact, your soul is an exchange, across which continually hurry the busy feet of those who make merchandise of the souls of humankind. You are buying and selling, but you little think that you are selling the truth and buying your soul's destruction. You have no time, you say, to think of religion. No, the road of your heart is such a crowded thoroughfare that there is no room for the wheat to spring up. If it did begin to germinate, some rough foot would crush the green blade before it could reach perfection. The seed has occasionally lain long enough to begin to sprout, but just then a new place of amusement has been opened, and you have entered there, and as with an iron heel, the germ of life that was in the seed was crushed. Corn could not grow in Cornhill or Cheapside, however excellent the seed might be. Your heart is just like those crowded thoroughfares, for so many cares and sins throng it, and so many proud, vain, evil, rebellious thoughts against God pass through it, that the seed of truth cannot grow.

We have looked at this hard roadside. Let us now describe what becomes of the good word when it falls upon such a heart. It would have grown if it had fallen on right soil, but it has dropped into the wrong place, and it remains as dry as when it fell from the sower's hand. The word of the gospel lies upon the surface of such a heart, but never enters it. Like the snow, which sometimes falls upon our streets, drops upon the wet pavement, melts, and is gone at once, so is it with this person. The word has not had time to quicken in their soul; it lies there an instant, but it never takes root or has the slightest effect.

Why do men and women come to hear if the word never enters their hearts? That has often puzzled us. Some hearers would not miss a Sunday on any account; they are delighted to come up with us to worship, but the tear never trickles down their cheek, their soul never mounts up to heaven on the wings of praise, nor do they truly join in our confessions of sin. They do not think of the wrath to come, nor of the future state of their souls. Their heart is as iron; the minister might as well speak to a heap of stones as preach to them. What brings these senseless sinners here? Surely, we are as hopeful of converting lions and leopards as these untamed, insensible hearts. Do these people come to our assemblies because it is respectable to attend a place of worship? Or is it that their coming helps to make them comfortable in their sins? If they stopped coming, perhaps their conscience would prick them, but they come so they may flatter themselves with the notion that they are religious.

My friends, your case is one that might make an angel weep! How sad to have the sun of the gospel shining on your faces, and yet to have blind eyes that never see the light! The music of heaven is lost upon you, for you have no ears to hear. You can catch the turn of a phrase, you can appreciate the poetry of an illustration, but the hidden meaning, the divine life, you do not perceive. You sit at the marriage feast, but you eat not of the dainties; the bells of heaven ring with joy over those who have been saved, but you live unsaved, without God, and without Christ. Though we plead with you, and pray for you, and weep over you, you still remain as hardened, as careless, and as thoughtless as ever you were. May God have mercy on you, and break up your hard hearts, that his Word may abide in you.

We have not, however, completed the picture. The passage tells us that the fowls of the air devoured the seed. Is there here a wayside hearer? Perhaps he did not mean to hear this sermon, and when he has heard it he will be asked by one of the wicked to come into company. He will go with the tempter, and the good seed will be devoured by the fowls of the air. Plenty of evil ones are ready to take away the gospel from the heart. The devil himself, that prince of the air, is eager at any time to snatch away a good thought. And then the devil is not alone—he has legions of helpers. He can set a man's wife, children, friends, enemies, customers, or creditors, to eat up the good seed, and they will do it completely. Oh, sorrow upon sorrow, that heavenly seed should become devil's meat; that God's corn should feed foul birds!

My friends, if you have heard the gospel from your youth, what wagonloads of sermons have been wasted on you! In your younger days you heard old Dr. So-and-so, and the dear old man was inspired to pray for his hearers until his eyes were red with tears! Do you recollect those many Sundays when you said to yourself, "Let me go to my chamber and fall on my knees and pray"? But you did not; the fowls of the air ate up the seed, and you went on to sin as you had sinned before. Since then, by some strange impulse, you are very rarely absent from God's house; but now the seed of the gospel falls into your soul as if it dropped upon an iron floor, and nothing comes of it. The law may be thundered at you; you do not sneer at it, but it never affects you. Jesus Christ may be lifted up; his dear wounds may be exhibited; his streaming blood may flow before your very eyes, and you may be bidden with all earnestness to look to him and live; but it is as if one should sow the seashore. What should I do for you? Should I stand here and rain tears upon this hard highway? No, my tears will not break it up; it is trodden too hard for that. Should I bring the gospel plow? No, the plowshare will not enter ground so solid. What should we do? O God, you know how to melt the hardest heart with the precious blood of Jesus. Do it now, we beseech you, and thus magnify your grace, by causing the good seed to live and to produce a heavenly harvest.

THE SECOND HEARERS—THOSE REPRESENTED BY THE STONY GROUND

"And some fell upon a rock; and as soon as it was sprung up, it withered away, because it lacked moisture." You can easily picture to yourselves that piece of rock in the midst of the field thinly veiled with soil; the seed falls there as it does everywhere else. It springs up, it hastens to grow, it withers, it dies. None but those who love the souls of others can tell what hopes, what joys, and what bitter disappointments these stony places have caused us. We have a class of hearers whose hearts are hard, and yet they are apparently the softest and most impressible of us. While others see nothing in the sermon, these individuals weep. Whether you preach the terrors of the law or the love of Calvary, they are alike stirred in their souls, and the liveliest impressions are apparently produced. Some of them may be listening now. They have resolved, but they have procrastinated. They are not the sturdy enemies of God who clothe themselves in steel, but they seem to bare their breasts, and lay them open to the minister. Rejoiced in heart, we shoot our arrows there, and they appear to penetrate; but a secret armor blunts every dart, and no wound is felt.

The parable speaks of this character: "Some fell upon stony places, where they had not much earth: and forthwith they sprung up, because they had no deepness of earth" (Matthew 13:5). Or as another passage explains it: "And these are they likewise which are sown on stony ground; who, when they have heard the word, immediately receive it with gladness; and have no root in themselves, and so endure but for a time: afterward, when affliction or persecution ariseth for the word's sake, immediately they are offended" (Mark 4:16–17). Are there not thousands of hearers who receive the word with joy? They have no deep convictions, but they leap suddenly to Christ and profess an instantaneous faith in him, and that faith has all the appearance of being genuine. When we look at it, the seed has really sprouted. There is a kind of life in it, there is apparently a green blade. We thank God that a sinner is brought back, a soul is born to God. But our joy is premature; they sprang up so suddenly and received the word with joy because they had no depth of earth, and the selfsame cause which hastened their reception of the seed also causes them, when the sun is risen with its fervent heat, to wither away.

These people we see every day in the week. They come to join the church; they tell us a story of how they heard us preach on such-and-such an occasion, and, oh, the word was so blessed to them, they never felt so happy in their lives! "Oh, sir, I thought I must leap from my seat when I heard about precious Christ, and I believed on him there and then; I am sure I did." We question them as to whether they were ever convinced of sin. They think they were; but one thing they know, they feel a great pleasure in religion. We ask them, "Do you think you will hold on?" They are confident that they will. They hate the things they once loved, they are sure they do. Everything has become new to them. And this happens all of a sudden. We inquire when the good work began. We find it began when it ended, that is to say, there was no previous work, no plowing of the soil, but suddenly they sprang from death to life, as if a field should be covered with wheat by magic. Perhaps we receive them into the church, but in a week or two they are not so regular as they used to be. We gently reprove them, and they explain that they meet with such opposition in religion that they are obliged to yield a little. Another month and we lose them altogether. The reason is that they have been laughed at or exposed to a little opposition, and they have gone back.

And what do you think are the feelings of the minister? He is like the gardener, who sees his field all green and flourishing, but at night a frost nips every shoot, and his hoped-for gains are gone. The minister goes to his chamber, falls on his face before God, and cries, "I have been deceived; my converts are fickle, their religion has withered as the green herb." In the ancient story Orpheus is said to have had such skill upon the lyre that he made the oaks and stones dance around him. It is a poetical fiction, and yet it sometimes happens to the minister, that not only have the godly rejoiced but men and women, like oaks and stones, have danced from their places. Alas, they have been oaks and stones still. Hushed is the lyre. The oak returns to its rooting place, and the stone casts itself heavily to the earth. The sinner, who like Saul was among the prophets, goes back to plan mischief against the Most High.

If it is bad to be a wayside hearer, I cannot think it is much better to be like the rock. This second class of hearers certainly gives us more joy than the first. A certain company always comes to join a new minister, and I have often thought it is an act of God's kindness that he allows these people to gather while the minister is young and has but few to stand by him. These people are easily moved, and if the minister preaches earnestly they feel it, and they love him and rally round him, much to his comfort. But time, which proves all things, proves them. They seemed to be made of true metal, but when they are put into the fire to be tested, they are consumed in the furnace. Some of the shallow kind are here now. I have looked at you when I have been preaching, and I have often thought, "That man one of these days will come out from the world, I am sure he will." I have thanked God for him. Alas, he is the same as ever. Years and years have we sowed him in vain, and it is to be feared it will be so to the end, for he is without depth, and without the moisture of the Spirit. Must it be so? Must I stand over the mouth of your open sepulcher, and think, "Here lies a shoot which never became an ear, a man in whom grace struggled but never reigned, who gave some hopeful spasms of life and then subsided into eternal death?" God save you! May the Spirit deal with you effectually, and may you yet bring forth fruit to God, that Jesus may have a reward for his sufferings.

The Third Hearers—Those Represented As Among Thorns

"And some fell among thorns; and the thorns sprang up with it, and choked it." Now, this was good soil. The two first characters were bad;

the wayside was not the proper place, the rock was not a congenial situation for the growth of any plant; but this is good soil, for it grows thorns. Wherever a thistle will spring up and flourish, there would wheat flourish too. This was fat, fertile soil; it was no marvel therefore that the gardener dealt largely there and threw handful after handful upon that corner of the field. See how happy the gardener is when in a month or two he visits the spot. The seed has sprung up. True, there's a suspicious little plant down there of about the same size as the wheat. "Oh," he thinks, "that's not much; the corn will outgrow *that*. When it is stronger, it will choke out these few thistles that have unfortunately mixed with it." Mr. Gardener, you do not understand the force of evil, or you would not dream so! The gardener comes again and sees that the seed has grown. There is even the corn in the ear, but thistles, thorns, and briers have become intertwined with one another, and the poor wheat can hardly get a ray of sunshine. It is so choked with thorns that it looks quite yellow; the plant is starved. Still, it perseveres in growing, and it does seem as if it would bring forth a little fruit. But sadly, it never comes to anything. With it the reaper never fills his arm.

We have this population very largely among us. These hear the word and understand what they hear. They take the truth home; they think it over; they even go the length of making a profession of religion. The wheat seems to sprout and grow; it will soon come to perfection. In no hurry, these men and women have a great deal to see after. Their establishment employs so many hundred hands; do not be deceived as to their godliness—they have no time for it. They will tell you that they must live, that they cannot neglect this world, that they must look out for the present, and as for the future, they will give it attention by-and-by. They continue to attend gospel-preaching, and the poor little stunted blade of religion keeps on growing after a fashion. Meanwhile they have grown rich, they come to the place of worship in a carriage, they have all their hearts can wish. Now the seed will grow, will it not? No, no. They have no cares now; the shop is given up; they live in the country. They do not have to ask, "Where will the money come from to meet the next bill?" or "How will I be able to provide for an increasing family?" Now they have too much instead of too little, for they have *riches*, and they are too wealthy to be gracious. "But," says one, "they might spend their riches for God." Certainly they might, but they do not, for riches are deceitful. They have to entertain much company, and chime in with the world, and so Christ and his church are left behind.

Yes, but they begin to spend their riches, and they have surely got over that difficulty, for they give largely to the cause of Christ. They are generous in charity; the little blade will grow, will it not? No, for now the thorns of pleasure have taken hold. Their liberality to others involves liberality to themselves—their pleasures, amusements, and vanities choke the wheat of true religion, and the good grains of gospel truth cannot grow because they have to attend that musical party, that ball, and that soirée, and so they cannot think of the things of God. I know several from this class. I knew one, high in court circles, who confessed to me that he wished he were poor, for then he might enter the kingdom of heaven. He said to me, "Ah! Sir, these politics, these politics, I wish I were rid of them, they are eating the life out of my heart. I cannot serve God as I would." I know another, overloaded with riches, who said to me, "Ah! Sir, it is an awful thing to be rich; one cannot keep close to the Savior with all this earth about him."

My dear readers, I will not ask for you that God may lay you on a bed of sickness, that he may strip you of all your wealth and bring you to beggary; but, oh, if he were to do it, and you were to save your souls, it would be the best bargain you could ever make. If those mighty ones who complain that the thorns choke the seed could give up all their riches and pleasures, if they who fare sumptuously every day could take the place of Lazarus at the gate, it would be a happy change for them if their souls might be saved. A man may be honorable and rich and yet go to heaven, but it will be hard work, for "It is easier for a camel to go through the eye of a needle, than for a rich man to enter into the kingdom of God" (Mark 10:25). God does allow some rich men to enter the kingdom of heaven, but hard is their struggle. Steady, young person, steady! Hurry not to climb to wealth! It is a place where many heads are turned. Do not ask God to make you popular; they that have popularity are wearied by it. Cry with Agur, "Give me neither poverty nor riches" (Proverbs 30:8). God allow me to tread the golden mean, and may I ever have in my heart that good seed, which shall bring forth fruit a hundredfold to his own glory.

THE FOURTH HEARERS—THOSE REPRESENTED BY THE GOOD GROUND

Of the GOOD GROUND, as you will note, we have but one in four. Will one in four of our hearers, with well-prepared heart, receive the Word?

The ground is described as "good"—not that it was good by nature, but it had been made good by grace. God had plowed it; he had stirred it up with the plow of conviction, and there it lay in ridge and furrow as it should lie. When the gospel was preached, the heart received it, saying, "That is just the blessing I want. Mercy is what a needy sinner requires." The preaching of the gospel was THE thing to give comfort to this disturbed and plowed soil. Down fell the seed to take good root. In some cases it produced fervency of love, largeness of heart, devotedness of purpose of a noble kind, like seed which produces a hundredfold. The man or woman became a mighty servant for God, they spent themselves and were spent. They took their place in the forefront of Christ's army, stood in the hottest of the battle, and did deeds of daring which few could accomplish—the seed produced a hundredfold. It fell into another heart of like character; the person could not do the most, but still, they did much. They gave themselves to God, and in their business they had a word to say for their Lord; in their daily walk they quietly adorned the doctrine of God their Savior—they brought forth sixtyfold. Then it fell on another, whose abilities and talents were but small; they could not be a star, but they would be a glowworm; they could not do as the greatest, but they were content to do something, however humble. The seed had brought forth in them tenfold, perhaps twentyfold.

How many are there of this sort here? Is there one who prays within, "God be merciful to me, a sinner"? The seed has fallen in the right spot. Soul, your prayer will be heard. God never sets a person longing for mercy without intending to give it. Does another whisper, "Oh, that I might be saved"? Believe on the Lord Jesus Christ, and you will be saved. Have you been the leader of sinners? Trust Christ, and your enormous sins will vanish as the millstone sinks beneath the flood. Is there no one here who will trust the Savior? Can it be possible that the Spirit is entirely absent? That he is not moving in one soul? That he is not producing life in one spirit? We will pray that he may now descend, that the Word may not be in vain.

EIGHT

THE PRINCIPAL WHEAT

"The principal wheat."

(Isaiah 28:25)

THE prophet mentions it as a matter of wisdom on the part of the gardener, that HE KNOWS WHAT IS THE PRINCIPAL THING TO CULTIVATE and makes it his principal care. The verse essentially says, "Does not the gardener cast in the principal wheat?" He does not go to the granary and take out wheat and cumin and barley and rye, and fling these about right and left, but he estimates the value of each grain and arranges them in his mind accordingly. He does not think that cumin and caraway, which he merely grows to give flavor to his meal, are of half such importance as his breadcorn, and though rye and barley have their values, he does not reason that even these are equal to what he calls "the principal wheat." He is a man of discretion; he arranges things. He places the most important crop in the front rank and gives it the most care.

THE GARDENER'S FIRST LESSON: KEEP THINGS DISTINCT IN YOUR MIND

Keep things distinct in your mind, not huddled and muddled by a careless thoughtlessness. Do not live a confused life, without care and discretion, running all things into one; but sort things out, and divide and distinguish between the precious and the vile. See what this is worth, and what the other is worth, and set your matters in rank and order, making some of them principal and others of them inferior. I suggest to young people especially that, in starting life, you say to yourselves, "What shall we live for? There is a principal thing for which we ought to live; what shall it be?" Have you asked yourselves that question, or have you gone at it hit or miss? What are you living for? What is your principal aim? Is it going to be that of the old gentleman in Horace who said to his boy, "Get money: get it honestly, if you can; but, by all means, get money"? Will you be a moneymaker? Will coin be your principal corn? Or will you choose a life of pleasure—"A short life and a merry one"—as many fools have said to their great sorrow? Is it in self-indulgence that your life is to be spent? Are thistles to be your principal crop? Because there is pleasure in looking at a Scotch thistle, do you intend to grow acres of pleasurable vice? And will you make your bed upon them when you come to die? Search and see what is worthy of being the principal object in life; and, when you have found it out, then ask the Holy Spirit to help you to choose that one thing and give all your powers and abilities to the cultivation of it. The farmer, who finds that wheat ought to be his principal crop, makes it so, and expends a great deal of effort with that end in view. Learn from this to have a main objective and to give your whole mind to it.

This farmer was wise, because *he counted that to be important which was the most necessary.* His family could do without cumin, which was but a flavoring. Perhaps his wife might complain, or the cook might grumble, but that was not as important as if the children cried for bread. They certainly must have wheat, for bread is the staff of life. It is bread that strengthens our hearts, and therefore the farmer must grow wheat if he does not grow anything else. That which is necessary he regarded as the principal thing. Is not this common sense? If we were wisely to sit down and estimate, should we not say, "To be forgiven my sins, to be right with God, to be holy, to be fit to live eternally in heaven, is the greatest, the most needful thing for me, and therefore I will make it the principal object of my pursuit"? A creature cannot be satisfied unless he is answering the question of why he has been created, and the purpose of every intelligent creature is first to glorify God, and next, to enjoy God. What bliss it must be to enjoy God himself forever and ever! Other things may be desirable, but this thing is necessary. A sufficient income, a measure of esteem among others, a degree of health—all these are the flavoring of life, but to be saved in the Lord with an everlasting salvation is life itself. Jesus Christ is the bread by which our soul's best life is sustained. Oh, that we were all wise enough to feel that to be one with Christ is the one thing necessary, that to be at peace with God is the principal thing, that to be brought into harmony with the Most High is the true music of our being. Other herbs may take their place in due order, but grace is the principal wheat, and we must cultivate it.

This farmer was wise because *he made that to be the principal thing which was the most fit to be so*. Of course, barley is useful as food, for nations have lived on barley bread, and lived healthily, too, and rye has been the nutriment of millions. Neither have they starved on oats and other grains. Still, give me a piece of wheat bread, for it is the best staff for life's journey. This farmer knew that wheat was the most fitting food for humankind, and so he did not put the inferior grain, which might act as a substitute, into the prominent place, but he gave wheat the preference. He did not say, "the principal barley," or "the principal rye," much less "the principal cumin," or "the principal fitches,"[19] but "the principal wheat."

And what is there, friends, that is so fit for the heart, the mind, the soul of humankind, as to know God and Christ? Other mental foods, such as the fruits of knowledge and the dainties of science, excellent though they may be—are inferior nutriment and unsuitable to build up inner strength. In my God and my Savior, I find my heaven and my all. My soul sits down to a crumb of truth about Jesus and finds great satisfaction in living upon it. The more we can know God and enjoy

God and become like God, and the more Christ is our daily bread, the more do we perceive the fitness of all this to our newborn natures. O beloved, make that to be your principal object which is the highest pursuit of an immortal mind.

> Religion is the chief concern
>> Of mortals here below.
> May I its great importance learn,
>> Its sovereign virtues know.
> More needful this than glitt'ring wealth
>> Or aught the world bestows;
> Nor reputation, food, or health
>> Can give us such repose.[20]

Moreover, this farmer was wise, because *he made that the principal thing which was the most profitable.* Under certain circumstances, wheat is not the most profitable thing which a farmer can grow, but ordinarily, it is the best crop that the earth yields, and therefore the verse speaks of "the principal wheat." Our grandfathers used to rely upon the wheatstack to pay their rent. They looked to their corn as the arm of their strength; and though it is not so now, it always was so of old, and perhaps it may yet be so again. Anyhow, the illustration works with regard to true religion. That is the most profitable thing. I am told that the rich find it very hard to get hold of anything which yields five percent, but this blessed fear of the Lord is an extraordinarily profitable investment, for it does not yield a hundred percent or a thousand percent, but a man begins with nothing, and all things become his by faith. Being freely relieved of our sins, we are by overflowing grace greatly enriched, so that we number among our possessions heaven itself, Christ himself, God himself. All things are ours. Oh, what a blessed crop to sow! What a harvest comes of it!

Godliness is profitable for the life that now is, and for that which is to come. Godliness is a blessing to a person's body; it keeps them from drunkenness and vice, and it is a blessing to their soul, for it makes them sweet and pure. It is a blessing to them in every way. If I had to die like a dog, I would like to live like a Christian. If there were no hereafter, yet still, for comfort and for joy, give me the life of one who strives to live like Christ. There is a practical everyday truth in the verse—

> 'Tis religion that can give
> Sweetest pleasures while we live,
> 'Tis religion must supply
> Solid comforts when we die.[21]

That religion must not be of the common sort; it must have for its root a hearty faith in Jesus Christ. Religion must be either everything or nothing, either first or nowhere. Make it "the principal wheat," and it will richly repay you.

The Gardener's Second Lesson: Give This Principal Thing the Principal Place

I find that the Hebrew is translated by some eminent scholars, "He puts the wheat into the principal place." That little handful of cumin for the flavoring of cakes is grown in a corner of the garden, and the various herbs are placed in their proper borders. The barley is set in its plot and the rye in its acre, but if there is a good bit of rich soil—the best available—the gardener appropriates it to the principal wheat. He gives his choicest fields to that which is to be the main means of his living.

Now, here is a lesson for you and for me. Let us give to true godliness our principal powers and abilities. Let us give to the things of God our best and *most intense thought*. I pray you, do not just take your religion from what I tell you, or from what somebody else tells you, but think it over. Read, mark, learn, and inwardly digest the Word of God. The thoughtful Christian is the growing Christian. Remember, the service of God deserves our first consideration and endeavor. We are poor things at our prime, but we ought to give the Lord nothing short of our best. God would not have us serve him heedlessly, but he would have us use all the brain and intellect and mind that we have in studying and practicing his Word. "Acquaint now thyself with him, and be at peace" (Job 22:21). "Meditate upon these things; give thyself wholly to them" (1 Timothy 4:15). If your mind is clearer and more active at a certain time than at another, then sow the principal wheat at that time. If you feel more alert and more inclined to think at one time of the day than at another, let your mind then go toward the best things.

Be sure, also, to yield to this subject *your most earnest love.* The best field in the little estate of manhood is not the head but the heart; sow the principal wheat there. Oh, to have true religion in the heart—to love what we know, to love it intensely, to hold it fast with the grip of life and death, never to let it go! The Lord says, "Give me your heart," and he will not be contented with anything less than our heart. When your zeal is most burning and your love is most fervent, let that warmth and fervency all go toward the Lord your God and to the service of him who has redeemed you with his precious blood. Let the principal wheat have the principal part of your nature. Toward God and Christ also turn your *most fervent desires.* When you enlarge your desire, desire Christ; when you become ambitious, let your ambition be all for God. Let your hunger and your thirst be after righteousness. Let your aspirations and your longings be all toward holiness and the things that will make you more like Christ. Give to this principal wheat your principal desires.

Then, let the Lord have *the attentive respect of your life.* Let the principal wheat be sown in every action. If we are truly Christians, we must be as much Christians outside the church as we are in it. We should try to make our eating and our drinking, and everything we do, tend to the glory of God. Draw no line between the secular and the religious parts of your life, but let the secular be made religious by a devout desire to glorify God in the one as much as in the other. Let us worship God in the most ordinary part of life, even as those do who stand before his throne. This is how it ought to be. Let us sow the principal wheat in all the fields of our conversation, in business, with our family, among our friends, and with our children. May each of us believe, "For me to live is Christ. I cannot live without Christ, or for anything but Christ." Let your whole nature yield itself to Jesus, and to no one else.

We should give to this principal wheat *our most earnest labors.* We should spend ourselves for the spread of the gospel. Christians ought to lay themselves out to serve Jesus. I hate to see a professing Christian zealous in politics and lukewarm in devotion—all on fire at a business meeting yet chill as winter at a prayer meeting. Some fly like eagles when they are serving the world, but they have a broken wing when they are in the service of God. This should not be. If anything should rouse us up, and make the lion within us roar in his strength, it should be when we confront the foes of Jesus or fight in his cause. Our Lord's service is the principal wheat; let us labor most in connection with it.

This, I think, should also affect *our greatest sacrifices.* The love of Christ ought to be so strong as to swallow up self and make sacrifice our daily joy. For Christ's name, we should be willing to endure poverty, reproach, slander, exile, death. Nothing should be as dear to a Christian as Christ. Now, I will ask you whether it is so in our own lives or not. Is the love of Jesus the principal wheat with us? Are we giving our religion the chief place or not? I am afraid some people treat religion as certain individuals treat a farm as a hobby; they hire someone to manage it and only give an eye to it now and then. Their minister is the manager, and they expect him to see to it for them. These hobby farms are perfunctory efforts in half-heartedness. Look at these half-and-half believers. Do they have religion? Certainly. But they are like the man whom the child spoke of at Sunday school. "Is your father a Christian?" said the teacher. "Yes," said the child, "but he has not worked much at it lately." I could point out several of this sort, who are sowing their wheat very sparingly and choosing the most barren patch to sow it in. They profess to be Christians, but religion is a tenth-rate matter on their farm. Some have a large acreage for the world and a poor little plot for Christ. They are growers of worldly pleasure and self-indulgence, and they sow a little religion by the roadside for the sake of appearance. This will not do. God will not be mocked in this way. If we despise him and his truth, we will be lightly esteemed. So let us give our principal time, talent, thought, and effort to that which is the chief concern of immortal spirits. May we imitate the gardener who gives the principal wheat the principal place in his farm.

The Gardener's Third Lesson: Select the Principal Seedcorn When You Are Sowing Your Wheat

When a farmer is setting aside wheat for sowing, he does not choose the tail-corn and the worst of his produce, but if he is a sensible man, he likes to sow the best wheat in the world. Many farmers search the country for a good sample of wheat for sowing, for they do not expect to get a good harvest out of bad seed. The gardener is taught by God to put into the ground "the principal wheat." If I am going to sow to the Lord and be a Christian, I should sow the best kind of Christianity.

I should try to do this, first, *by believing the most important doctrines.* I would believe not this "ism," nor that, but the unadulterated truth which Jesus taught, for a holy character will only grow by the Spirit of God out of true doctrine. Falsehood breeds sin: truth produces and fosters holiness. You and I therefore ought to select our seed carefully, and cast out all error. If we are wise, we will focus most on the most important truths, for I have known people who attach the greatest importance to the smallest things. They fight over the lowly fitch seeds while leaving the wheat to the crows. There are those who will disagree about vessels and trumpets, but I will focus on preaching the doctrine of the precious blood and the glorious truths of Christ. These doctrines are the principal wheat, and therefore these will be what I choose to focus on.

Next to that, we ought to sow *the noblest examples*. Many are stunted in their faith because they choose a bad model to start with. They imitate dear old Mr. So-and-so until they grow wonderfully like him, only with the best of him left out. A minister happens to be of a gloomy turn of mind, and he preaches the deep experience of the children of God, and consequently a group of good people think it is their duty to be melancholy. Why do they need to fall into a ditch because their leader has splashed himself? We should never copy anyone's weaknesses. To be like Paul, there is no need to have weak eyes; to be like Thomas, there is no necessity to doubt. If you copy any good person, there is a point at which you ought to stop short. If I must have a human model, I would prefer one of the bravest of the saints of God, but how much better to follow that perfect pattern which we have in Christ Jesus!

We should sow the best wheat by seeing that we have *the purest spirit*. Sadly, many of us have become soiled by self or pride, or despondency or sloth, or some earthly taint. But what a grand thing it is to live in the spirit of Christ! May we be humble, lowly, bold, self-sacrificing, pure, chaste, and holy.

And then there is one more method of sowing selected seed. We should endeavor to live in *the closest communion with God*. A dear brother prayed just now that we might have as much grace as we were capable of receiving, and that God would bring us into such a state that we might not hinder him in anything which he wills us to do. This is a good prayer. It should be our desire to rise to the highest form of spiritual life. If you sow this principal wheat, get the best sort of it. There is a spirit and a spirit; there are doctrines and doctrines. The best is the best for you. Friends, if you mean to be devout, go in for it thoroughly. Do not sneak through the world as if you were ashamed of your Lord. If you are Christ's, show your colors. Rally to his banner, gather to his trumpet call, and then stand up, stand up for Jesus. If there is any humanity in you, this great cause calls for it all. Exhibit it, and may the Spirit of God help you to do so.

THE GARDENER'S FOURTH LESSON: GROW THE PRINCIPAL WHEAT WITH THE PRINCIPAL CARE

Some critics say the proper translation is that the farmer plants his wheat in rows. It is said that in olden times, the large crops in Palestine were the result of how they planted the wheat. They set it in lines, so that it was not checked or suffocated by being too thick in one place; neither was there any fear of its being too thin in another. The wheat was planted, and then streams of water were given to each particular plant. No wonder that the land brought forth abundantly.

We should give our principal care to the principal thing. Our godliness should be carried out with discretion and care. Friends, are we careful enough as to our religious walk? Have you ever searched to the bottom of your profession? Why do you happen to be members of a certain church? Your mother was so. Well, there is some good in that reason, but not enough to justify you in the sight of God. I pray you judge your standing. If any Christian minister is afraid to urge you to this duty, I stand in doubt of him. I beg you to examine all that I teach you, for I would not like to be responsible for another's creed. Like the Bereans, search and see whether these things line up with Scripture or not. One of the greatest blessings that the church could have would be a searching spirit which would refer everything to the Holy Scriptures. If they do not speak according to this word, it is because there is no light in them. Do your service to God as carefully as the eastern farmer planted his wheat when he set it in rows with great orderliness and exactness. You serve a precise God; therefore serve him precisely. He is a jealous God; therefore be careful of the least bit of error or worship according to one's fancy.

Take care, also, that you water every part of your religion, as the farmer watered each plant. Pray for grace from on high that you may never be parched and dried up. Give to your faith, to your hope, to your love, and to all the plants that are in your soul every other service which the farmer gives to his wheat. Give grace your principal care, for it deserves it.

THE GARDENER'S FIFTH LESSON: FROM YOUR PRINCIPAL ACTIONS, YOU MAY EXPECT YOUR PRINCIPAL CROP

With this I close. If religion is the principal thing, you may look to religion for your principal reward. The harvest will come to you in various ways. You will have the greatest success in this life if you live completely to the glory of God. Success or failure depends upon the fitness of our object. It is of no use *my* attempting to sing, for I will never be able to conduct a choir. I could not succeed in that, but if I preach, I may succeed, for that is my work. Now you, Christian man or woman, if you try to live to the world, you will not prosper, for you are not fitted for it. Grace has spoiled you for sin. If you live to God with all your heart, you will succeed in it, for God has made you on purpose for it. As he made the fish for the water, and the birds for the air, so he made the believer for holiness and the service of God, and you will be out of your element—a fish out of water, a bird in the stream—if you leave the service of God. The Eastern farmer's prosperity hinges on his wheat, and yours upon your devotion to God. It is to godliness that you must look for your joy. Is there any bliss like the bliss of knowing that you are in Christ and are the beloved of the Lord? It is to your religion that you must look for comfort on a sick and dying bed, and you may be there very soon.

In the world to come what a crop, what a harvest, will come of serving the Lord! What will come out of all else? What but mere smoke? A woman has made millions in money, and she is dead. What has she gotten by her wealth? A man's fame rings throughout the earth as a great and successful warrior, and he is dead. What has he received as the result of all his honors? To live to the world is like playing with boys in the street for halfpence, or with babies for bits of oyster shell. Life for God is real and substantial, but all else is waste. Let us believe this, and prepare ourselves for the challenges of serving the Lord. May the divine Spirit help us to sow "the principal wheat" and to live in joyful expectation of reaping a happy harvest according to the promise, "They that sow in tears shall reap in joy" (Psalm 126:5).

NINE

SPRING IN THE HEART

Thou waterest the ridges thereof abundantly: thou
settlest the furrows thereof: thou makest it soft with
showers: thou blessest the springing thereof.

(PSALM 65:10)

Though other seasons excel in fullness, spring must always bear the palm for freshness and beauty. We thank God when the harvest hours draw near and the golden grain invites the sickle, but we ought equally to thank him for the rougher days of spring, for these prepare the harvest. April showers are the mothers of the sweet May flowers, and the wet and cold of winter are the parents of the splendor of summer. God blesses the spring, or else it could not be said, "Thou crownest the year with thy goodness" (Psalm 65:11). There is as much necessity for divine benediction in spring as there is for heavenly bounty in summer; therefore, we should praise God all the year round.

Spiritual spring is a very blessed season in a church. It is then that we see youthful devotion developed, and we hear the joyful cry of those who say, "We have found the Lord." Our sons and daughters are springing up as the grass and willows by the watercourses. We hold up our hands in glad astonishment and cry, "Who are these that fly as a cloud and as doves to their windows?" In the revival days of a church, when God is blessing her with many conversions, she has great cause to rejoice in God and to sing, "Thou blessest the springing thereof."

Now we will take the verse in reference and apply it to individual cases. There is a time of springing of grace, when it is just in its bud, just breaking through the dull, cold earth of unregenerate nature. I desire to talk a little about that, and concerning the blessing which the Lord grants to the green blade of newborn godliness, to those who are beginning to hope in the Lord.

The Work Previous to the Springing Thereof

It appears from the verse that there is work for God alone to do before the springing comes, and we know that there is work for God to do through us as well.

There is work for us to do. Before there can be a springing up in the soul, there must be *plowing*, harrowing, and sowing. There must be a plowing, and we do not expect that as soon as we plow we shall harvest the sheaves. Blessed be God—in many cases the harvester overtakes the plowman, but we must not always expect it. In some hearts God is long in preparing the soul by conviction; the law with its ten black horses drags the plowshare of conviction up and down the soul until there is no one part of it left unfurrowed. Conviction goes deeper than any plow to the very core and center of the spirit, until the spirit is wounded. The plowers make deep furrows indeed when God puts his hand to the work: the soil of the heart is broken in pieces in the presence of the Most High.

Then comes the *sowing*. Before there can be a springing up, something must be put into the ground, so that after the preacher has used the plow of the law, he applies to his Master for the seed basket of the gospel. Gospel promises, gospel doctrines—especially a clear exposition of free grace and the atonement—these are the handfuls of corn which we scatter in all directions. Some of the grain falls on the highway and is lost, but other handfuls fall where the plow has been, and there abide.

Then comes the *harrowing* work. We do not expect to sow seed and then leave it: the gospel has to be prayed over. The prayer of the preacher and the prayer of the Church make up God's harrow to rake in the seed after it is scattered, and so it is covered up within the clods of the soul, and is hidden in the heart of the hearer.

Now there is a reason why I dwell upon this; namely, that I may exhort my dear brothers and sisters who have not seen success, not to give up the work but to hope that they have been doing the plowing and sowing and harrowing work, and that the harvest is to come. I mention this for yet another reason, and that is to warn those who expect to have a harvest without this preparatory work. I do not believe that much good will come from attempts at sudden revivals made without previous prayerful labor. To be permanent, a revival must be a matter of growth and the result of much holy effort, longing, pleading, and watching. The servant of God is to preach the gospel whether others are prepared for it or not; but in order for it to work, the hearers must be prepared. Upon some hearts warm, earnest preaching drops like an unusual thing which startles but does not convince. In other congregations, where good gospel preaching has long been the rule and much prayer has been offered, the words fall into the hearers' souls and bring forth speedy fruit. We must not expect to have results without work. There is no hope of a church having an extensive revival in its midst unless there is continued and importunate waiting upon God, together with earnest laboring, intense anxiety, and hopeful expectation.

But there is also a work to be done which is beyond our power. After plowing, sowing, and harrowing, there must come the shower from heaven. "Thou visitest the earth, and waterest it," says Psalm 65:9. All our efforts are in vain unless God blesses us with the rain of his Holy Spirit's influence. O Holy Spirit! You, and you alone, work wonders in the human heart, and you come from the Father and the Son to do the Father's purposes, and to glorify the Son.

Three effects are spoken of here. First, we are told that *he waters the ridges*. As the ridges of the field become well saturated through and through with the abundant rain, so God sends his Holy Spirit until the whole heart of humankind is moved and influenced by his divine operations. The understanding is enlightened, the conscience is quickened, the will is controlled, the affections are inflamed; all these powers, which I may call the ridges of the heart, come under the divine working. It is ours to deal with people as individuals, to influence them with the gospel truth and to set before them motives that are suitable to move rational creatures. But after all, it is the rain from on high which alone can water the ridges: there is no hope of the heart being savingly affected except by divine operations.

Next, it is added, "*Thou settlest the furrows*," by which some think it is meant that the furrows are drenched with water. Others think there is an allusion here to the beating down of the earth by heavy rain until the ridges become flat, with the soaking of the water settling the soil into a more compact mass. It is certain that the influences of God's Spirit have a humbling and settling effect upon us. We were once unsettled like the earth that is dry and crumbly, blown about and carried away with every wind of doctrine; but as the earth when soaked with rain becomes compacted and knit together, so the heart becomes solid and serious under the power of the Spirit. As the high parts of the ridge are beaten down into the furrows, so the lofty ideas, the grand schemes, and carnal boastings of the heart begin to decrease when the Holy Spirit comes to work upon the soul. Genuine humility is a very gracious fruit of the Spirit. To be broken in heart is the best means of preparing the soul for Jesus. "A broken and a contrite heart, O God, thou wilt not despise" (Psalm 51:17). Friends, always be thankful when you see the high thoughts of someone brought down; this settling the furrows is a very gracious preparatory work of grace.

It is added, *"Thou makest it soft with showers."* Our hearts are naturally hardened against the gospel; like the Eastern soil, they are as hard as iron if there has been no gracious rain. How sweetly and effectively does the Spirit of God soften us through and through! We are no longer toward the Word what we used to be: we feel everything, whereas once we felt nothing. The rock flows with water; the heart is dissolved in tenderness; the eyes are melted into tears.

All this is God's work. I have said already that God works through us, but still, it is God's immediate work to send down the rain of his grace from on high. Perhaps he is at work in some of you, though as yet there is no springing up of spiritual life in your souls. Though your condition is still a sad one, we will hope for you that before long there shall be seen the living seed of grace sending up its tender green shoot above the soil, and may the Lord bless the springing thereof.

A Brief Description of the Springing Thereof

After the workings of the Holy Spirit have been quietly going on for a certain season as pleases the great Master and Gardener, then there are signs of grace. Remember the apostle's words: "First the blade, then the ear, after that the full corn in the ear" (Mark 4:28). Some of our friends are greatly disturbed because they cannot see the full corn in the ear in themselves. They suppose that, if they were the subjects of a divine work, they would be precisely like certain advanced Christians with whom it is their privilege to commune, or of whom they may have read about in biographies. Beloved, this is a very great mistake. When grace first enters the heart, it is not a great tree covering with its shadow whole acres, but it is the least of all seeds, like a grain of mustard seed. When it first rises upon the soul, it is not the sun shining at high noon, but it is the first dim ray of dawn. Are you so simple as to expect the harvest before you have passed through the springtime? I hope that by a very brief description of the earliest stage of Christian experience, you may be led to say, "I have gone as far as that," and then I hope you may be able to take the comfort of the verse to yourself: "Thou blessest the springing thereof."

What then is the springing up of piety in the heart? We think it is first seen in *sincerely earnest desires after salvation*. The individual is not saved in their own understanding, but they long to be. That which was once a matter of indifference is now a subject of intense concern. Once they despised Christians and thought them needlessly earnest; they thought religion a mere trifle, and they looked upon the things of time and sense as the only substantial matters—but now how changed they are! They envy the poorest Christian and would change places with the least fortunate believer if they might but be able to one day reach a mansion in the skies. Now worldly things have lost power over them, and spiritual things are uppermost. Once they cried to others, "Who will show us any good?" but now they cry, "Lord, lift up the light of your countenance upon me." Once it was the corn and the wine to which they looked for comfort, but now they look to God alone. Their rock of refuge must be God, for they find no comfort elsewhere. Their holy desires, which they had years ago, were like smoke from the chimney, soon blown away; but now their longings are permanent, though not always operative to the same degree. At times these desires amount to a hungering and a thirsting after righteousness, and yet they are not satisfied with these desires, but wish for a still more anxious longing after heavenly things. These desires are among the first springings of divine life in the soul.

"The springing thereof" shows itself next in *prayer*. It *is* prayer now. Once it was the mocking of God with holy sounds unattended by the heart; but now, though the prayer is such that the individual would not like a human ear to hear them, yet God approves it, for it is the talking of a spirit to a Spirit, and not the muttering of lips to an unknown God. Their prayers, perhaps, are not very long: they do not amount to more than this, "Oh!" "Ah!" "Would to God!" "Lord, have mercy upon me, a sinner!" and such short exclamations, but they *are* prayers. "Behold he prayeth" (Acts 9:11) does not refer to a long prayer; it is quite as sure proof of spiritual life within, if it only refers to a sigh or to a tear. These "groanings which cannot be uttered" (Romans 8:26) are among "the springings thereof."

There will also be manifest *a hearty love for the means of grace*, and the house of God. The Bible, long unread, which was thought to be of little more use than an old almanac, is now treated with great consideration. And though the reader finds little in it that comforts them just now, and much that alarms them, they still feel that it is the book for them, and they turn to its pages with hope. When they go up to God's house, they listen eagerly, hoping that there may be a message for them. Before, they attended worship as a sort of pious necessity which was expected of all respectable people; but now they go up to God's house that they may find the Savior. Once there was no more religion in them than in the door which turns upon its hinges; but now they enter the house praying, "Lord, meet with my soul," and if they receive no blessing, they go away sighing, "Oh, that I knew where I might find him, that I might come even to his seat." This is one of the blessed signs of "the springing thereof."

The soul in this state has *faith in Jesus Christ*, at least in some degree. It is not a faith which brings great joy and peace, but still, it is a faith which keeps the heart from despair and prevents it from sinking under a sense of sin. I have known a time when I did not believe that anyone living could see faith in me, and when I could scarcely perceive any in myself, and yet I was bold to say with Peter, "Lord, thou knowest all things; thou knowest that I love thee" (John 21:17). What others cannot see, Christ can see.

Many people have faith in the Lord Jesus Christ, but they are so engaged in looking at it that they do not see it. If they would look to Christ and not to their own faith, they would not only see Christ but see their own faith too; but they measure their faith, and it seems so little when they contrast it with the faith of full-grown Christians, that they fear it is not faith at all. If you have faith enough to receive Christ, remember the promise, "But as many as received him, to them gave he power to become the sons of God" (John 1:12). Poor, simple, weakhearted, and troubled one, look to Jesus and answer: Can such a Savior suffer in vain? Can such an atonement be offered in vain? Can you trust him, and yet be cast away? It cannot be. It never was in the Savior's heart to shake off one who clung to his arm. However feeble the faith, he blesses "the springing thereof." The difficulty comes partly from misunderstanding and partly from lack of confidence in God.

If like some Londoners, you had never seen corn when it is green, you would cry out, "What! Do you say that yonder green stuff is wheat?" "Yes," the farmer says, "that is wheat." You look at it again and you reply, "Why, man alive, that is nothing but grass. You do not mean to tell me that this grassy stuff will ever produce a loaf of bread such as I see in the baker's window; I cannot conceive it." No, you could not conceive it, but when you get accustomed to it, it is not at all wonderful to see the wheat go through certain stages—first the blade, then the ear, and finally the full ear of corn. Some of you have never seen growing grace and do not know anything about it. When you are newly converted, you meet with Christians who are like ripe golden ears and you say, "I am not like them." True, you are no more like them than that grassy stuff in the furrows is like full-grown wheat; but you will grow like them one of these days. You must expect to go through the blade period before you get to the ear period, and in the ear period you will have doubts whether you will ever come to the full ear of corn, but you will arrive at perfection in due time. Thank God that you are in Christ at all. Whether I have much faith or little faith, whether I can do much for Christ or little for Christ, is not the first question. I am saved, not on account of what I am but on account of what Jesus Christ is; and if I am trusting him, however little in Israel I may be, I am as safe as the brightest of the saints.

I have said, however, that mixed with misunderstanding there is a great deal of unbelief. I cannot put it all down to an ignorance that may be forgiven, for there is sinful unbelief too. Friend, why do you not trust Jesus Christ? Poor, quickened, awakened conscience, God gives you his word that those who trust in Christ will not be condemned, and yet you are afraid that you are condemned! But this is not the truth. You should never doubt the truthfulness of God. All your other sins do not grieve Christ so much as the sin of thinking that he is unwilling to forgive you, or the sin of suspecting that if you trust him, he will cast you away. Do not slander his gracious character. Do not disbelieve the generosity of his tender heart. He says, "Him that cometh to me I will in no wise cast out" (John 6:37). Come in the faith of his promise, and he will receive you just now.

I have now given you some description of "the springing thereof."

The Lord Blesses the Springing Thereof

Thirdly, according to the verse, there is one who sees this springing. Thou, Lord—thou blessest the springing thereof. I wish that some of us had quicker eyes to see the beginnings of grace in the souls of others, for we let slip away many opportunities to help others. If a woman had the charge of a number of children that were not her own, I do not suppose she would notice all the initial stages of illness. But when a mother nurses her own dear children, as soon as there is upon the cheek or in the eye the smallest sign of approaching sickness, she perceives it at once. I wish we had just as quick an eye and just as tender a heart toward precious souls. I do not doubt that many young people are weeks and even months in distress, who need not be, if we who know the Lord were a little more eager to help them in their times of sorrow. Shepherds are up all night at lambing time to catch the lambs as soon as they are born and take them in and nurse them. We, who ought to be shepherds for God, should be looking out for all the lambs, especially in the seasons when many are born into God's great fold, for tender nursing is always wanted in the first stages of the new life. God, however, when his servants do not see "the springing thereof," sees it all.

Now, you silent friends, who dare not speak to father or mother, or brother or sister, this verse ought to be a sweet morsel to you: "*Thou blessest the springing thereof.*" This proves that God sees you and your newborn grace. The Lord sees the first sign of penitence. Though you only say to yourself, "I will arise and go to my Father," your Father hears you. Though it is nothing but a desire, your Father registers it. "Put thou my tears into thy bottle: are they not in thy book?" (Psalm 56:8). He is watching your return; he runs to meet you, and puts his arms about you and kisses you with the kisses of his accepting love. Oh, friend, be encouraged with that thought, that up in the chamber or down by the hedge, or wherever it is that you have sought secrecy, God is there. Dwell on the thought, "Thou God seest me" (Genesis 16:13). This is a precious passage: "All my desire is before thee" (Psalm 38:9). And here is another sweet one: "The LORD taketh pleasure in them that fear him, in those that hope in his mercy" (Psalm 147:11). He can see you when you only hope in his mercy, and he takes pleasure in you if you have only begun to fear him. Here is yet another helpful truth: "The LORD will perfect that which concerneth me" (Psalm 138:8).

Have you a concern about these things? Is it a matter of soul-concern with you to be reconciled to God, and to have an interest in Jesus' precious blood? It is only "the springing thereof," but he blesses it. It is written, "A bruised reed shall he not break, and the smoking flax shall he not quench: he shall bring forth judgment unto truth" (Isaiah 42:3). There will be victory for you, even before the judgment seat of God, though as yet you are only like the flax that smokes and gives no light, or like the reed that is broken and yields no music. God sees the first springing of grace.

WHAT A MISERY TO HAVE THIS SPRINGING THEREOF WITHOUT GOD'S BLESSING!

The verse says, "Thou *blessest* the springing thereof." We must, just for a moment and by way of contrast, think of how the springing would have been without the blessing. Suppose we were to see a revival among us without God's blessing. It is my conviction that there are revivals which are not of God at all, but are produced merely by excitement. If there is no blessing from the Lord, it will be all a delusion, a bubble blown into the air for a moment, then gone to nothing. We will only see the people stirred, to become the more dull and dead afterwards, and this is a great harm to the church.

In the individual heart, if there should be a springing up without God's blessing, there would be no good in it. Suppose you have good desires, but no blessing on these desires. They will only tantalize and worry you, and then, after a time, they will be gone, and you will be more impervious than you were before to religious convictions. If religious desires are not of God's sending, but are caused by excitement, they will probably prevent you from seriously hearing the Word of God in times to come. If convictions do not soften, they will certainly harden. To what ends have some been driven who have had springings of a certain sort which have not led them to Christ! Some have been crushed by despair. They tell us that religion crowds the madhouse: it is not true; but there is no doubt whatever that religiousness of a certain kind has driven many an individual out of their mind. The poor souls have felt their wound but have not seen the balm. They have not known Jesus. They have had a sense of sin and nothing more. They have not fled for refuge to the hope which God has set before them. Marvel not if people do go mad when they refuse the Savior. It may come as a trial upon those who, when in great distress of mind, will not fly to Christ. I believe it is with some just this—you must either fly to Jesus, or else your burden will become heavier and heavier until your spirit will utterly fail. This is not the fault of religion; it is the fault of those who will not accept the remedy which religion presents. A springing up of desires without God's blessing would be an awful thing, but we thank him that this is not the case.

THE COMFORTING THOUGHT THAT GOD DOES BLESS THE SPRINGING THEREOF

I wish to deal with you who are tender and troubled; I want to show that God *does* bless your springing. He does it in many ways.

Frequently he does it by the cordials which he brings. You have a few very sweet moments: you cannot say that you are Christ's, but at times the bells of your heart ring very sweetly at the mention of his name. The means of grace are very precious to you. When you gather to the Lord's worship, you feel a holy calm, and you go away from the service wishing that there were seven Sundays in the week instead of one. By the blessing of God, the Word has spoken to you, as if the Lord had sent his servants on purpose to you. You lay aside your crutches for awhile, and you begin to run. Though these things have been sadly transient, they are tokens for good.

On the other hand, if you have had none of these comforts, or few of them, and the means of grace have not been consolations to you, I want you to see that as a blessing. It may be the greatest blessing God can give us to take away all comforts on the road, in order to quicken our running toward the end. When someone is flying to the City of Refuge to be protected from the enemy, it may be an act of great consideration to stop them for a moment to allow them to quench their thirst and run more swiftly afterwards. But perhaps, in a case of imminent peril, it may be the kindest thing neither to give them anything to eat or to drink, nor invite them to stop for a moment, in order that they may fly with undiminished speed to the place of safety.

The Lord may be blessing you in the uneasiness which you feel. If you cannot say that you are in Christ, it may be the greatest blessing which heaven can give to take away every other blessing from you, in order that you may be compelled to fly to the Lord. You perhaps have a little of your self-righteousness left, and while it is so you cannot get joy and comfort. The royal robe which Jesus gives will never shine brilliantly upon us until every rag of our own goodness is gone. Perhaps you are not empty enough, and God will never fill you with Christ until you are. Fear often drives us to faith. Have you never heard of a person walking in the fields into whose bosom a bird has flown because it had been pursued by the hawk? Poor, timid thing, it would not have ventured there had not a greater fear compelled it. All this may be so with you; your fears may be sent to drive you more swiftly and closer to the Savior, and if so, I see in these present sorrows the signs that God is blessing "the springing thereof."

In looking back on my own "springing," I sometimes think God blessed me then in a lovelier way than he does now. Though I would not willingly return to that early stage of my spiritual life, there were many joys about it. An apple tree when loaded with apples is a very comely sight, but give me, for beauty, the apple tree in bloom. The whole world does not present a lovelier sight than an apple blossom. A full-grown Christian laden with fruit is a comely sight, but still there is a peculiar loveliness about the young Christian. Let me tell you what that blessedness is: You have probably now a greater horror of sin than believers who have known the Lord for years; they might wish that they felt your tenderness of conscience. You have now a graver sense of duty, and a more solemn fear of the neglect of it, than some who are farther advanced. You have also a greater zeal than many; you are now doing your first works for God and burning with your first love, and nothing is too hot or too heavy for you. I pray that you may never decline, but always advance.

Three Lessons for Us to Learn

First, *let older saints be very gentle and kind to young believers*. God blesses the springing thereof—mind that you do the same. Do not throw cold water upon young desires; do not snuff out young believers with hard questions. While they are babes and need the milk of the Word, do not be choking them with your strong meat; they will eat strong meat by-and-by, but not just yet. Remember, Jacob would not overwork the lambs; be equally prudent. Teach and instruct them, but let it be with gentleness and tenderness, not as their superiors, but as tender caregivers for Christ's sake. God, you see, blesses the springing thereof—may he bless it through you!

The next thing I have to say is, *fulfill the duty of gratitude*. Beloved, if God blesses the springing thereof we ought to be grateful for a little grace. If you have only seen the first shoot peeping up through the soil, be thankful and you shall see the green blade waving in the breeze. Be thankful for the ankle-deep verdure and you shall soon see the commencement of the ear. Be thankful for the first green ears and you shall see the flowering of the wheat, and by-and-by its ripening, and the joyous harvest.

The last lesson is one of *encouragement*. If God blesses "the springing thereof," dear beginners, what will he not do for you in later days? If he gives you such a meal when you break your fast, what dainties will be on your table when he says to you, "Come and dine"; and what a banquet will he furnish at the supper of the Lamb! O troubled one! let the storms which howl and the snows which fall, and the wintry blasts that nip your springing, all be forgotten in this one consoling thought: that God blesses your springing, and whom God blesses none can curse. Over your head, dear, desiring, pleading, languishing soul, the Lord of heaven and earth pronounces the blessing of the Father, and the Son, and the Holy Spirit. Take that blessing and rejoice in it evermore. Amen.

TEN

FARM LABORERS

I have planted, Apollos watered; but God gave the increase. So then neither is he that planteth any thing, neither he that watereth; but God that giveth the increase. Now he that planteth and he that watereth are one: and every man shall receive his own reward according to his own labour. For we are labourers together with God: ye are God's husbandry.

(1 CORINTHIANS 3:6–9)

I will begin at the end of this passage, because I find it to be the easiest way of mapping out my discourse. We will first remark that *the church is God's farm*: "Ye are God's husbandry." In the margin of the revised version we read, "Ye are God's tilled ground," and that is the very expression for me. "Ye are God's tilled ground," or farm. After we have spoken of the farm, we will next say a little about the fact that *the Lord employs laborers* on his estate. And when we have looked at the laborers—such poor fellows as they are—we will remember that *God himself is the great worker*: "We are labourers together with God."

THE CHURCH IS GOD'S FARM

The Lord has made the church his own by his sovereign *choice*. He has also secured it to himself by *purchase*, having paid for it a price immense. "The LORD's portion is his people; Jacob is the lot of his inheritance" (Deuteronomy 32:9). Every acre of God's farm cost the Savior an extraordinary effort; indeed, the blood of his heart. He loved us and gave himself for us: that is the price he paid. Henceforth the church is God's property, and he holds the title deed of it. It is our joy to feel that we are not our own; we are bought with a price. The church is God's farm by choice and purchase.

And now he has made it his by *enclosure*. Previously it lay exposed as part of an open common, bare and barren, covered with thorns and thistles, and the haunt of every wild beast; for we were "by nature the children of wrath, even as others" (Ephesians 2:3). Divine foreknowledge surveyed the waste, and electing love marked out its portion with a full line of grace, setting us apart to be the Lord's own estate forever. In due time effectual grace came forth with power and separated us from the rest of humankind, as fields are hedged and ditched to part them from the open heath. Has not the Lord declared that he has chosen his vineyard and fenced it?

> We are a garden wall'd around,
> Chosen and made peculiar ground;
> A little spot, enclosed by grace
> Out of the world's wide wilderness.[22]

The Lord has also made this farm plainly his own by *cultivation*. What more could he have done for his farm? He has totally changed the nature of the soil: from being barren, he has made it a fruitful land. He has plowed it, and cultivated it, and expanded it, and watered it, and planted it with all manner of flowers and fruits. It has already brought forth to him many a pleasant cluster, and there are brighter times to come, when angels shall shout the harvest home, and Christ "shall see of the travail of his soul, and shall be satisfied," (Isaiah 53:11).

This farm is preserved by the Lord's continual *protection*. Not only did he enclose it and cultivate it by his miraculous power to make it his own farm, but he continually maintains possession of it. "I the LORD do keep it; I will water it every moment: lest any hurt it, I will keep it night and day" (Isaiah 27:3). If it were not for God's continual power, her hedges would soon be thrown down and wild beasts would devour her fields. Wicked hands are always trying to break down her walls and lay her waste, so that there should be no true Church in the world, but the Lord is jealous for his land and will not allow it to be destroyed. A church would not long remain a church if God did not preserve it for himself. What if God should say, "I will take away the hedge thereof, and it shall be eaten up; and break down the wall thereof, and it shall be trodden down" (Isaiah 5:5)? What a wilderness it would become. What does he say? "But go ye now unto my place which was in Shiloh, where I set my name at the first, and see what I did to it for the wickedness of my people Israel" (Jeremiah 7:12).

Go to Jerusalem, which once was the city of his glory and the shrine of his indwelling; what is left there today? Go to Rome, where Paul once preached the gospel with power; what is it now but the center of idolatry? The Lord may remove the candlestick and leave a place that was bright as day to become black as darkness itself. God's farm remains a farm because he is ever in it to prevent its returning to its former wildness. Omnipotent power is as necessary to keep the fields of the church under cultivation as it is to first reclaim them.

Since the church is God's own farm, *he expects to receive a harvest from it*. The world is waste, and he looks for nothing from it; but we are tilled land, and therefore a harvest is due from us. Barrenness suits the moorland, but to a farm it would be a great discredit. Love looks for returns of love; grace given demands gracious fruit. Watered with the drops of the Savior's blood, should we not bring forth a hundredfold to his praise? Kept by the eternal Spirit of God, should there not be produced in us fruits to his glory? The Lord's cultivation of us has shown a great expenditure of cost, and labor, and thought; should there not be a proportionate return? Should the Lord not get from us a harvest of obedience, a harvest of holiness, a harvest of usefulness, a harvest of praise? Should it not be so?

I think some churches forget that an increase is expected from every field of the Lord's farm, for they never have a harvest or even look for one. Farmers do not plow their lands or sow their fields for amusement; they mean business, and plow and sow because they desire a harvest. If this fact could but enter into the heads of some believers, surely they would look at things in a different light; but lately it has seemed as if we thought that God's church was not expected to produce anything, but instead existed for her own comfort and personal benefit. Friends, it must not be so; the great Gardener must have some reward for his work. Every field must yield its increase, and the whole estate must sing forth his praise. We join with the bride in the Song in saying, "My vineyard, which is mine, is before me: thou, O Solomon, must have a thousand, and those that keep the fruit thereof two hundred" (Song of Solomon 8:12).

But I come back to the place from which I started. This farm is, by choice, by purchase, by enclosure, by cultivation, by preservation, entirely the Lord's. It would be unjust to allow any of the laborers to call even a part of the estate their own. When a great man has a large farm of his own, what would he think if Hodge the plowman should say, "Look here, I plow this farm, and therefore it is mine: I shall call this field Hodge's Acres"? "No," says Hobbs, "I reaped that land last harvest, and therefore it is mine, and I shall call it Hobbs's Field." What if all the other laborers became Hodgeites and Hobbsites, and so parceled out the farm among them? I think the landlord would soon dismiss the lot of them. The farm belongs to its owner, and let it be called by his name; it is absurd to call it by the names of those who labor upon it. Should insignificant nobodies rob God of his glory?

Remember how Paul put it: "Who then is Paul, and who is Apollos?" (1 Corinthians 3:5). "Is Christ divided? was Paul crucified for you? or were ye baptized in the name of Paul?" (1 Corinthians 1:13).

The entire church belongs to him who has chosen it in his sovereignty, bought it with his blood, fenced it by his grace, cultivated it by his wisdom, and preserved it by his power. There is but one church on the face of the earth, and those who love the Lord should keep this truth in mind. Paul is a laborer, Apollos is a laborer, Cephas is a laborer; but the farm is not Paul's, not so much as a rood of it. Nor does a single parcel of land belong to Apollos or the smallest allotment to Cephas, for "Ye are Christ's" (1 Corinthians 3:23). The fact is that in this case, the laborers belong to the land, not the land to the laborers: "For all things are your's; whether Paul, or Apollos, or Cephas" (1 Corinthians 3:21–22). And "We preach not ourselves, but Christ Jesus the Lord; and ourselves your servants for Jesus' sake" (2 Corinthians 4:5).

THE GREAT GARDENER EMPLOYS LABORERS

By human agency God ordinarily works out his designs. He can, if he pleases, by his Holy Spirit get directly at our hearts, but that is his business and not ours. We must listen to such words as these: "It pleased God by the foolishness of preaching to save them that believe" (1 Corinthians 1:21). The Master's commission is not, "Sit still and see the Spirit of God convert the nations;" but "Go ye into all the world, and preach the gospel to every creature" (Mark 16:15). Observe God's method in supplying us with food. In answer to the prayer, "Give us this day our daily bread," he might have told the clouds to drop manna, morning by morning, at each one's door; but he sees that it is for our good to work, and so he uses the hands of the plowman and the sower for our supply. God might cultivate his chosen farm, the church, by miracle or by angels; but in great condescension he blesses her through her own sons and daughters. He employs us for our own good, for we who are laborers in his fields receive much more good for ourselves than we bestow. Labor develops our spiritual muscle and keeps us in health. "Unto me," says Paul, "who am less than the least of all saints, is this grace given, that I should preach among the Gentiles the unsearchable riches of Christ" (Ephesians 3:8).

Our great Master means for every laborer on his farm to receive some benefit from it, for he never muzzles the mouth of the ox that treads out the corn. The laborer's daily bread comes out of the soil. Though he works not for himself, but for his Master, he still has his portion of food. In the Lord's granary there is seed for the sower, but there is also bread for the eater. However disinterestedly we may serve God in the cultivating of his church, we are ourselves partakers of the fruit. It is a wonder that he uses us at all, for we are poor tools at the best, and more hindrance than help.

The laborers employed by God are all *occupied by necessary work*. Notice: "I have planted, Apollos watered." Who beat the big drum, or blew his own trumpet? Nobody. On God's farm none are kept for ornamental purposes. I have read some sermons which could only have been meant for show, for there was not a grain of gospel in them. They were plows with the share left out, drills with no wheat in the box, clod-crushers made of butter. I do not believe that our God will ever pay wages to those who only walk about his grounds to show themselves off. Orators who display their eloquence in the pulpit are more like wanderers who stray onto the farm to pick up chickens than honest laborers who work to bring forth a crop for their master. Many of the members of our churches live as if their only business on the farm was to pluck blackberries or gather wildflowers. They are great at finding fault with other people's plowing and mowing, but not a bit of work will they do themselves. Come, my good friends. Why do you stand idle all day? The harvest is plentiful, and the laborers are few.

You who think yourselves more cultivated than ordinary people, if you are indeed Christians, you must not strut about and look down upon those who are hard at work. If you do, I will say, "That person has mistaken his master; he may probably be employed by some gentle-man farmer, who cares more for show than profit; but our great Lord is practical, and on his estate his laborers attend to needful labor." When you and I preach or teach it will be well if we say to ourselves, "What will be the use of what I am going to do? I am about to teach a difficult subject; will it do any good? I have chosen a challenging point of theology; will it serve any purpose?" Brothers and sisters, a laborer may work very hard at a whim of his own, and yet it may be all for nothing. Some messages do little more than show the differ-ence between tweedle-*dum* and tweedle-*dee*, and what is the use of that? Suppose we sow the fields with sawdust, or sprinkle them with rosewater, what of that? Will God bless our moral essays and fine com-positions and pretty passages? Friends, we must aim at usefulness: we must as laborers together with God be occupied with something that is worth doing. "I," says one, "have planted." It is well, for planting must be done. "I," answers another, "have watered." That also is good and necessary. See to it that each of you brings in a solid report, but let no one be content with the mere child's play of oratory, or the getting up of entertainments and such like.

On the Lord's farm *there is a division of labor.* Even Paul did not say, "I have planted and watered." No, Paul planted. And certainly Apollos could not say, "I have planted as well as watered." No, it was enough for him to attend to the watering. No person has all gifts. How foolish, then, are they who say, "I enjoy So-and-so's ministry because he edifies the saints in doctrine, but when he was away the other Sunday, I could not learn from the preacher because all he talked about was the conversion of sinners." Yes, he was planting; you have been planted a good while and do not need planting again, but you ought to be thankful that others are hearing that message. One sows and another reaps, and therefore instead of grumbling at the honest plowman because he did not bring a sickle with him, you ought to have prayed for him that he might have strength to plow deep and break up hard hearts.

Observe that, on God's farm, *there is unity of purpose* among the laborers. Read the verse: "Now he that planteth and he that watereth are one." One Master has employed them, and though he may send them out at different times, and to different parts of the farm, they are all being used for one end—to work for one harvest. In England we do not understand what is meant by watering, because the farmer could not water all his farm, but in other places a farmer waters almost every inch of his ground. He would have no crop if he did not use all means available for irrigating the fields. If you have ever been in Italy, Egypt, or Palestine, you will have seen a complete system of wells, pumps, wheels, buckets, channels, little streamlets, pipes, and so on, by which the water is carried all over the garden to every plant; otherwise, in the extreme heat of the sun, it would be dried up. Planting needs wisdom, watering needs quite as much, and the piecing of these two works together requires the laborers to be of one mind. It is a bad thing when laborers are at cross purposes and work against each other, and this evil is worse in the church than anywhere else. How can I plant with success if my helper will not water what I have planted? What is the use of my watering if nothing is planted? Farming is spoiled when foolish people undertake it and quarrel over it; for from sowing to reaping the work is one, and all must be done to one end. Let us pull together all our days, for strife brings barrenness.

We are called upon to notice that *all the laborers put together are nothing at all*: "Neither is he that planteth any thing, neither he that watereth." The workmen are nothing at all without their master. All the laborers on a farm could not manage it if they had no one at their head, and all the preachers and Christian workers in the world can do nothing unless God be with them. Remember that every laborer on God's farm has derived all his qualifications from God. No man knows how to plant or water souls except what the Lord teaches him from day to day. All these holy gifts are grants of free grace. All the laborers work under God's direction and arrangement, or they work in vain. They would not know when or how to do their work if their

Master did not guide them by his Spirit, without whose help they cannot even think a good thought. All God's laborers must go to him for
their seed, or else they will scatter tares. All good seed comes out
of God's granary. If we preach, it must be the true Word of God, or
nothing can come of it. More than that, all the strength that is in the
laborer's arm to sow the heavenly seed must be given by the Master.
We cannot preach except God be with us. A sermon is vain talk and
dreary word-spinning unless the Holy Spirit enlivens it. He must give
us both the preparation of the heart and the answer of the tongue, or
we shall be as men who sow the wind. When the good seed is sown,
the whole success of it rests with God. If he withholds the dew and
the rain, the seed will never rise from the ground; and unless he shall
shine upon it, the green ear will never ripen. The human heart will
remain barren, even though Paul himself should preach, unless God
the Holy Ghost works with Paul and blesses the word to those that
hear it. Therefore, since the increase is of God alone, put the laborers
into their place. Do not make too much of us; for in the end, we are
all unprofitable servants.

Though inspiration calls the laborers nothing, it says that *they
shall be rewarded*. God works our good works in us and then rewards
us for them. Here we have mention of a personal service and a personal reward: "Every man shall receive his own reward according to
his own labour." The reward is proportionate—not to the success,
but to the labor. Many discouraged workers may be comforted by
that expression. You are not to be paid by results, but by endeavors.
You may have a stiff bit of clay to plow or a dreary plot of land to
sow, where stones, birds, thorns, and travelers, and a burning sun,
may all be aligned against the seed; but you are not accountable
for these things, for your reward shall be according to your work.
Some put a great deal of labor into a little field and make much out
of it. Others use a great deal of labor throughout a long life, and yet
they see but small result, for it is written, "One soweth, and another
reapeth" (John 4:37). But the harvester will not get all the reward; the

sower will receive their portion of the joy. The laborers are nobodies, but they will enter into the joy of their Lord.

Unitedly, according to the passage, *the workers have been successful*, and that is a great part of their reward. "I have planted, Apollos watered; but God gave the increase." Frequently believers say in their prayers, "A Paul may plant, an Apollos may water, but it is all in vain unless God gives the increase." This is quite true, but another truth is often overlooked; namely, that when Paul plants and Apollos waters, God does give the increase. We do not labor in vain. There would be no increase without God; but then we are not without God. When such men as Paul and Apollos plant and water, there is sure to be an increase—they are the right kind of laborers, they work with a right spirit, and God is certain to bless them. This is a great part of the laborer's wages.

GOD HIMSELF IS THE GREAT WORKER

He may use what laborers he pleases, but the increase comes alone from him. Brothers and sisters, you know it is so in natural things: the most skillful farmer cannot make the wheat germinate and grow and ripen. He cannot even preserve a single field until harvest time, for the farmer's enemies are many and mighty. In farming there's many a slip 'twixt the cup and the lip, and when the farmer thinks that he will soon harvest his crop, there are blights and mildews lingering about to rob him of his gains. God must give the increase. If any man is dependent on God it is the gardener, and through him we are all of us dependent upon God from year to year for the food by which we live. Even the king must live by the produce of the field. God gives the increase in the barn and the hayrick, and in the spiritual farm it is even more so, for what can individuals do in this business? If any of you think that it is an easy thing to win a soul, I should like you to attempt it. Suppose that without divine aid you should try to save a soul—you might as well attempt to make a world. Why, you cannot create a fly—how can you create a new heart and a right spirit? Spiritual renewal is a great mystery; it is out of your reach. "The wind bloweth where it listeth, and thou hearest the sound thereof, but canst not tell whence it cometh, and whither it goeth: so is every one that is born of the Spirit" (John 3:8).

What can you and I do in this matter? It is far beyond our line. We can speak of the truth of God, but to apply that truth to the heart and conscience is quite another thing. I have preached Jesus Christ with my whole heart, and yet I know that I have never produced a saving effect upon a single unsaved man or woman unless the Spirit of God has opened the heart and placed the living seed of truth within it. Experience teaches us this. Equally is it the Lord's work to keep the seed alive when it springs up. We think we have converts, but it is not long before we are disappointed in them. Many are like blossoms on our apple trees; they are fair to look upon, but they do not come to anything. Others are like the many little apples which fall off long before they have come to any size. One who presides over a great church and feels an agony for the souls of men will soon be convinced that if God does not work, there will be no work done. We will see no conversion, no sanctification, no final perseverance, no glory brought to God, no satisfaction for the passion of the Savior, unless the Lord be with us. Well said our Lord, "Without me ye can do nothing" (John 15:5).

Briefly I would draw certain practical lessons out of this important truth. The first is, if the whole farm of the church belongs exclusively to the great Master Worker, and the laborers are worth nothing without him, *let this promote unity among all whom he employs*. If we are all under one Master, do not let us quarrel. It is a miserable business when we cannot bear to see good being done by those of a different denomination who work in ways of their own. If a new laborer comes on the farm, and he uses a hoe of a new shape, should I become his enemy? If he does his work better than I do mine, should I be jealous? Do you not remember reading in the Scriptures that, upon one occasion, the disciples could not cast out a devil? This ought to have made them humble, but to our surprise we read a few verses later that they saw someone casting out devils in Christ's name, and they forbade him to do so because he followed not with their company. *They* could not cast out the devil themselves, and they forbade those who could. A certain band of people are going about winning souls, but because they are not doing it in our fashion, we do not like it. It is true they have odd ways, but they do really save souls, and that is the main point. Instead of raising trivial objections, let us encourage all on Christ's side. Wisdom is justified of her children, though some of them are far from attractive. The laborers ought to be satisfied with the new plowman if their Master smiles upon him. Friend, if the great Lord has employed you, it is no business of mine to question his choice. Can I lend you a hand? Can I show you how to work better? Or can you show me how I can improve? This is the proper behavior of one worker to another.

This truth, however, ought to *keep all the laborers very dependent*. Are you going to preach, young friend? "Yes, I am going to do a great deal of good." Are you? Have you forgotten that you are nothing? "Neither is he that planteth any thing." A divine is coming brimful of the gospel to comfort the saints. If he is not coming in strict dependence on God, he, too, is nothing. "Neither [is] he that watereth." Power belongs to God. Humankind is vanity and their words are wind; to God alone belongs power and wisdom. If we keep our places in all lowliness our Lord will use us; but if we exalt ourselves he will leave us to our nothingness.

Next, notice that *this fact elevates everybody who labors in God's garden*. My soul is lifted up with joy when I mark these words, "For we are labourers together with God." We are mere laborers on his farm, and yet laborers *with him*. Does the Lord work with us? We know he does by the signs following. "My Father worketh hitherto, and I work" (John 5:17), is language for all the children of God as well as for the great Firstborn. God is with you, my friends, when you are serving him with all your heart. When you speak about Jesus, it is God who speaks by you, picking up that stranger on the way and telling him of salvation by faith. Christ is speaking through you even as he spoke with the woman at the well. If you are preaching pardon through the atoning blood of Jesus, it is the God of Peter who is testifying of his Son, even as he did on the day of Pentecost.

Lastly, *how this should drive us to our knees.* Since we are nothing without God, let us cry mightily to him for help in this our holy service. Let both sower and harvester pray together, or they will never rejoice together. If the blessing is withheld, it is because we do not cry for it and expect it. Brother and sister laborers, come to the mercy seat, and we will yet see the harvesters return from the fields bringing their sheaves with them, though perhaps they went forth weeping to the sowing. To our Father, who is the great Gardener, be all glory, forever and ever. Amen.

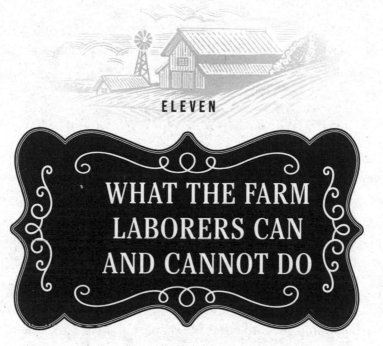

ELEVEN

WHAT THE FARM LABORERS CAN AND CANNOT DO

And he said, So is the kingdom of God, as if a man should cast seed into the ground; and should sleep, and rise night and day, and the seed should spring and grow up, he knoweth not how. For the earth bringeth forth fruit of herself; first the blade, then the ear, after that the full corn in the ear. But when the fruit is brought forth, immediately he putteth in the sickle, because the harvest is come.

[Mark 4:26–29]

There is a lesson for "labourers together with God" (1 Corinthians 3:9). It is a parable for all who are concerned in the kingdom of God. It will be of little value to those who are in the kingdom of darkness, for they are not asked to sow the good seed: "Unto the wicked God saith, What hast thou to do to declare my statutes?" (Psalm 50:16). But all who are commissioned to scatter seed for the Royal Gardener will be glad to know how the harvest is preparing for him whom they serve. Listen, you who sow beside all waters, you who with holy diligence seek to fill the garners of heaven—listen, and may the Spirit of God speak into your ears as you are able to bear it.

What We Can Do and What We Cannot Do

"So is the kingdom of God, as if a man should cast seed into the ground"—this the gracious worker can do. "And the seed should spring and grow up, he knoweth not how"—this is what he cannot do, for seed once sown is beyond human jurisdiction, and we can neither make it spring nor grow. Before long the worker comes in again—"When the fruit is brought forth, immediately he putteth in the sickle." We can harvest in due season, and it is both our duty and our privilege to do so. You see, then, that there is a place for the worker at the beginning, and though there is no room for them in the middle passage, yet another opportunity is given them further on when that which they sowed has actually yielded fruit.

Notice, then, that *we can sow*. Anyone who has received the knowledge of the grace of God in their heart can teach others. We cannot all teach alike, for all have not the same gifts; to one is given one talent, and to another ten. Neither have we all the same opportunities, for one lives in obscurity and another has far-reaching influence; yet there is not within the family of God an infant hand which may not drop its own tiny seed into the ground. There is not a man among us who needs to stand idle in the marketplace, for work suitable to his strength is waiting for him. There is not a saved woman who is left without a holy task; let her do it and win the approving word, "She hath done what she could" (Mark 14:8).

We need never quarrel with God because we cannot do everything, if he only permits us to do this one thing; for sowing the good seed is a work which will need all our wit, our strength, our love, our care. Holy seed sowing should be adopted as our highest pursuit, and it will be no inferior purpose for the noblest life. You will need heavenly teaching that you may carefully select the wheat, and keep it free from the weeds of error. You will require instruction to winnow out of it your own thoughts and opinions, for these may not be according to the mind of God. People are not saved by our word, but by God's Word. We need grace to learn the gospel correctly, and to teach the whole of it. To different men and women, we must, with discretion, bring forward that part of the Word of God which will best bear upon their consciences, for much may depend upon the Word being *in season.*

Having selected the seed, we will have plenty of work to do if we go forth and sow it everywhere, for every day brings its opportunity, and every company furnishes its occasion. "In the morning sow thy seed, and in the evening withhold not thine hand" (Ecclesiastes 11:6). And "Sow beside all waters" (Isaiah 32:20).

Still, wise sowers discover favorable opportunities for sowing, and gladly seize upon them. There are times when it would clearly be a waste to sow, for the soil could not receive it; it is not in a fit condition. After a shower, or before a shower, or at some such time as those who have studied agriculture prefer, those are the times we must be up and laboring. While we are to work for God always, there are seasons when it would be like casting pearls before swine to talk of holy things, and there are other times when to be silent would be a great sin. Sluggards in the time for plowing and sowing are sluggards indeed, for they not only waste the day but also throw away the year. If you watch for souls, and use hours of happy vantage, and moments of sacred softening, you will not complain of the limited space allowed for laboring. Even if you are never called to water or to harvest, your position is important if you fulfill the work of the sower.

For little though it seems you teach the simple truth of the gospel, your work is still essential. How will others hear without a teacher? Servants of God, the seed of the Word is not like thistledown, which is borne by every wind. The wheat of the kingdom needs a human hand to sow it, and without such work it will not enter into the hearts of others, neither can it bring forth fruit to the glory of God. The preaching of the gospel is the necessity of every age; God grant that we may never be deprived of it. Even if the Lord should send us a famine of bread and water, may he never send us a famine of the word of God. Faith comes by hearing, and how can there be hearing if there is no teaching? Scatter the seed of the kingdom, for this is essential to the harvest.

This seed should be sown often, for many are the foes of the wheat, and if you repeat not your sowing you may never see a harvest. The seed must be sown everywhere, too, for there are no choice corners of the world that you can afford to let alone, in the hope that they will be self-productive. You may not leave the rich and intelligent under the notion that surely the gospel will be found among them, for it is not so: the pride of life leads them away from God. You may not leave the poor and illiterate, and say, "Surely they will of themselves feel their need of Christ." Not so: they will sink from degradation to degradation unless you lift them up with the gospel. No tribe of people, no particular constitution of the human mind, may be neglected by us; but everywhere we must preach the Word, in season and out of season. I have heard that the celebrated circumnavigator Captain Cook, in whatever part of the earth he landed, took with him a little packet of English seeds and scattered them in suitable places. He would leave the boat and wander up from the shore. He said nothing, but quietly scattered the seeds wherever he went, so that he belted the world with the flowers and herbs of his native land. Imitate him wherever you go; sow spiritual seed in every place that your foot treads upon.

Let us now think of what you cannot do. *You cannot, after the seed has left your hand, cause it to put forth life.* I am sure you cannot make it grow, for you do not know how it grows. The passage says, "And the seed should spring and grow up, he knoweth not how." That which is beyond the range of our knowledge is certainly beyond the reach of our power. Can you make a seed germinate? You may place it under conditions of damp and heat which will cause it to swell and break forth with a shoot, but the germination itself is beyond you. How is it done? We know not. After the germ has been put forth, can you make it further grow and develop its life into leaf and stem? No; that, too, is out of your power. And when the green, grassy blade has been succeeded by the ear, can you ripen it? It will be ripened; but can *you* do it? You know you cannot; you can have no part in the actual process, though you may promote the conditions under which it can grow. Life is a mystery; growth is a mystery; ripening is a mystery: and these three mysteries are as fountains sealed against all intrusion.

How is it that there is within the ripe seed the preparations for another sowing and another growth? What is this vital principle, this secret reproducing energy? Do you know anything about this? The philosopher may talk about chemical combinations, and he may proceed to quote analogies from this and that, but still the growth of the seed remains a secret. It springs up, and nobody knows how. Certainly this is true of the rise and progress of the life of God in the heart. It enters the soul and roots itself we know not how. Naturally men and women hate the Word, but it enters in, and it changes their hearts so that they come to love it, yet we know not how. Their whole nature is renewed, so that instead of producing sin it yields repentance, faith, and love, but we know not how. How the Spirit of God deals with the mind, how he creates the new heart and the right spirit, how we are begotten again unto a lively hope, we cannot tell. The Holy Ghost enters into us—we hear not his voice, we see not his light, we feel not his touch; yet he works an effective work upon us, which we are not long in perceiving. We know that the work of the Spirit is a new creation, a resurrection, a quickening from the dead, but all these words are only covers to our utter ignorance of the mode of his working, with which it is not in our power to meddle. We do not know how he performs his miracles of love, and, not knowing how he works, we may be quite sure that we cannot take the work out of his hands. We cannot create, we cannot quicken, we cannot transform, we cannot convert, we cannot save.

This work of God having proceeded in the growth of the seed, what next? *We can reap the ripe ears.* After a season God the Holy Spirit uses his servants again. As soon as the living seed has produced first of all the blade of thought, and afterwards the green ear of conviction, and then faith—which is as a full ear of corn—then the Christian worker comes in for further service, for *he or she can reap.* "When the fruit is brought forth, immediately he putteth in the sickle." This is not the reaping of the last great day, for that does not come within the scope of the parable, which evidently relates to a human sower and harvester. The kind of harvesting which the Savior here intends is that which he referred to when he said to his disciples, "Lift up your eyes, and look on the fields; for they are white already to harvest" (John 4:35). After he had been sowing the seed in the hearts of the Samaritans, and it had sprung up so that they began to reveal faith in him, the Lord Jesus cried, "They are white already to harvest." The apostle said, "One soweth, and another reapeth" (John 4:37). Our Lord said to the disciples, "I sent you to reap that whereon ye bestowed no labour" (John 4:38). Is there not a promise, "In due season we shall reap, if we faint not" (Galatians 6:9)?

Christian workers begin their harvest work by watching for signs of faith in Christ. They are eager to see the blade, and delighted to mark the ripening ear. They often hope that men and women are believers, but they long to be sure of it; and when they judge that at last the fruit of faith is put forth, they begin to encourage, to congratulate, and to comfort. They know that the young believer needs to be housed in the barn of Christian fellowship, that he or she may be saved from a thousand perils. No wise farmer leaves the fruit of the field long exposed to the hail which might beat it out, or to the mildew which might destroy it, or to the birds which might devour it. No believers should be left outside of the gathering of holy fellowship; they should be carried into the midst of the church with all the joy which attends the home-bringing of sheaves. Workers for Christ watch carefully, and when they discern that their time is come, they begin at once to fetch in the converts, that they may be cared for by the congregation, separated from the world, screened from temptation, and laid up for the Lord. They are diligent to do it at once, because the Scripture says, "immediately he putteth in the sickle." They do not wait for months in cold suspicion; they are not afraid that they will encourage too soon when faith is really present. They come with the word of promise and the smile of godly love at once, and they say to the new believer, "Have you confessed your faith? Is not the time come for an open confession? Has not Jesus bidden the believer to be baptized? If you love him, keep his commandments." They do not rest until they have introduced the convert to the communion of the faithful. For our work, beloved, is but half done when men and women are made disciples and baptized. We have then to encourage, to instruct, to strengthen, to console, and to help in all times of difficulty and danger. What does the Savior say? "Go ye therefore, and teach all nations, baptizing them in the name of the Father, and of the Son, and of the Holy Ghost: teaching them to observe all things whatsoever I have commanded you" (Matthew 28:19–20).

Observe, then, the sphere and limit of agency. We can introduce the truth to others, but that truth the Lord himself must bless; the living and growing of the Word within the soul is of God alone. When the mystic work of growth is done, we are able to gather the saved ones in the church. For Christ to form in others the hope of glory is not of our working; that remains with God. But, when Jesus Christ is formed in them, to discern the image of the Savior and say, "Come in, thou blessed of the LORD; wherefore standest thou without?" (Genesis 24:31), this is our duty and delight. To create the divine life is God's; to cherish it is ours. To cause the hidden life to grow is the work of the Lord; to see the uprising and development of that life and to harvest it is the work of the faithful, even as it is written, "When the fruit is brought forth, immediately he putteth in the sickle, because the harvest is come."

This, then, is our first lesson—we see what we can do and what we cannot do.

WHAT WE CAN KNOW AND WHAT WE CANNOT KNOW

First, *what we can know*. We can know when we have sown the good seed of the Word that it will grow, for God has promised that it will do so. Not every grain in every place—for some will go to the bird, and some to the worm, and some to be scorched by the sun—but, as a general rule, God's Word will not return to him void; it will prosper where he has sent it. This we can know. And we can know that the seed will continue to grow once it takes root; that it is not a dream or a picture that will disappear, but a thing of force and energy, which will advance from a grassy blade to corn in the ear, and under God's blessing will develop to actual salvation and be as the "full corn in the ear." God helping and blessing it, our work of teaching will not only lead men and women to thought and conviction but to conversion and eternal life.

We also can know, because we are told so, that the reason for this is mainly because there is life in the Word. In the Word of God itself there is life, for it is written, "The word of God is quick, and powerful" (Hebrews 4:12)—that is, "living and powerful." It is the "incorruptible" seed . . . "which liveth and abideth for ever" (1 Peter 1:23). It is the nature of living seeds to grow, and the reason the Word of God grows in our hearts is because it is the living Word of the living God, and where the word of a king is, there is power. We know this because the Scriptures teach us so. Is it not written, "Of his own will begat he us with the word of truth" (James 1:18)?

Moreover, the earth "bringeth forth fruit of herself." We must mind what we are saying here, for human hearts do not produce faith of themselves; they are as hard rock on which the seed perishes. But it means this—that as the earth under the blessing of the dew and the rain is, by God's secret working upon it, made to take up and embrace the seed, so the hearts of men and women are made ready to receive and enfold the gospel of Jesus Christ within itself. The awakened heart wants exactly what the Word of God supplies. Moved by a divine influence, the soul embraces the truth and is embraced by it, and so the truth lives in the heart and is quickened by it. Our love accepts the love of God; our faith wrought in us by the Spirit of God believes the truth of God; our hope wrought in us by the Holy Ghost lays hold of the things revealed, and so the heavenly seed grows in the soil of the soul. The life comes not from you who preach the Word, but it is placed within the Word which you preach by the Holy Spirit. The life is not in your hand, but in the heart, which is led to take hold of the truth by the Spirit of God. Salvation comes not from the personal authority of the preacher, but through the personal conviction, personal faith, and personal love of the hearer. So much as this we may know, and is it not enough for all practical purposes?

Still, there is *a something which we cannot know*, a secret into which we cannot pry. I repeat what I have said before: you cannot look into an individual's inward parts and see exactly how the truth takes hold of the heart or the heart takes hold of the truth. Many have watched their own feelings until they have become blind with despondency, and others have watched the feelings of the young until they have done them more harm than good by their rigorous supervision. In God's work there is more room for faith than for sight. The heavenly seed grows secretly. You must bury it out of sight, or there will be no harvest. Even if you keep the seed above ground, and it does sprout, you cannot discover *how* it grows; even though you microscopically watched its swelling and bursting, you could not see the inward vital force which moves the seed. We know not the way of the Spirit. His work is wrought in secret. "Explain the new birth," says somebody. My answer is, "Experience the new birth, and you shall know what it is." There are secrets into which we cannot enter, for their light is too bright for mortal eyes to endure. As humans, we cannot become omniscient, for we are creatures, not the Creator. For us there must ever be a region not only unknown but also unknowable. So far shall our knowledge go, but no farther; and we may thank God it is so, for this is how he leaves room for faith and gives cause for prayer. Cry mightily to the Great Worker to do what we cannot attempt to perform, that so, when we see others saved, we may give the Lord all the glory evermore.

What We May Expect If We Work for God and What We May Not Expect

According to this parable *we may expect to see fruit*. The farmer casts his seed into the ground: the seed springs and grows, and he naturally expects a harvest. I wish I could say a word to stir up the expectations of Christian workers, for I fear that many work without faith. If you have a garden or a field and you sow seed in it, you would be very greatly surprised and grieved if it did not come up at all; but many Christians seem quite content to work on without expectation of result. This is a pitiful kind of working—pulling up empty buckets by the year together. Surely, I must either see some result for my labor and be glad, or else, failing to see it, I must be ready to break my heart if I am a true servant of the great Master. We ought to have expected results; if we had expected more we should have seen more, but a lack of expectation has been a great cause of failure in God's workers.

But we may not expect to see all the seed that we sow spring up the moment we sow it. Sometimes, glory be to God, we have but to deliver the Word, and straightway others are converted: the reaper overtakes the sower, in such instances, but it is not always so. Some sowers have been diligent for years upon their plots of ground, and yet apparently all has been in vain; at last the harvest has come, a harvest which would had never been reaped if they had not persevered to the end. This world, as I believe, is to be converted to Christ—but not today, nor tomorrow, perhaps not for many an age, but the sowing of the centuries is not being lost; it is working on toward the grand ultimatum. A crop of mushrooms may soon be produced; but a forest of oaks will not reward the planter until generations of his children have crumbled into dust. It is ours to sow and to hope for quick harvesting, but still, we ought to remember that "the husbandman waiteth for the precious fruit of the earth, and hath long patience for it, until he receive the early and latter rain" (James 5:7), and so must we. We are to expect results but not to be dispirited if we have to wait for them.

We are also to expect to see the good seed grow, but *not always after our fashion*. Like children, we are apt to be impatient. Your little boy sowed mustard and cress yesterday in his garden. This afternoon Johnny will be turning over the ground to see if the seed is growing. There is no probability that his mustard and cress will come to anything, for he will not let it alone long enough for it to grow. So is it with hasty workers; they must see the result of the gospel directly, or else they distrust the blessed Word.

Certain preachers are in such a hurry that they allow no time for thought, no space for counting the cost, no opportunity for men and women to consider their ways and turn to the Lord with full purpose of heart. All other seeds take time to grow, but the seed of the Word must grow before the speaker's eyes like magic, or he thinks nothing has been done. Such good believers are so eager to produce blade and ear there and then, that they roast their seed in the fire of fanaticism, and it perishes. They make others think that they are converted, and thus effectually hinder them from coming to a saving knowledge of the truth. Some are prevented from being saved by being told that they are saved already, and by being puffed up with a notion of perfection when they are not even broken in heart. Perhaps if such people had been taught to look for something deeper, they might not have been satisfied with receiving seed on stony ground; but now they exhibit a rapid development and an equally rapid decline and fall. Let us believingly expect to see the seed grow, but let us look to see it advance after the manner of the preacher—firstly, secondly, thirdly: first the blade, then the ear, then the full ear of corn.

We may expect also to see the seed ripen. Our works will by God's grace lead up to real faith in those he has formed by his Word and Spirit; but *we must not expect to see it perfect at first*. How many mistakes have been made here. Here is a young, impressionable person, and some good, sound brother or sister talks with the trembling beginner and asks profound questions. They shake their experienced head and knit their furrowed brow. They go into the cornfield to see how the crops are prospering, and though it is early in the year, they lament that they cannot see an ear of corn; indeed, they perceive nothing but mere grass. "I cannot see a trace of corn," they say. No, of course they cannot, for they will not be satisfied with the blade as an evidence of life but must insist upon seeing everything at full growth at once. If you had looked for the blade, you would have found it; and it would have encouraged you. For my own part I am glad even to perceive a faint desire, a feeble longing, a degree of uneasiness, or a measure of weariness of sin, or a craving after mercy. Will it not be wise for you, also, to allow things to begin at the beginning, and to be satisfied with their being small at the first? See the blade of desire, and then watch for more. Soon you shall see a little more than desire, for there shall be conviction and resolve, and after that a feeble faith, small as a mustard seed, but bound to grow.

Do not despise the day of small things. Do not examine the newborn babe to see whether he is sound in doctrine after your idea of soundness; ten to one he is a long way from understanding and you will only worry the dear heart by introducing difficult questions. Speak to him about his being a sinner and Christ a Savior, and you will in this way water him so that grace will eventually become the full ear of corn. It may be that there is not much that looks like wheat about him yet, but by-and-by you will say, "Wheat! That it is, if I know wheat. This man is a true ear of corn, and gladly will I place him among my Master's sheaves." If you cut down the blades, where will the ears come from? Expect grace in your converts, but do not look to see glory in them just yet.

What Sleep Workers May Take and What They May Not Take

It is said of the sower that he sleeps and rises night and day, and the seed springs and grows up, he knows not how. They say a farmer's trade is a good one because it is going on while he is in bed and asleep; and surely ours is a good trade, too, when we serve our Master by sowing good seed, for it is growing even while we are asleep.

But how may a good worker for Christ lawfully go to sleep? I answer, first, he may sleep the sleep of *restfulness* born of confidence. You are afraid the kingdom of Christ will not come, are you? Who asked you to tremble for the ark of the Lord? Afraid for the infinite Jehovah that his purposes will fail? Shame on you! Your anxiety dishonors your God. Shall Omnipotence be defeated? You had better sleep than wake to play the part of Uzzah. Rest patiently; God's purpose will be accomplished, his kingdom will come, his chosen will be saved, and Christ will see of the travail of his soul. Take the sweet sleep which God gives to his beloved, the sleep of perfect confidence, such as Jesus slept in the rear part of the ship when it was tossed with tempest. The cause of God never was in jeopardy, and never will be; the seed sown is insured by Omnipotence and must produce its harvest. In patience possess your soul, and wait until the harvest comes, for the pleasure of the Lord must prosper in the hands of Jesus.

Also take that sleep of *joyful expectancy* which leads to a happy waking. Get up in the morning and feel that the Lord is ruling all things for the attainment of his own purposes and the highest benefit of all who put their trust in him. Look for a blessing by day, and close your eyes at night calmly expecting to meet with better things tomorrow. If you do not sleep, you will not wake up in the morning refreshed and ready for more work. If it were possible for you to sit up all night and eat the bread of carefulness, you would be unfit to attend to the service which your Master appoints for the morning; therefore take your rest and be at peace, and work with calm dignity, for the matter is safe in the Lord's hands. Is it not written, "So he giveth his beloved sleep" (Psalm 127:2)?

Take your rest because you have consciously resigned your work into God's hands. After you have spoken the Word, resort to God in prayer and commit the matter into his hand, and then do not fret about it. It cannot be in better keeping; leave it with he who works all in all.

But do not sleep the sleep of unwatchfulness. The farmer sows his seed, but he does not forget about it. He has to mend his fences, to drive away birds, to remove weeds, or to prevent floods. He does not watch the growth of the seed, but he has plenty else to do. He sleeps, but it is only in due time and measure and is not to be confused with the sluggard's slumbers. He never sleeps the sleep of indifference, or even of inaction, for each season has its demand upon him. He has sown one field, but he has another to sow. He has sown, but he has also to reap; and if reaping is done, he has to thresh and to winnow. A farmer's work is never done, for in one part or the other of the farm he is needed. His sleep is but a pause that gives him strength to continue his occupation. The parable teaches us to do all that lies within our power, but not to intrude into the domain of God. We are to labor diligently, but with regard to the secret working of truth upon another's mind, we are to pray and rest, looking to the Lord for the inward power.

TWELVE

THE SHEEP BEFORE
THE SHEARERS

As a sheep before her shearers is dumb, so he
openeth not his mouth.

(ISAIAH 53:7)

Our Lord Jesus so took our place that we are in this chapter compared to sheep: "All we like sheep have gone astray" (v. 6), and
he is compared to a sheep also—"As a sheep before her shearers is
dumb." It is wonderful how complete was the interchange of positions
between Christ and his people, so that he became what they were in
order that they might become what he is. We can well understand
how we should be the sheep and he the shepherd; but to liken the
Son of the Highest to a sheep would have been an unpardonable presumption had not his own Spirit employed the condescending figure.

Though the emblem is very gracious, its use in this place is by no
means singular, for our Lord had been before Isaiah's day typified by
the lamb of the Passover. Since then, he has been proclaimed as "the
Lamb of God, which taketh away the sin of the world" (John 1:29); and
indeed, even in his glory, he is the Lamb in the midst of the throne.

OUR SAVIOR'S PATIENCE

In opening up this divine passage, I would invite you to consider, first, our Savior's patience, set forth under the figure of a sheep dumb before her shearers.

Our Lord was brought to the shearers that he might be shorn of his comfort and of his honor, shorn even of his good name, and shorn at last of his life itself; but when under the shearers, he was as silent as a sheep. How patient he was before Pilate, and Herod, and Caiaphas, and on the cross! We have no record of his uttering any exclamation of impatience at the pain and shame which he received at the hands of these wicked men. We hear not one bitter word. Pilate cries, "Answerest thou nothing? behold how many things they witness against thee" (Mark 15:4); Herod is woefully disappointed, for he expected to see some miracle wrought by him. All that our Lord does say is in submissive tones, like the bleating of a sheep, though infinitely more full of meaning. He utters sentences like these: "To this end I was born, and for this cause came I into the world, that I should bear witness unto the truth" (John 18:37), and "Father, forgive them; for they know not what they do" (Luke 23:34). Otherwise, he is all patience and silence.

Remember, first, that our Lord was silent and did not open his mouth *against his adversaries* and did not accuse one of them of cruelty or injustice. They slandered him, but he replied not; false witnesses arose, but he answered them not. One would have thought he must have spoken when they spat in his face. Might he not have said, "Friend, why do you do this? For which of all my works do you insult me?" But the time for such expostulations was over. When they smote him on the face with the palms of their hands, it would not have been wonderful if he had said, "Why do you smite me so?" But no; it is as though he did not hear their revilings. He brings no accusation to his Father. He needed only to have lifted his eye to heaven, and legions of angels would have chased away the ribald soldiery; one flash of a seraph's wing and Herod would have been eaten by worms and Pilate died the death he well deserved as an unjust judge. The hill of the cross might have become a volcano's mouth to swallow up the whole multitude who stood there jesting and jeering at him: but no, there was no display of power—or rather, there was so great a display of power over himself that he restrained Omnipotence itself with a strength which never can be measured.

Again, as our Lord did not utter a word against his adversaries, so he did not say a word *against any one of us*. You remember how Zipporah said to Moses, "Surely a bloody husband art thou to me" (Exodus 4:25), as she saw her child bleeding; and surely Jesus might have said to his church, "You are a costly spouse to me, to bring me all this shame and bloodshed." But he gave liberally, he opened the very fountain of his heart, and he did not reproach anyone. He had reckoned on the uttermost expenditure, and therefore he endured the cross, despising the shame.

> This was compassion like a God,
>> That when the Savior knew
> The price of pardon was His blood,
>> His pity ne'er withdrew.[23]

No doubt he looked across the ages; for that eye of his was not dim, even when bloodshot on the tree. He must have foreseen your indifference and mine, our coldness of heart, and base unfaithfulness, and he might have left on record some such words as these: "I am suffering for those who are utterly unworthy of my regard; their love will be a miserable return for mine. Though I give my whole heart for them, how lukewarm is their love to me! I am sick of them, I am weary of them, and it is woe to me that I should be laying down my heart's blood for such a worthless race as these my people are." But there is not a hint of such a feeling. No. "Having loved his own which were in the world, he loved them unto the end" (John 13:1), and he did not utter a syllable that looked like murmuring at his suffering on their behalf or regretting that he had commenced the work.

And again, as there was not a word against his adversaries, nor a word against you or me, so there was not a word *against his Father*, nor a syllable of complaining at the severity of the chastisement laid upon him for our sakes. You and I have murmured when under a comparatively light grief. We have dared to cry out against God, "My face is foul with weeping, and on my eyelids is the shadow of death; not for any injustice in mine hands: also my prayer is pure" (Job 16:16–17). But not so the Savior; in his mouth were no complaints. It is quite impossible for us to conceive how the Father pressed and bruised him, yet was there no repining. "My God, my God, why hast thou forsaken me?" (Matthew 27:46) is an exclamation of astonished grief, but it is not the voice of complaint. It shows humanity in weakness, but not humanity in revolt. Many are the lamentations of Jeremiah, but few are the lamentations of Jesus. Jesus wept, and Jesus sweated great drops of blood, but he never murmured nor felt rebellion in his heart.

Behold your Lord and Savior lying in passive resignation beneath the shearers, as they take away everything that is dear to him, and yet he opens not his mouth. I see in this our Lord's *complete submission*. He gives himself up; there is no reserve about it. The sacrifice did not need binding with cords to the horns of the altar. How different from your case and mine! He stood there willing to suffer, to be spit upon, to be shamefully entreated, and to die, for in him there was a complete surrender. He was wholly given to do the Father's will, and to work out our redemption. There was *complete self-conquest* too. In him no faculty arose to plead for liberty and ask to be exempted from the general strain; no limb of the body, no portion of the mind, no faculty of the spirit started, but all submitted to the divine will: the whole Christ gave up his whole being unto God, that he might perfectly offer himself without spot for our redemption.

There was not only self-conquest but *complete absorption in his work*. The sheep, lying there, thinks no more of the pastures; it yields itself up to the shearer. The zeal of God's house did eat up our Lord in Pilate's hall as well as everywhere else, for there he witnessed a good confession. No thought had he but for the clearing of the divine honor and the salvation of God's elect. Friends, I wish we could arrive at this, to submit our whole spirit to God, to learn self-conquest, and the delivering up of the conquered self entirely to God.

The wonderful serenity and submissiveness of our Lord are still better set forth by our passage, if it be indeed true that sheep in other places are even more docile than they are with us. Those who have seen the noise and roughness of many of our washings and shearings will hardly believe the testimony of that ancient writer Philo-Judaeus when he affirms that the sheep came voluntarily to be shorn. He says: "Woolly rams laden with thick fleeces put themselves into the shepherd's hands to have their wool shorn, being thus accustomed to pay their yearly tribute to man, their king by nature. The sheep stands in a silent inclining posture, unconstrained under the hand of the shearer. These things may appear strange to those who do not know the docility of the sheep, but they are true." Marvelous indeed was this submissiveness in our Lord's case; let us admire and imitate it.

View Our Own Case Under the Same Metaphor As That Reference to Our Lord

Did I not begin by saying that because we were sheep, he deigns to compare himself to a sheep? Let us look from another point of view; our Lord was a sheep under the shearers, and as he is, so are we also in this world. Though we will never be offered up like lambs in the temple by way of atonement, yet the saints for ages were the flock of slaughter, as it is written: "For thy sake we are killed all the day long; we are accounted as sheep for the slaughter" (Romans 8:36). Jesus sends us forth as sheep in the midst of wolves, and we are to regard ourselves as living sacrifices, ready to be offered up. I dwell, however, more particularly upon the second symbol: we are brought as sheep under the shearers' hands.

Just as a sheep is taken by the shearer, and its wool is all cut off, so does the Lord take his people and shear them, taking away all their earthly comforts and leaving them bare. I wish when it came our turn to undergo this shearing operation, it could be said of us as of our Lord, "As a sheep before her shearers is dumb, so he openeth not his mouth." I fear that we open our mouths a great deal, and make no end of complaining without any apparent cause, or with the very slenderest reason. But now to the illustration.

First, remember that *a sheep rewards its owner for all his care and trouble by being shorn*. There is nothing else that I know of that a sheep can do. It yields food when it is killed, but while it is alive the one payment that the sheep can make to the shepherd is to yield its fleece in due season. Some of God's people can give to Christ a tribute of gratitude by active service, and they should do so gladly every day of their lives. But many others cannot do much in active service, and about the only reward they can give to their Lord is to render up their fleece by suffering when he calls on them to suffer, submissively yielding to be shorn of their personal comfort when the time comes for patient endurance.

Here comes the shearer; he takes the sheep and begins to cut, cut, cut, cut, taking away the wool wholesale. Affliction is often used as the big shears. The husband, or perhaps the wife, is removed, little children are taken away, property is shorn off, and health is gone. Sometimes the shears cut off the man's good name; slander follows; comforts vanish. Well, this is your shearing time, and it may be that you are not able to glorify God to any very large extent except by undergoing this process. If this is true, do you not think that we, like good sheep of Christ, should surrender ourselves cheerfully, feeling, "I lay myself down with this intent, that you should take from me anything and everything, and do what you will with me; for I am not my own, I am bought with a price"?

Notice that the sheep is itself *benefited by the operation of shearing*. Before they begin to shear the sheep, the wool is long and old, and every bush and brier tears off a bit of the wool until the sheep looks ragged and forlorn.

If the wool were left, when the heat of summer came the sheep would not be able to bear itself, it would be so overloaded with clothing that it would be as uncomfortable as we are when we have kept on our borrowed wool, our flannels and broadcloths, too late. So, brothers and sisters, when the Lord shears us, we do not like the operation any more than the sheep do; but first, it is for *his glory*; and secondly, it is for *our benefit*, and therefore we are bound most willingly to submit. There are many things that we should have liked to have kept which, if we had kept them, would not have proved blessings but curses. A stale blessing is a curse. The manna, though it came from heaven, was only good so long as God's command made it a blessing, but when they kept it too long, it bred worms and stank, and then it was no blessing. Many people would keep their mercies until they turn to corruption; but God will not have it so. Up to a certain point being wealthy was a blessing; it would not have been a blessing any longer, and so the Lord took your riches away. Up to that point your child was a blessing, but it would have been no longer so, and therefore it fell sick and died. You may not be able to see it, but it is so, that God, when he withdraws a blessing from his people, takes it away because it would not be a blessing any longer.

Before sheep are shorn, *they are always washed*. Were you ever present at the scene when they drive them down to the brook? Men are placed in rows, leading to the shepherd who stands in the water. The sheep are driven down, and the men seize them and throw them into the pool, keeping their faces above water, and swirl them round and round and round to wash the wool before they clip it off. You see them come out on the other side frightened to death, poor things, wondering whatever is coming. I want to suggest to you, friends, that whenever a trial threatens to overtake you, you should entreat the Lord to sanctify it to you. If the Good Shepherd is going to clip your wool, ask him to wash it before he takes it off; ask to be cleansed in spirit, soul, and body. It is a very good custom Christian people have of asking a blessing on their meals before they eat bread. Do you not think it is even more necessary to ask a blessing on our troubles before we get into them? Here is your dear child likely to die; will you not, dear parents, meet together and ask God to bless the death of that child, if it is to happen? The harvest fails; would it not be well to say, "Lord, sanctify this poverty, this loss, this year's bad harvest: cause it to be a means of grace to us." Why not ask a blessing on the cup of bitterness as well as upon the cup of thanksgiving? Ask to be washed before you are shorn, and if the shearing must come, let it be your chief concern to yield clean wool.

After the washing, when the sheep has been dried, it actually *loses what was its comfort*. The sheep is thrown down, and the shearers get to work; the poor creature is losing its comfortable fleece. You also will have to part with your comforts. Will you remember this? The next time you receive a fresh blessing, call it a loan. Poor sheep, there is no wool on your back but what will have to come off; child of God, there is no earthly comfort in your possession but what will either leave you, or you will leave it. Nothing is our own except our God. "Why," says one, "not our sin?" Sin was our own, but Jesus has taken it upon himself, and it is gone. There is nothing our own but our God, for all his gifts are held on lease, terminable at his sovereign will. We foolishly consider that our mercies belong to us, and when the Lord takes them away we half grumble. A loan, they say, should go laughing home, and so we should rejoice when the Lord takes back that which he had lent us. All our possessions are but brief favors borrowed for the hour. As the sheep yields up its wool and so loses its comfort, so must we yield up all our earthly properties; or if they remain with us till we die, we shall part with them then, and we shall not take so much as one of them across the stream of death.

The shearers *take care not to hurt the sheep*; they clip as close as they can, but they do not cut the skin. If possible, they will not draw blood, even in the smallest degree. When they do make a gash, it is because the sheep does not lie still; but a careful shearer has bloodless shears. Of this Thomson sings in his "Seasons," and the passage is so good an illustration of the whole subject that I will adorn my discourse with it:

> How meek, how patient, the mild creature lies!
> What softness in its melancholy face,
> What dumb complaining innocence appears!
> Fear not, ye gentle tribes! 'tis not the knife
> Of horrid slaughter that is o'er you waved;
> No, 'tis the tender swain's well guided shears,
> Who having now, to pay his annual care,
> Borrow'd your fleece, to you a cumbrous load,
> Will send you bounding to your hills again.[24]

It is the kicking and the struggling that make the shearing work difficult, but if we are silent before the shearers, no harm can come. The Lord may clip wonderfully close; I have known him to clip some so close that they did not seem to have a bit of wool left, for they were stripped entirely, even as Job when he cried, "Naked came I out of my mother's womb, and naked shall I return thither" (Job 1:21). Still, like Job, they have added, "The LORD gave, and the LORD hath taken away; blessed be the name of the LORD" (Job 1:21).

Notice that the shearers always *shear at a suitable time*. It would be a very wicked, cruel, and unwise thing to begin sheep-shearing in wintertime. There is a proverb which talks about God "tempering the wind to the shorn lamb." It may be so, but it is a very cruel practice to shear lambs while winds need tempering. Sheep are shorn when it is warm, genial weather, when they can afford to lose their fleeces, and are all the better for being relieved of them. As the summer comes on, sheep-shearing time comes. Have you ever noticed that whenever the Lord afflicts us, he selects the best possible time? There is a prayer that he puts into his disciples' mouths: "Pray ye that your flight be not in the winter" (Matthew 24:20); the spirit of that prayer may be seen in the seasonableness of our sorrows. He will not send us our worst troubles at our worst times. If your soul is depressed, the Lord does not send you a very heavy burden; he reserves such a load for times when you have joy in the Lord to be your strength. It has come to be a kind of feeling with us that when we have much delight, a trial is near, but when sorrow thickens, deliverance is approaching. The Lord does not send us two burdens at a time; or, if he does, he sends double strength. His shearing time is chosen with tender discretion.

There is another thing to remember. It is with us, as it is with the sheep, that *there is new wool coming*. Whenever the Lord takes away our earthly comforts with one hand, one, two, three, he restores with the other hand six, a score, a hundred; we are crying and whining about the little loss, and yet it is necessary in order that we may be able to receive the great gain. Yes, it will be so, we shall have cause for rejoicing, and "joy cometh in the morning" (Psalm 30:5). If we have lost one position, there is another for us; if we have been driven out of one place, a better refuge is prepared. Providence opens a second door when it shuts the first. If the Lord takes away the manna, as he did from his people Israel, it is because they have the old corn of the land of Canaan to live upon. If the water of the rock did not follow the tribes any longer, it was because they drank of the Jordan, and of the brooks. O sheep of the Lord's fold, there is new wool coming; therefore, do not fret at the shearing. I have given these thoughts in brief, that we may come to the last word.

IMITATE THE EXAMPLE OF OUR BLESSED LORD WHEN OUR TURN COMES TO BE SHORN

Let us be silent before the shearers, submissive, tranquilly at rest, even as he was. I have been giving, in everything I have said, a reason for so doing. I have shown that our shearing by affliction glorifies God, rewards the Shepherd, and benefits ourselves. I have shown that the Lord measures and tempers our affliction, and sends the trial at the right time. I have shown you in many ways that it will be wise to submit ourselves as the sheep does to the shearer, and that the more completely we do so, the better.

We struggle far too much, and we are apt to make excuses for so doing. Sometimes we say, "Oh, this is so painful, I cannot be patient! I could have borne anything else but this." When a father is going to correct his child, does he select something pleasant? No. The painfulness of the punishment is the essence of it, and even so the bitterness of our sorrow is the soul of our chastening. By the blueness of the wound, the heart will be made better. Do not complain because your trial seems strange and sharp. That would in fact be saying, "If I have it all my own way, I will, but if everything does not please me, I will rebel"; and that is not a fit spirit for a child of God.

Sometimes we complain because of our great weakness. "Lord, if I were stronger, I would not mind this heavy loss, but I am frail as a dry leaf driven of the tempest." But who is to be the judge of the suitability of your trial? You or God? Since the Lord judges this trial to be suitable to your weakness, you may be sure that it is so. Lie still! Lie still! "Alas," you say, "my grief comes from the most cruel quarter; this trouble did not arise directly from God, it came through my cousin or my brother who ought to have treated me with gratitude. It was not an enemy; then I could have borne it." My friend, let me assure you that in reality, trial comes not from an enemy after all. God is at the bottom of all your tribulation; look through the second causes to the great First Cause. It is a great mistake when we fret over the human instrument which smites us, and forget the hand which uses the rod. If I strike a dog, he bites my stick; poor creature, he knows no better; but if he could think a little he would bite *me*, or else take the blow submissively. Now, you must not begin biting the stick. After all, it is your heavenly Father that uses the staff; though it be of ebony or of blackthorn, it is in his hand. It is well to have done with picking and choosing our trials, and to leave the whole matter in the hand of infinite wisdom. A sweet singer has put this matter very prettily; let me quote the lines:

Yet when my Lord did ask me on what side
    I were content,
The grief, whereby I must be purified,
    To me was sent,

As each imagined anguish did appear,
    Each withering bliss,
Before my soul, I cried, "Oh! spare me here,
    Oh, no, not this!—"

Like one that having need of, deep within,
    The surgeon's knife,
Would hardly bear that it should graze the skin,
    Though for his life.

Till He at last, who best doth understand
    Both what we need,
And what can bear, did take my case in hand,
    Nor crying heed.[25]

This is the core of my sermon: Oh, believer, yield yourself! Lie passive in the hands of God! Yield, and struggle not! There is no use in struggling, for our great Shearer, if he means to shear, will do it. Did I not say just now that the sheep, by struggling, might be cut by the shears? So you and I, if we struggle against God, will get two strokes instead of one; and after all there is not half so much trouble in a trouble as there is in kicking against the trouble. The plowman has a rod and pricks the ox to make it move more actively; he does not hurt it much by his gentle prodding, but suppose the ox flings out its leg the moment it touches him, driving the rod into himself, and bleeds. So it is with us—we will find it hard to kick against the pricks; we will endure much more pain by rebelling than would have come if we had yielded to the divine will. What good comes of fretting? We cannot make one hair white or black. You that are troubled, rest with us, for you cannot make shower or shine, foul or fair, with all your groaning. Did you ever bring a penny into the till by fretting, or put a loaf on the table by complaint? Murmuring is wasted breath, and fretting is wasted time. To lie passive in the hand of God brings a blessing to the soul. I would myself be more quiet, calm, and self-possessed. I long to cry habitually, "Lord, do what you will, when you will, as you will, with me, your servant; appoint me honor or dishonor, wealth or poverty, sickness or health, exhilaration or depression, and I will take all right gladly from your hand." One is not far from the gates of heaven when they are fully submissive to the Lord's will.

You who have been shorn have, I hope, received comfort through the ever-blessed Spirit of God. May God bless you. Oh, that sinners, too, would humble themselves under the mighty hand of God! Submit yourselves unto God, let every thought be brought into captivity to him, and the Lord send his blessing, for Christ's sake. Amen.

THIRTEEN

IN THE HAYFIELD

He causeth the grass to grow for the cattle.

(Psalm 104:14)

A T the appointed season all the world is busy with gathering in the grass crop, and you can scarcely ride a mile in the country without scenting the delicious fragrance of the new-mown hay, and hearing the sharpening of the mower's scythe. There is a gospel in the hayfield, and that gospel we intend to bring out as we may be enabled by the Holy Spirit.

Our verse guides us at once to the spot, and we shall need no preface. "He causeth the grass to grow for the cattle"—three things we will notice: first, that *grass is in itself instructive*; second, that *grass is far more so when God is seen in it*; and third, that *by the growth of grass for the cattle, the ways of grace may be illustrated*.

THE GRASS IS INSTRUCTIVELY SYMBOLIC

First, then, "He causeth the grass to grow for the cattle." Here we have *something which is in itself instructive*. Scarcely any emblem, with the exception of water and light, is more frequently used by inspiration than the grass of the field.

In the first place, the grass may be instructively looked upon as *the symbol of our mortality*. "All flesh is as grass" (1 Peter 1:24). The whole history of humankind may be seen in the meadow. We spring up green and tender, subject to the frosts of infancy, which imperil our young lives; we grow, we come to maturity, we put on beauty even as the grass is adorned with flowers; but after a while our strength departs and our beauty is wrinkled, even as the grass withers and is followed by a fresh generation, which withers in its turn. Like ourselves, the grass ripens but to decay. We all come to maturity in due time, and then decline and wither as the green herb. Some of the grass is not left to come to ripeness at all, but the mower's scythe removes it, even as swift-footed death overtakes the careless children of Adam. "In the morning it flourisheth, and groweth up; in the evening it is cut down, and withereth. For we are consumed by thine anger, and by thy wrath are we troubled" (Psalm 90:6–7). "As for man, his days are as grass: as a flower of the field, so he flourisheth. For the wind passeth over it, and it is gone; and the place thereof shall know it no more" (Psalm 103:15–16). This is very humbling, and we need frequently to be reminded of it, or we dream of immortality beneath the stars. We ought never to tread upon the grass without remembering that whereas the green sod covers our graves, it also reminds us of them, and preaches by every blade a sermon to us concerning our mortality, of which Scripture says, "All flesh is grass, and all the goodliness thereof is as the flower of the field" (Isaiah 40:6).

In the second place, grass is frequently used in Scripture as *an emblem of the wicked*. David tells us from his own experience that the righteous man is apt to grow envious of the wicked when he sees the prosperity of the ungodly. We have seen them spreading themselves like green bay trees, fixed and rooted in their places; and when we have smarted under our own troubles, and felt that all the day long we were chastened every morning, we have been apt to say, "How can this be consistent with the righteous government of God?" We are reminded by the psalmist that in a short time we shall pass by the place of the wicked, and he will not be; we will diligently gaze up his place, and it will not be; for he is soon cut down as the grass, and withers as the green herb. The grass withers, the flowers fade away, and so shall pass away forever the glory of those who build upon the estate of time and dig for lasting comfort in the mines of the earth. As the gardener gathers up the green herb and, despite its former beauty, casts it into the fire, such must be the fate of boastful sinners. The judge will command his angels, "Bind them in bundles to burn" (Matthew 13:30). Where now is their merriment? Where now is their confidence? Where now is their pride and your pomp? Where now are their boastings and their loud-mouthed blasphemies? They are silent forever, for, as thorns crackle under a pot but are speedily consumed and leave nothing except a handful of ashes, so shall it be with the wicked as to this life; the fire of God's wrath shall devour them.

It is more pleasing to recollect that the grass is used in Scripture as *a picture of the elect of God*. The wicked are comparable to the dragons of the wilderness, but God's own people will spring up in their place, for it is written, "In the habitation of dragons, where each lay, shall be grass with reeds and rushes" (Isaiah 35:7). The elect are compared to grass, because of their number as they shall be in the latter days, and because of the rapidity of their growth. You remember the passage, "There shall be an handful of corn in the earth upon the top of the mountains; the fruit thereof shall shake like Lebanon: and they of the city shall flourish like grass of the earth" (Psalm 72:16). Oh, that the long-expected day might soon come, when God's people will no longer be like a lone tuft of grass, but when they will spring up as among the grass, as "willows by the water courses" (Isaiah 44:4). Grass and willows are two of the fastest-growing things we know of; so will a nation be born in a day, so will crowds be converted at once. For when the Spirit of God is mightily at work in the midst of the church, men and women will fly to Christ as doves fly to their dovecotes, so that the astonished church will exclaim, "These, where had they been?" Oh, that we might live to see the age of gold, the time which prophets have foretold, when the company of God's people will be as innumerable as the blades of grass in the meadows, and grace and truth shall flourish.

How like the grass are God's people for this reason, that they are absolutely dependent on the influences of heaven! Our fields are parched if spring showers and gentle dews are withheld, and what are our souls without the gracious visitations of the Spirit? Sometimes through severe trials, our wounded hearts are like the mown grass, and then we have the promise, "He shall come down like rain upon the mown grass: as showers that water the earth" (Psalm 72:6). Our sharp troubles have taken away our beauty, but the Lord visits us, and we revive again. Thank God for that old saying, which is a gracious doctrine as well as a true proverb: "Each blade of grass has its own drop of dew." God is pleased to give his own special mercies to each one of his own servants. "Thy blessing is upon thy people" (Psalm 3:8).

Once again, grass is comparable to *the food with which the Lord supplies the necessities of his chosen ones.* Take the twenty-third Psalm, and you have the metaphor worked out in the sweetest form of pastoral song: "He maketh me to lie down in green pastures: he leadeth me beside the still waters" (Psalm 23:2). Just as the sheep has nourishment according to its nature—and this nourishment is abundantly found for it by its shepherd so that it not only feeds but then lies down in the midst of the fodder, satiated with plenty, and per-fectly content and at ease—even so are the people of God when Jesus Christ leads them into the pastures of the covenant and opens up to them the precious truths upon which their souls will be fed. Beloved, have we not proved that promise true, "In this mountain shall the Lord of hosts make unto all people a feast of fat things, a feast of wines on the lees, of fat things full of marrow, of wines on the lees well refined" (Isaiah 25:6)? My soul has sometimes fed upon Christ until I have felt as if I could receive no more, and then I have laid myself down in the bounty of my God to take my rest, satisfied with favor, and full of the goodness of the Lord.

Thus, you see, the grass itself is not without instruction for those who will incline their ear.

GOD IS SEEN IN THE GROWING OF THE GRASS

He is seen first as a worker, "He *causeth* the grass to grow." He is seen secondly as a caretaker, "He causeth the grass to grow *for the cattle*."

1. First, as a *worker*, God is to be seen in every blade of grass, if we have but eyes to discern him. This is a blind world, which always talks about "natural laws," and "the effects of natural causes," but forgets that laws cannot operate of themselves, and that natural causes, so called, are not causes at all unless the First Cause has set them in motion. The old Romans used to say, *God* thundered; *God* rained. We say *it* thunders; *it* rains. What "it"? All these expressions are subterfuges to escape from the thought of God. We commonly say, "How wonderful are the works of *nature!*" What is "nature"? Do you know what *nature* is? I remember a lecturer in the street speaking about nature, and he was asked by a Christian man standing by whether he would tell him what nature was. He never gave a reply. The production of grass is not the result of natural law apart from the actual work of God; mere law would be inoperative unless the great Master himself sent a thrill of power through the matter which is regulated by the law—unless, like the steam engine, which puts force into all the spinning jennies and wheels of a cotton mill, God himself were the motive power to make every wheel revolve. I find rest on the grass as on a royal couch, now that I know that my God is there at work for his creatures.

Having asked you to see God as a worker, I now bid you to see God in *common things*. He makes the grass to grow—grass is a common thing. You see it everywhere, yet God is in it. Dissect it and pull it to pieces; the attributes of God are illustrated in every single flower of the field, and in every green leaf. In like manner, see God in your common matters, your daily afflictions, your common joys, your everyday mercies. Do not say, "I must see a miracle before I see God." In truth everything teems with marvel. See God in the bread of your table and the water of your cup. It will be the happiest way of living if you can say in each providential circumstance, "My Father has done all this." See God also in *little things*. The little things of life are the greatest troubles. A man will hear that his house is burned down more quietly than he will see an ill-cooked joint of meat upon his table, when he counted upon its being properly prepared. It is the *little* stone in the shoe which makes the pilgrim limp. To see God in little things, to believe that there is as much the presence of God in a limb falling from the elm as in the avalanche which crushes a village; to believe that the guidance of every drop of spray, when the wave breaks on the rock, is as much under the hand of God, as the steerage of the mightiest planet in its course; to see God in the little as well as in the great—all this is true wisdom.

Think, too, of God working among *solitary things*; for grass does not merely grow where we take care of it, but it also grows up there on the side of the lone Alp, where no traveler has ever passed. Where only the eye of the wild bird has beheld their lonely verdure, moss and grass display their beauty, for God's works are fair to other eyes than those of mortals. And you, solitary child of God, dwelling, unknown and obscure, in a remote hamlet; you are not forgotten by the love of heaven. He makes the grass grow all alone, and will he not make you flourish despite your loneliness? He can bring forth your graces and educate you for the skies in solitude and neglect. The grass, you know, is a thing we tread upon; nobody thinks of its being crushed by the foot, and yet God makes it grow. Perhaps you are oppressed and downtrodden, but let not this depress your spirit, for God executes righteousness for all those who are oppressed. He makes the grass to grow, and he can make your heart flourish under all the oppressions and afflictions of life, so that you will still be happy and holy though all the world marches over you; still living in the immortal life which God himself bestows on you, though hell itself set its heel upon you. Poor and needy one, unknown, unobserved, oppressed and downtrodden, God makes the grass to grow, and he will take care of you.

2. But I said we should see in the text God also as a great *caretaker.* "He causeth the grass to grow *for the cattle.*" "Doth God take care for oxen? Or saith he it altogether for our sakes?" (1 Corinthians 9:9–10). "Thou shalt not muzzle the mouth of the ox that treadeth out the corn" (1 Corinthians 9:9) shows that God has cares for the beasts of the field—but it shows much more than that, namely that he would have those who work for him feed as they work. God cares for the beasts, and makes grass to grow for them. Though sometimes we have said with David, "So foolish was I, and ignorant: I was as a beast before thee" (Psalm 73:22), yet God cares for us. "He giveth to the beast his food, and to the young ravens which cry" (Psalm 147:9)—there you have an instance of his care for birds, and here we have his care for beasts; and though you, my hearer, may seem to yourself to be as black and defiled as a raven, and as far from anything spiritually good as the beasts, yet take comfort from this verse. He gives grass to the cattle, and he will give grace to you, though you think yourself to be as a beast before him.

Observe that he cares for these beasts who are *helpless* as to caring for themselves. The cattle could not plant the grass, nor cause it to grow. Though they can do nothing in the matter, he does it all for them; *he* causeth the grass to grow. You who are as helpless as cattle to help yourselves, who can only stand and moan out your misery, but know not what to do, God can prevent you in his loving-kindness, and favor you in his tenderness. Let the bleatings of your prayer go up to heaven, let the meanings of your desires go up to him, and help will come to you though you cannot help yourselves. Beasts are *silent, speechless things*, yet God makes the grass grow for them. Will he hear those that cannot speak, and will he not hear those who can? Since our God views with kind consideration the cattle in the field, he will surely have compassion upon his own sons and daughters when they desire to seek his face.

There is this also to be said: God not only cares for cattle, but *the food* which he provides for them is fit food—he causeth *grass* to grow for the cattle, just the sort of food which ruminants require. The Lord God also provides fit sustenance for his people. Depend upon him by faith and wait upon him in prayer, and you will have food perfect for you. You will find in God's mercy just that which your nature demands, suitable supplies for your own needs.

This "convenient" food the Lord takes care to reserve for the cattle, for no one eats the cattle's food but the cattle. There is grass for them, and nobody else cares for it, and thus it is kept for them; even so God has a special food for his own people: "The secret of the LORD is with them that fear him; and he will shew them his covenant" (Psalm 25:14). Though the grass be free to all who choose to eat it, no creature cares for it except the cattle for whom it is prepared; and though the grace of God is free to all men, no man cares for it except the elect of God, for whom he prepared it, and whom he prepares to receive it. There is as much reserve of the grass for the cattle as if there were walls around it; and so, though the grace of God be free, and there is no boundary set about it, yet it is as much reserved as if it were restricted.

God is seen in the grass as the worker and the caretaker; then *let us see his hand in providence at all times.* Let us see it, not only when we have abundance but even when we have scant supplies; for the grass is preparing for the cattle even in the depth of winter. In our trials and troubles, we are still cared for by God. He will accomplish his own divinely gracious purposes in us; we need only to be still and see the salvation of God. Every winter's night has a direct connection with the joyous days of mowing and harvesting, and each time of grief is linked to future joy.

GOD'S WORKING IN THE GRASS ILLUSTRATES GRACE

I will soliloquize, and say to myself as I read the text,

> He causeth the grass to grow for the cattle. In this I perceive a satis-
> fying provision for that form of creature. I am also a creature, but I
> am a nobler creature than the cattle. I cannot imagine for a moment
> that God will provide all that the cattle need and not provide for
> me. But naturally I feel uneasy; I cannot find in this world what I
> want—if I were to win all its riches, I should still be discontented;
> and when I have all that heart could wish of time's treasures, yet
> still my heart feels as if it were empty. There must be somewhere or
> other something that will satisfy me as a person with an immortal
> soul. God altogether satisfies the ox; he must therefore have some-
> thing or other that would altogether satisfy me if I could get it. There
> is the grass, the cattle get it, and when they have eaten their share,
> they lie down and seem perfectly contented; now, all I have ever
> found on earth has never satisfied me so that I could lie down and
> be satisfied. There must, then, be something somewhere that would
> content me if I could get at it.

Is not this good reasoning? I ask both the Christian and the unbeliever to go with me so far; but then let us proceed another step: The
cattle do get what they want—not only is the grass provided, but they
get it. Why should not I obtain what I want? I find my soul hungering
and thirsting after something more than I can see with my eyes or
hear with my ears; there must be something to satisfy my soul, why
should I not find it? The cattle pasture upon that which satisfies them;
why should not I obtain satisfaction too? Then I begin to pray, "O Lord,
satisfy my mouth with good things, and renew my youth."

While I am praying, I also meditate and think—God has provided
for cattle that which is agreeable to their nature; they are nothing
but flesh, and flesh is grass—there is therefore grass for their flesh.

I also am flesh, but I am something else besides; I am spirit, and to satisfy me I need spiritual meat. Where is it? When I turn to God's Word, I find there that though the grass withers, the word of the Lord endures forever, and the word which Jesus speaks to us is spirit and life. "Oh!" I say, "Here is spiritual food for my spiritual nature; I will rejoice therein." May God help me to know what that spiritual meat is, and enable me to lay hold of it, for I perceive that though God provides the grass for the cattle, *the cattle must eat it themselves.* They are not fed if they refuse to eat. I must imitate the cattle and receive that which God provides for me. What do I find provided in Scripture? I am told that the Lord Jesus came into this world to suffer, and bleed, and die instead of me, and that if I trust in him, I shall be saved. And, being saved, the thoughts of his love will give solace and joy to me and be my strength. What have I to do but to feed on these truths? I do not find the cattle bringing any preparation to the pasture except hunger, but they enter it and partake of their portion. Even so must I by an act of faith live upon Jesus. Lord, give me grace to feed upon Christ; make me hungry and thirsty after him; give me the faith by which I may be a receiver of him, that so I may be satisfied with favor, and full of the goodness of the Lord.

This passage, though it looked small, grows as we meditate on it. I want to introduce you to a few more illustrations of divine grace. *Preventing grace may here be seen in a symbol.* Grass grew before cattle were made. We find in the first chapter of Genesis that God provided the grass before he created the cattle. And what a mercy that covenant supplies, for God's people were prepared before they were born. God had given his Son Jesus Christ to be the Savior of his chosen before Adam fell; long before sin came into the world the everlasting mercy of God foresaw the ruin of sin, and provided a refuge for every elect soul. What a thought it is for me, that, before I hunger, God has prepared the manna; before I thirst, God has caused the rock in the wilderness to send forth crystal streams to satisfy the thirst of my soul! See what sovereign grace can do! Before the cattle come to the pasture, the grass has grown for them, and before I feel my need of divine mercy, that mercy is provided for me. Then I perceive an illustration of free grace, for *when the ox comes into the field he brings no money with him.* I, a poor, needy sinner, having nothing, come and receive Christ without money and without price. The Lord makes the grass to grow for the cattle, and so does he provide grace for my needy soul, though I have no money, no virtue, no excellence of my own.

And why is it, my friends, why is it that God gives the cattle the grass? The reason is, *because they belong to him*: "The silver and the gold are mine, and the cattle upon a thousand hills" (Haggai 2:8 and Psalm 50:10). God provides grass for his own cattle, and grace is provided for God's people. Of every herd of cattle in the world, God could say, "They are mine." Long before the rancher puts his brand on the bullock, God has set his creating mark on it. Before the stamp of Adam's fall was set upon our brow, the stamp of electing love was set there: "In thy book all my members were written, which in continuance were fashioned, when as yet there was none of them" (Psalm 139:16).

God also feeds cattle because *he has entered into a covenant with them to do so.* "What! A covenant with the cattle?" says somebody. Yes, it is true, for when God spoke to his servant Noah, in that day when all the cattle came out of the ark, we find him saying, "I establish my covenant with you, and with your seed after you; and with every living creature that is with you, of the fowl, of *the cattle*, and of every beast of the earth with you" (Genesis 9:9–10). A covenant was made with the cattle, and the covenant was that seedtime and harvest should not fail; therefore the earth brings forth for them, and for them the Lord causes the grass to grow. Does Jehovah keep his covenant with cattle, and will he not keep his covenant with his own beloved? It is because his chosen people are his covenanted ones in the person of the Lord Jesus, that he provides for them all things that they will need in time and in eternity, and satisfies them out of the fullness of his everlasting love.

Once again, God feeds the cattle, and then *the cattle praise him.* We find David saying, in the hundred and forty-eighth Psalm, "Praise ye the LORD . . . Beasts, and all cattle" (vv. 1, 10). The Lord feeds his people to the end that their glory may sing praise to him and not be silent. While other creatures give glory to God, let the redeemed of the Lord especially say so, whom he has redeemed out of the hand of the Enemy.

Nor even yet is our verse exhausted. Turning one moment from the cattle, I want you to notice the grass. It is said of the grass, "*He causeth* the grass to grow." Here is a doctrinal lesson, for if grass does not grow without God's causing it to grow, how could grace arise in the human heart apart from divine operations? Surely grace is a much more wonderful product of divine wisdom than the grass can be! And if grass does not grow without a divine cause, it is certain that grace does not dwell in us without a divine implantation. If I have so much as one blade of grace growing within me, I must trace it all to God's divine will and give him all the glory.

Again, if God thinks it worth his while to make grass and take care of it, much more will he think it to his honor to cause his grace to grow in our hearts. If the great invisible Spirit, whose thoughts are high and lofty, condescends to look after that humble thing which grows by the hedge, surely he will condescend to watch over his own nature, which he calls the incorruptible seed, "which liveth and abideth for ever" (1 Peter 1:23).

Mungo Park, in the deserts of Africa, was much comforted when he picked up a little piece of moss and saw the wisdom and power of God in that lonely piece of verdant loveliness. When you see the fields ripe and ready for the mower, your hearts should leap for joy to see how God has produced the grass, caring for it all through the rigorous cold of winter and the chill months of spring, until at last he sent the genial rain and sunshine and brought the fields into their best condition. And so, my soul, though you may endure many a frost of sorrow and a long winter of trial, the Lord will still cause you to grow in grace, and in the knowledge of our Lord and Savior Jesus Christ; to whom be glory forever. Amen.

FOURTEEN

THE JOY OF HARVEST

They joy before thee according to the joy in harvest.

(Isaiah 9:3)

The other day I kept the feast with a company who shouted, "Harvest Home." I was glad to see the rich and poor rejoicing together; and when the cheerful meal was ended, I was glad to turn one of the tables into a pulpit, and in the large barn preach the gospel of the ever-blessed God to an earnest audience. My heart was merry in harmony with the occasion, and I will now keep in the same key and talk to you a little about the joy of harvest. Londoners forget that it is harvest time; living in this great desert of dingy bricks, we hardly know what an ear of wheat is like, except as we see it dry and white in the window of a corn dealer's shop; yet let us all remember that there is such a season as harvest, when by God's goodness the fruits of the earth are gathered in.

WHAT IS THE JOY OF HARVEST?

The joy of harvest is here taken as the simile of the joy of the saints before God. I am afraid that to the mere selfish order of spirits, the joy of harvest is simply that of personal gratification at the increase of wealth. Sometimes the farmer only rejoices because *he sees the reward of his toils*, and is so much the richer man. I hope that with many there mingles the second cause of joy; namely, gratitude to God that an abundant harvest will give bread to the poor, and remove complaining from our streets. There is a lawful joy in harvest, no doubt, to the person who is enriched by it; for all who work hard have a right to rejoice when at last they gain their desire. It would be well if we would always recollect that our last and greatest harvest will be to us according to their labor. The individual who sows to the flesh will of the flesh reap corruption, and only the one who sows to the spirit will of the spirit reap life everlasting. Many a young person commences life by sowing what they call their *wild oats*, which they had better never have sown, for they will bring them a terrible harvest. They expect that from these wild oats they will gather a harvest of true pleasure, but it cannot be; the truest pleasures of life spring from the good seed of righteousness, and not from the hemlock of sin. As a farmer who sows thistles in his furrows must not expect to reap the golden wheatsheaf, so those who follow the ways of vice must not expect happiness. On the contrary, if they sow the wind, they will reap the whirlwind. When a sinner feels the pangs of conscience, they may well say, "This is what I sowed." When they will at last receive the punishment of their evil deeds, they will blame no one but themselves; they sowed tares and they must reap tares. On the other hand, Christians, though their salvation is not of works, but of grace, will have a gracious reward given to them by their Master. Sowing in tears, they shall reap in joy. Putting out their talents to interest, they shall enter into his Master's joy, and hear him say, "Well done, thou good and faithful servant" (Matthew 25:21). The joy of harvest in part consists of the reward of labor; may such be our joy in serving the Lord.

The joy of harvest has another element in it; namely, that of *gratitude to God for favors bestowed*. We are singularly dependent on God—far more so than most of us imagine. When the children of

Israel were in the wilderness, they went forth every morning and gathered the manna. Our manna does not come to us every morning, but it comes once a year. It is as much a heavenly supply as if it lay like a frost round about the camp. If we went out into the field and gathered food which dropped from the clouds, we should think it a great miracle, and is it not as great a marvel that our bread should come up from the earth as that it should come down from the sky? The same God who bade the heavens drop with angels' food bids the dull earth in its due season to yield corn for humankind. Therefore, whenever we find that harvest comes, let us be grateful to God, and let us not suffer the season to pass over without psalms of thanksgiving. I believe I shall be correct if I say that there is never in the world, as a rule, more than sixteen months' supply of food; that is to say, when the harvest is gathered in, there may be sixteen months' supply. But at the time of harvest there is not usually enough wheat in the whole world to last the population more than four or five months, so that if the harvest did not come, we should be on the verge of famine. We live still from hand to mouth. Let us pause and bless God, and let the joy of harvest be the joy of gratitude.

To the Christian it should be great joy, by means of the harvest, *to receive an assurance of God's faithfulness*. The Lord has promised that seedtime and harvest, summer and winter, shall never cease; and when you see the loaded wain carrying in the crop, you may say to yourself, "God is true to his promise. Despite the dreary winter and the damp spring, autumn has come with its golden grain." Depend upon it, that as the Lord keeps this promise, he will keep all the rest. All his promises are true in Christ Jesus; if he keeps his covenant to the earth, much more will he keep his covenant with his own people, whom he has loved with an everlasting love. Go, Christian, to the mercy seat with the promise on your lips and plead it. Be assured it is not something that has lost its power. Do not let unbelief cause you to stammer when you mention the promise before the throne, but say it boldly: "Remember the word unto thy servant, upon which thou hast caused me to hope" (Psalm 119:49). Shame on us that we so little believe our God. The world is full of proofs of his goodness. Every rising sun, every falling shower, every revolving season certifies his faithfulness. Why do we doubt him? If we never doubt him until we have cause for it, we will never know distrust again. Encouraged by the return of harvest, let us resolve in the strength of the Spirit of God that we will not waver, but will believe in the divine Word and rejoice in it.

Once more. To the Christian, in the joy of harvest there will always be *the joy of expectation.* As there is a harvest to the gardener for which he waits patiently, so there is a harvest for every faithful individual who is looking for the coming and the appearing of our Lord and Savior Jesus Christ. The mature Christian, like the ripe ear of corn, hangs down his head with holy humility. When he was but green in the things of God, he stood erect and was somewhat boastful, but now that he has become full of the blessing of the Lord, he is humbled and bows himself down. He is waiting for the sickle, and he dreads it not, for no common reaper shall come to gather Christ's people—he himself will reap the harvest of the world. The Lord leaves the destroying angel to reap the vintage and to cast it into the wine-vat to be trodden with vengeance; but as for the grain which he himself has sown, he will gather it himself with his own golden sickle. We are looking for this. We are growing among the tares—and sometimes we are half afraid lest the tares be stronger than ourselves and choke the wheat— but we shall be separated by-and-by, and when the corn is sifted well and stored in the granary, we shall be there. It is this expectation which even now makes our hearts throb with joy. We have gone to the grave with precious sheaves that belonged to our Master, and when we were there we thought we could almost say, "Lord, if they sleep they will do well. Let us die with them." Our joy of harvest is the hope of being at rest with all the saints, and forever with the Lord. A view of these shadowy harvests upon earth should make us exceedingly glad, because they are the image and foreshadowing of the eternal harvest above.

What Joys Equal the Joy of the Harvest for the Believer?

So much about the joy of harvest; but I hasten onward. It is a common notion that Christians are an unhappy people. It is true that we are tried, but it is false that we are miserable. With all their trials, believers have such a compensation in the love of Christ that they are still a blessed generation, and it may be said of them, "Happy art thou, O Israel" (Deuteronomy 33:29).

One of the first seasons in which we knew a joy equal to the joy of harvest—a season which has continued with us ever since it commenced—was *when we found the Savior*, and so obtained salvation. You recollect for yourselves, brothers and sisters, the time of the plowing of your souls. My heart was fallow and covered with weeds, but on a certain day the great Gardener came and began to plow my soul. Ten black horses were his team, and it was a sharp plowshare that he used, and the plowers made deep furrows. The ten commandments were those black horses, and the justice of God, like a plowshare, tore my spirit. I was condemned, undone, destroyed, lost, helpless, hopeless—I thought hell was before me. Then there came a cross plowing, for when I went to hear the gospel, it did not comfort me; it made me wish I had a part in it, but I feared that such a blessing was out of the question. The choicest promises of God frowned at me, and his threatenings thundered at me. I prayed, but found no answer of peace. It was long this way with me. After the plowing came the sowing. God who plowed the heart made it conscious that it needed the gospel, and the gospel seed was joyfully received.

Do you recollect that auspicious day when at last you began to have some little hope? It was very little—like a green blade that peeps up from the soil; you scarce knew whether it was grass or corn, whether it was presumption or true faith. It was a little hope, but it grew very pleasantly. But then a frost of doubt came; snow of fear fell; cold winds of despondency blew on you; and you said, "There can be no hope for me." But what a glorious day was that when at last the wheat which God had sown ripened, and you could say, "I have looked to him and have been lightened; I have laid my sins on Jesus, where God laid them of old, and they are taken away, and I am saved." I remember well that day, and so, no doubt, do many of you. Oh, friends, no gardener ever shouted for joy as our heart shouted when precious Christ became ours and we could grasp him with full assurance of salvation in him. Many days have passed since then, but the joy of it is still fresh with us. And, blessed be God, it is not the joy of the first day only that we look back upon; it is the joy of every day since then, more or less; for our joy nobody can take from us; still we are walking in Christ, even as we received him. Even now all our hope on him is stayed, all our help from him we bring; and our joy and peace continue with us because they are based upon an immovable foundation. We rejoice in the Lord, yes, and we will rejoice.

The joy of harvest generally shows itself by the farmer giving a feast to his friends and neighbors; and, usually, those who find Christ express their joy by telling their friends and their neighbors about the great things the Lord has done for them. The grace of God is communicative. A person cannot be saved and always hold their tongue about it; as well look for silent choirs in heaven as for a silent church on earth. If a man has been thirsty, and has come to the living stream, his first impulse will be to cry, "Look, every one that thirsts!" Do you feel the joy of harvest, the joy that makes you wish that others should share with you? If so, do not repress the impulse to proclaim your happiness. Speak of Christ to brothers and sisters, to friends and kinsfolk; and, if the language is stammering, the message in itself is so important that the words in which you couch it will be a secondary consideration. Tell it, tell it out far and wide—that there is a Savior, that you have found him, and that his blood can wash away our transgressions. Tell it everywhere, and the joy of harvest will spread over land and sea, and God shall be glorified.

We have another joy which is like the joy of harvest. We frequently have it too. It is *the joy of answered prayer.* I hope you know what it is to pray in faith. Some prayer is not worth the words used in presenting it, because there is no faith mixed with it. "With all your sacrifices, you should offer salt," and the salt of faith is needful if we would have our sacrifices accepted. Those who are familiar with the mercy seat know that prayer is a reality, and that the doctrine of divine answers to prayer is no fiction. Sometimes God will delay to answer for wise reasons; then his children must cry, and cry, and cry again. They are in the condition of the gardener who must wait for the precious fruits of the earth; and when at last the answer to prayer comes, they are then in the gardener's position when he receives the harvest. Remember Hannah's wail and Hannah's word. In the bitterness of her soul she cried to God, and when her child was given to her she called it "Samuel," meaning, "Asked of God;" for, said she, "For this child I prayed" (1 Samuel 1:27). He was a dear child to her, because he was a child of prayer. Any mercy that comes to you in answer to prayer will be your Samuel mercy, your darling mercy. You will say of it, "For this mercy I prayed," and it will bring the joy of harvest to your spirit. If the Lord desires to surprise his children, he has only to answer their prayers; most of them would be astonished if an answer came to their petitions. I know how they speak about answers to prayer. They say, "How remarkable! How wonderful!" as if it were anything remarkable that God should be true, and that the Most High should keep his promise. Oh, for more faith to rest upon his word! And we should have more of these harvest joys.

We have another joy of harvest in ourselves *when we conquer a temptation*. We know what it is to get under a cloud sometimes; sin within us rises with a darkening force, or an external adversity beclouds us, and we miss the plain path we were accustomed to walk in. A child of God at such times will cry mightily for help; for he is fearful of himself and fearful of his surroundings. Some of God's people have been by the week and month together exposed to double temptation, from without and from within, and have cried to God in bitter anguish. It has been a very hard struggle; the sinful action has been painted in very fascinating colors, and the siren voice of temptation has almost enchanted them. But when at last they have gone through the valley of the shadow of death without having slipped with their feet; when, after all, they have not been destroyed by Apollyon, but have come forth again into the daylight, they feel a joy unspeakable, compared with which the joy of harvest is mere childish merriment. Those know deep joy who have felt bitter sorrow. As the man feels that he is the stronger for the conflict, as he feels that he has gathered experience and stronger faith from having passed through the trial, he lifts up his heart, and rejoices, not in himself, but before his God, with the joy of harvest. Brothers and sisters beloved, you know what that means.

Again, there is such a thing as the joy of harvest *when we have been rendered useful*. The master passion of every Christian is to be useful. There should be a burning zeal within us for the glory of God. When the man who desires to be useful has laid his plans and set about his work, he begins to look out for the results; but perhaps it will be weeks, or years, before results will come. The worker is not to be blamed that there are no fruits as yet, but he is to be blamed if he is content to be without fruits. A preacher may preach without conversions, and who will blame him? But if he be happy, who will excuse him? It is ours to break our own hearts if we cannot by God's grace break others' hearts; if others will not weep for their sins, it should be our constant habit to weep for them. When the heart becomes earnest, warm, zealous, God usually gives a measure of success, some fiftyfold, some a hundredfold. When the success comes, it is the joy of harvest indeed.

I cannot help being egotistical enough to mention the joy I felt when first I heard that a soul had found peace through my youthful ministry. I had been preaching in a village some few Sabbaths with an increasing congregation, but I had not heard of a conversion, and I thought, "Perhaps I am not called of God. He does not mean me to preach, for if he did he would give me spiritual children." One Sabbath my good deacon said, "Don't be discouraged. A poor woman was saved last Sabbath." How long do you suppose it was before I saw that woman? It was just as long as it took me to reach her cottage. I was eager to hear from her own lips whether it was a work of God's grace or not. I always looked upon her with interest, though she was only a poor laborer's wife, until she was taken away to heaven, after having lived a holy life. Many since then have I rejoiced over in the Lord, but that first seal to my ministry was particularly dear to me. It gave me a sip of the joy of harvest. If somebody had left me a fortune, it would not have caused me one-hundredth part of the delight I had in discovering that a soul had been led to the Savior. I am sure Christian people who have not this joy have missed one of the choicest delights that a believer can know this side of heaven. In fact, when I see souls saved, I do not envy Gabriel his throne nor the angels their harps. It shall be our heaven to be out of heaven for a season if we can but bring others to know the Savior and so add fresh jewels to the Redeemer's crown.

I will mention another delight which is as the joy of harvest, and that is *fellowship with the Lord Jesus Christ*. This is not so much a matter for speech as for experience and delight. If we try to speak of what communion with Christ is, we fail. Solomon, the wisest of men, when inspired to write of the fellowship of the church with her Lord, was compelled to write in allegories and emblems, and though to the spiritual mind the book of Canticles is always delightful, yet to the carnal mind it seems a mere love song. The natural man discerns not the things that are of God, for they are spiritual, and can only be spiritually discerned. But, oh, the bliss of knowing that Christ is yours, and of entering into nearness of communion with him. To thrust your hand into his side, and your finger into the print of the nails—these be not everyday joys; but when such near and dear communings come to us on our high days and holy days, they make our souls like the chariots of Amminadib, or, if you will, they cause us to tread the world beneath our feet and all that earth calls good or great. Our condition matters nothing to us if Christ is with us—he is our God, our comfort, and our all, and we rejoice before him as with the joy of harvest.

I have no time to expand on this, for I want to close with one other practical word. Many of us are anxiously desiring a harvest which would bring to us an intense delight. Of late, people have communicated to me in many ways the strong emotion they feel of pity for the souls of humankind. Others of us have felt a mysterious impulse to pray more than we did, and to be more anxious than ever we were that Christ would save poor perishing sinners. We will not be satisfied until there is a thorough awakening in this land. We did not raise the feeling in our own minds, and we do not desire to repress it. We do not believe it can be repressed; but others will feel the same heavenly affection, and will sigh and cry to God day and night until the blessing comes. This is the sowing, this is the plowing, this is the harrowing—may it go on to harvesting. I long to hear my brothers and sisters universally saying, "We are full of anguish, we are in agony until souls be saved." The cry of Rachel, "Give me children, or else I die" (Genesis 30:1), is the cry of your minister this day, and the longing of thousands more besides. As that desire grows in intensity, a revival is approaching. We must have spiritual children born to Christ, or our hearts will break for the longing that we have for their salvation. Oh, for more of these longings, yearnings, cravings, laborings! If we plead until the harvest of revival comes, we shall partake in the joy of it.

Who will have the most joy? Those who have been the most concerned about it. You who do not pray in private, or come out to prayer meetings, will not have the joy when the blessing comes, and the church is increased. You had no share in the sowing, therefore you will have little share in the reaping. You who never speak to others about their souls, who take no part in Sunday school or mission work, but simply eat the fat and drink the sweet—you shall have none of the joy of harvest, for you do not put your hands to the work of the Lord. And who would wish that idlers should be happy? Rather in our zeal and jealousy we feel inclined to say, "Curse ye Meroz . . . curse ye bitterly the inhabitants thereof; because they came not to the help of the LORD, to the help of the LORD against the mighty" (Judges 5:23). If you come to the help of the Lord by his own divine Spirit, you will share the joy of harvest. Perhaps none will have more of that joy than those who will have the privilege of seeing their own dear ones brought to God. Some of you have children who are a trial to you whenever you think of them; let them be such a trial to you that they drive you to incessant prayer for them, and, if the blessing comes, why should it not drop on them? If a revival comes, why should not your daughter be converted, and that wild boy of yours be brought in, or even your gray-headed father, who has been skeptical and unbelieving—why should not the grace of God come to him? And, oh, what a joy of harvest you will have then! What bliss will thrill your spirit when you see those who are united to you in ties of blood united to Christ your Lord! Pray much for them with earnest faith, and you will yet have the joy of harvest in your own house, a shout of harvest home in your own family.

Possibly, my friend, you have not much to do with such joy, for you are yourself unsaved. Yet it is a grand thing for an unconverted person to be under a ministry that God blesses, and with a people that pray for conversions. It is a happy thing for you, young man, to have a Christian mother. It is a great blessing for you, unconverted woman, that you have a godly sister. These make us hopeful for you. While your relations are prayerful, we are hopeful for *you*. May the Lord Jesus be yours yet. But, oh! If you remain unbelieving, however rich a blessing comes to others, it will leave *you* none the better for it. "If ye be willing and obedient, ye shall eat the good of the land" (Isaiah 1:19), but there are some who may cry in piteous accents, "The harvest is past, the summer is ended, and we are not saved" (Jeremiah 8:20). It has been remarked that those who pass through a season of revival and remain unconverted are more hardened and unimpressed than before. I believe it to be so, and I pray the Divine Spirit to come with such energy that none of you may escape his power. May you be led to pray,

> Pass me not, O mighty Spirit!
>> Thou canst make the blind to see;
> Witnesser of Jesus' merit,
>> Speak the Word of power to me;
>>> Even me, even me,
>> Speak the Word of power to me.

> Have I been in sin long sleeping,
>> Long been slighting, grieving Thee?
> Has the world my heart been keeping?
>> O forgive and rescue me;
>>> Even me, even me,
>> O forgive and rescue me.[26]

Oh, for earnest, urgent prayer from all believers throughout the world! If our churches could be stirred up to incessant, vehement crying to God, so as to give him no rest until he makes Zion a praise in the earth, we might expect to see God's kingdom come and the power of Satan fall. As many of you as love Christ, I charge you by his dear name to be much in prayer; as many of you as love the Church of God, and desire her prosperity, I beseech you not to hold back in this time of supplication. The Lord grant that you may be led to plead until the harvest joy is granted. Do you remember one Sabbath my saying, "The Lord deals with you as you deal with his work during this next month." I feel as if it will be so with many of you—that the Lord will deal with you as you will deal with his church. If you scatter little, you will have little; if you pray little, you will have little favor. But if you have zeal and faith, and plead much and work much for the

Lord, good measure, pressed down and running over, will the Lord return to you. If you water others with drops, you shall receive drops in return; but if the Spirit helps you to pour out rivers of living water from your own soul, then floods of heavenly grace will flow into your spirit. God, bring in the unconverted, and lead them to a simple trust in Jesus; then shall they also know the joy of harvest. We ask it for his name's sake. Amen.

FIFTEEN

SPIRITUAL GLEANING

Let her glean even among the sheaves, and reproach her not.

(Ruth 2:15)

Country friends need no explanation of what is meant by gleaning. I hope the custom will never be banished from the land, but that the poor will always be allowed their little share of the harvest. I am afraid that many who see gleaning every year in the fields of their own parish are not yet wise enough to understand the heavenly art of spiritual gleaning. That is the subject which I have chosen on this occasion, and my verse is taken from the charming story of Ruth, which is known to every one of you. I will use the story as setting forth our own case, in a simple but instructive way. In the first place, we shall observe that there is *a great Gardener*; it was Boaz in Ruth's case, and it is our heavenly Father who is the Gardener in our case. Secondly, we will notice *a humble gleaner*; the gleaner was Ruth in this instance, but she may be looked upon as the representative of every believer. And, in the third place, here is a *gracious permission given* to Ruth: "Let her glean even among the sheaves, and reproach her not," and the same permission is spiritually given to us.

GOD OF THE WHOLE EARTH IS A GREAT GARDENER

This is true in *natural* things. As a matter of fact, all farm operations are carried on by his power and prudence. We may plow the soil and sow the seed, but as Jesus said, "My Father is the husbandman" (John 15:1). He appoints the clouds and allots the sunshine; he directs the winds and distributes the dew and the rain; he also gives the frost and the heat, and so by various processes of nature he brings forth food for man and beast. All the farming, however, which God does, is for the benefit of others and never for himself. He has no need of any of our works of agriculture. If he were hungry, he would not tell us. "The cattle upon a thousand hills," says he, ". . . are mine" (Psalm 50:10–11). The purest kindness and benevolence are those which dwell in the heart of God. Though all things are God's, his works in creation and in providence are not for himself, but for his creatures. This should greatly encourage us in trusting to him.

In *spiritual* matters God is the great Gardener; and there, too, all his works are done for his children, that they may be fed upon the finest of the wheat. Permit me to speak of the wide gospel fields which our heavenly Father farms for the good of his children. There is a great variety of these fields, and they are all fruitful: "The fountain of Jacob shall be upon a land of corn and wine; also his heavens shall drop down dew" (Deuteronomy 33:28). Every field which our heavenly Father tills yields a plentiful harvest, for there are no failures or famines with him.

The Doctrine Field

One part of his farm is called *Doctrine Field*. What full sheaves of finest wheat are to be found there! He who is permitted to glean in it will gather bread enough to spare, for the land brings forth by handfuls. Look at that large sheaf of election; full indeed of heavy ears of corn, such as Pharaoh saw in his first dream—ears full and strong. There is the great sheaf of final perseverance, where each ear is a promise that the work which God has begun he will assuredly complete. If we do not have enough faith to partake of either of these sheaves, we may glean around the choice sheaves of redemption by the blood of Christ. Many a poor soul who could not feed on electing love, nor realize his perseverance in Christ, can yet feed on the atonement and rejoice in the sublime doctrine of substitution. Many and rich are the sheaves which stand thick together in Doctrine Field; these, when threshed by meditation and ground in the mill of thought, furnish royal food for the Lord's family.

I wonder why it is that some of our Master's stewards are so prone to locking the gate of this field, as if they thought it dangerous ground. For my part, I wish my people would not only glean here but also carry home the sheaves by the wagonload, for they cannot be too well fed when truth is the food. Are my fellow laborers afraid that Jeshurun will wax fat and kick (Deuteronomy 32:15), if he has too much food? I fear there is more likelihood of his dying of starvation if the bread of sound doctrine is withheld. If we have a love for the precepts and warnings of the Word, we need not be afraid of the doctrines; on the contrary, we should search them out and feed upon them with joy. The doctrines of distinguishing grace are to be set forth in due proportions to the rest of the Word, and those are poor pulpits from which these grand truths are excluded. We must not keep the Lord's people out of this field. I say, swing the gate open and come in, all of you who are children of God! I am sure that in my Master's field nothing grows which will harm you. Gospel doctrine is always safe doctrine. You may feast upon it until you are full, and no harm will come of it. Be afraid of no revealed truth. Be afraid of spiritual ignorance, but not of holy knowledge. Grow in grace and in the knowledge of your Lord and Savior Jesus Christ. Everything taught in the Word of God is meant to be the subject of a Christian's study, therefore neglect nothing. Visit the doctrine field daily, and glean in it with the utmost diligence.

The Promise Field

The great Gardener has another field called *Promise Field*; of that I shall not need to speak, for I hope you often enter it and glean from it.

Just let us take an ear or two out of one of the sheaves and show them to you, that you may be induced to stay there the livelong day and carry home a rich load at night. Here is an ear: "The mountains shall depart, and the hills be removed; but my kindness shall not depart from thee, neither shall the covenant of my peace be removed" (Isaiah 54:10). Here is another: "When thou passest through the waters, I will be with thee; and through the rivers, they shall not overflow thee: when thou walkest through the fire, thou shalt not be burned; neither shall the flame kindle upon thee" (Isaiah 43:2). Here is another; it has a short stalk, but a heavy ear: "My grace is sufficient for thee" (2 Corinthians 12:9). Another is long in the straw, but very rich in corn: "Let not your heart be troubled: ye believe in God, believe also in me. In my Father's house are many mansions: if it were not so, I would have told you. I go to prepare a place for you. And if I go and prepare a place for you, I will come again, and receive you unto myself; that where I am, there ye may be also" (John 14:1–3). What a word is that! "I will come again." Yes, beloved, we can say of the Promise Field what cannot be said of a single acre in all of England; namely, that it is so rich a field that it could not be richer, and that it has so many ears of corn in it that you could not insert another. As the poet sings:

> What more can he say than to you he has said,
> to you who for refuge to Jesus have fled?[27]

Glean in that field, poor and needy ones, and never think that you are intruding. The whole field is your own, every ear of it; you may draw out from the sheaves themselves, and the more you take, the more you may.

The Ordinance Field

Then there is *Ordinance Field*; a great deal of good wheat grows in this field. The field of baptism has been exceedingly fruitful to some of us, for it has set forth to us our death, burial, and resurrection in

Christ, and thus we have been cheered and instructed. It has been good for us to declare ourselves on the Lord's side, and we have found that in keeping our Lord's commandments there is great reward. But I will not detain you long in this field, for some of our friends think it has a damp soil: I wish them more light and more grace. However, we will pass on to the field of the Supper, where grows the very best of our Lord's corn. What rich things have we fed upon in this choice spot! Have we not there tasted the sweetest and most sustaining of all spiritual food? In all the estate no field is to be found to rival this center and crown of all the domain; this is the King's Acre. Gospel gleaner, abide in that field; glean in it on the first day of every week, and expect to see your Lord there; for it is written, "He was known of them in breaking of bread" (Luke 24:35).

The Fellowship and Communion with Christ Field

The heavenly Gardener has one field upon a hill which equals the best of the others, even if it does not surpass them. You cannot really and truly go into any of the other fields unless you pass into this one, for the road to the other fields lies through this hill farm; it is called *Fellowship and Communion with Christ.* This is the field for the Lord's choicest ones to glean in. Some of you have only run through it; you have not stopped long enough in it, but those who know how to stay here—to live here—will spend their hours most profitably and pleasantly. It is only in proportion as we hold fellowship with Christ, and commune with him, that either ordinances, or doctrines, or promises can profit us. All other things are dry and barren unless we are enjoying the love of Christ, unless we bear his likeness, unless we dwell continually with him and rejoice in his love. I am sorry to say that few Christians think much of this field; it is enough for them to be sound in doctrine, and tolerably correct in practice. They care far less than they should about intimate communion with Christ Jesus, their Lord, by the Holy Ghost. I am sure that if we gleaned in this field, we should not have half so many naughty tempers nor a tenth as much pride, nor a hundredth part so much sloth. This is a field hedged and sheltered, and in it you will find better food than that which angels feed upon; indeed, you will find Jesus himself as the bread which came down from heaven. Blessed, blessed field, may we visit it every day. The Master leaves the gate wide open for every believer; let us enter in and gather the golden ears until we can carry no more. We have seen the great Gardener in his fields; let us rejoice that we have such a great Gardener near, and such fields to glean in.

A HUMBLE GLEANER

And now, in the second place, we have *a humble gleaner*. Ruth was a gleaner, and may serve as an illustration of what every believer should be in the fields of God.

The Gleaner Is Favored

The believer is a favored gleaner, for she *may take home a whole sheaf if she likes*; she may bear away all that she can possibly carry, for all things are freely given by the Lord. I use the figure of a gleaner because I believe that few Christians ever go much beyond it, and yet they are free to do so if they are able. Some may ask, "Why does not the believer reap all the field, and take all the corn home with them?" I answer that they are welcome to do so if they can, for no good thing will the Lord withhold from those who walk uprightly. If your faith is like a great wagon, and you can carry the whole field of corn, you have full permission to take it. Sadly, our faith is so little that we would rather glean than harvest; we are restricted in ourselves, not in our God. May you all outgrow the metaphor and come home, bringing your sheaves with you.

The Gleaner Has to Endure Much Toil and Fatigue

She rises early in the morning, and she trudges off to a field; if that be closed, she hastens to another; and if that be shut up, or gleaned already, she hurries farther still. All day long, while the sun is shining upon her, she seldom sits down to refresh herself, but still she goes on, *stoop*, *stoop*, *stoop*, gathering the ears one by one. She does not return to her home until nightfall, for she desires, if the field is good, to do much business that day, and she will not go home until she is loaded down. Beloved, let each one of us do so when we seek spiritual food. Let us not be afraid of a little fatigue in the Master's fields; if the gleaning is good, we must not soon weary in gathering the precious spoil, for the gains will richly reward our pains. I have a friend who walks five miles every Sunday to hear the gospel, and has the same distance to return. Another thinks little of a ten-miles journey; and these are wise, for to hear the pure Word of God no labor is extravagant. To stand in the aisle until ready to drop, listening all the while with strained attention, is a toil which meets a full reward if the gospel is heard, and the Spirit of God blesses it to the soul. A gleaner does not expect that the ears will come to her themselves; she knows that gleaning is hard work. We must not expect to find the best field next to our own house. We may have to journey to the far end of the parish, but what of that? Gleaners must not be choosers, and where the Lord sends the gospel, there he calls us to be present.

The Gleaner Must Stoop for Every Ear She Gets

We remark, next, that *every ear the gleaner gets she has to stoop for.* Why is it that proud people seldom profit under the Word? Why is it that certain "intellectual" folk cannot get any good out of our soundest ministers? If they need to have the corn lifted up for them and if the wheat is held so high over their heads they can hardly see it, they are pleased and cry, "Here is something wonderful!" They admire the extraordinary ability of the individual who can hold up the truth so high that nobody can reach it; but truly that is a sorry feat. The preacher's business is to place truth within the reach of all—children as well as adults. He is to let handfuls fall on purpose for poor gleaners, who will never mind stooping to collect the ears. If we preach to the educated people only, the wise ones can understand, but the illiterate cannot. But when we preach in all simplicity to the poor, other classes can understand it if they like, and if they do not like, they had better go somewhere else. Those who cannot stoop to pick up plain truth had better give up gleaning. For my part, I would be taught by a child if that is how I could know and understand the gospel better. The gleaning in our Lord's field is so rich that it is worth the hardest labor to be able to carry home a portion of it. Hungry souls know this and are not to be hindered in seeking their heavenly food. We will go down on our knees in prayer, and stoop by self-humiliation and confession of ignorance, and so gather with the hand of faith the daily bread of our hungering souls.

What the Gleaner Gets, She Must Win Ear by Ear

Next, note that what a gleaner gets *she wins ear by ear*; occasionally she picks up a handful at once, but as a rule it is straw by straw. In the case of Ruth, handfuls were let fall on purpose for her, but she was highly favored. The gleaner stoops and gets one ear, and then she stoops again for another. Now, beloved, where there are handfuls to be picked up at once, there is the place to go and glean; but if you cannot meet with such abundance, be glad to gather ear by ear. I have heard of certain people who have been in the habit of hearing a favorite minister, and when they go to another place, they say, "I cannot hear anybody after my own minister; I shall stay at home and read a sermon." Please remember the passage, "Not forsaking the assembling of ourselves together, as the manner of some is" (Hebrews 10:25). Let me also entreat you not to be so foolishly partial as to deprive your soul of its food. If you cannot get a handful at one stoop, do not refuse to gather an ear at a time. If you are not content to learn here a little and there a little, you will soon be half-starved, and then you will be glad to get back again to the other minister and pick up what his field will yield you. It is a sorry ministry which yields nothing. Go and glean where the Lord has opened the gate for you. The Scripture alone is worth the journey; do not miss it.

What the Gleaner Picks Up, She Keeps in Her Hand

She does not drop the corn as fast as she gathers it. There is a good thought at the beginning of the sermon, but the hearers are so eager to hear another that the first one slips away. Toward the end of the sermon a large handful falls their way, and they forget all that went before in their eagerness to retain this last and richest portion. The sermon is over, and, alas, it is nearly all gone from the memory, for many are about as wise as a gleaner would be if she should pick up one ear and drop it, then pick up another and drop it, and so on all day. The net result of such a day's work is a bad backache, and I fear that all our hearers will get by their hearing will be a headache. Be attentive, but be retentive too. Gather the grain and tie it up in bundles for carrying away with you, and mind you do not lose it on the road home. Many a person with a fair hold of the sermon loses it on the way home by engaging in idle talk with vain companions. I have heard of a Christian man who was seen hurrying home with all his might one Sunday. A friend asked him why he was in such haste. "Oh!" he said, "Two or three Sundays ago, our minister gave us a most blessed discourse, and I greatly enjoyed it. But when I got outside, two deacons were discussing it, and one pulled the sermon one way, and the other the other, until they had pulled it all to pieces and I lost all the meaning of it." Those must have been very bad deacons; let us not imitate them; and if we know any who are of their type, let us walk home alone in dogged silence sooner than lose all our gleanings by their controversies. After a good sermon, go home with your ears and your mouth shut. Act like the miser who not only gets all he can, but also keeps all he can. Do not lose by trifling talk that which may make you rich for all eternity.

The Gleaner Takes the Wheat Home and Threshes It

It is a wise thing to thresh a sermon, whoever may have been the preacher, for it is certain that there is a portion of straw and chaff about it. Many thresh the preacher by finding needless fault, but that is not half so good as threshing the sermon to get out of it the pure truth. Take a sermon, beloved, when you get one which is worth having, and lay it down on the floor of meditation, and beat it out with the flail of prayer, and you will get breadcorn from it. This threshing by prayer and meditation must never be neglected. If a gleaner should stow away her corn in her room and leave it there, the mice would get at it; but she would have no food from it if she did not thresh out the grain. Some get a sermon and carry it home, then allow Satan and sin and the world to eat it all up, and it becomes unfruitful and worthless to them. But those who know how to flail a sermon well, so as to clear out all the wheat from the straw—that is what makes a good hearer and feeds the soul on the truth that is heard.

After Threshing the Corn, the Gleaner Winnows It

Ruth did all this in the field; but you can scarcely do so. You must do some of the work at home. And observe, she did not take the chaff home; she left it behind her in the field. It is a prudent thing to winnow all the discourses you hear so as to separate the precious from the vile; but pray do not fall into the silly habit of taking home all the chaff and leaving the corn behind. I think I hear you say, "I will remember that unusual expression; I will make an anecdote out of that odd remark." Listen, for I have a word for you—if you hear a person retell nothing about a minister except his oddities, just stop them and say, "We have all our faults, and perhaps those who are most ready to speak of the faults of others are not quite perfect themselves; can you tell us what the preacher said that was worth hearing?" In many cases the answer will be, "Oh, I don't recollect that." They have sifted the corn, thrown away the good grain, and brought home the chaff. Follow the opposite rule: drop the straw and retain the good corn. Separate between the precious and the vile, and let the worthless material go where it may—you have no use for it, and the sooner you are rid of it, the better. Judge with care, reject false teaching with decision, and retain true doctrine with earnestness; this is how you will practice the enriching art of heavenly gleaning. May the Lord teach us wisdom, so that we may become "rich to all the intents of bliss," so our mouths will be satisfied with good things and our youth will be renewed like the eagle's.

GRACIOUS PERMISSION GIVEN

"Let her glean even among the sheaves, and reproach her not." Ruth had no right to go among the sheaves until Boaz gave her permission by saying, "Let her do it." For her to be allowed to go among the sheaves, in that part of the field where the wheat was newly cut and none of it carted, was a great favor: but Boaz whispered that handfuls were to be dropped on purpose for her, and that was a greater favor still. Boaz had a secret love for the maiden, and even so, beloved, it is because of our Lord's eternal love for us that he allows us to enter his best fields and glean among the sheaves. His grace permits us to lay hold upon doctrinal blessings, promise blessings, and experience blessings: the Lord favors us and gives us these kindnesses. We have no right to any heavenly blessings of ourselves; our portion is due to free and sovereign grace.

Boaz Loved Ruth

I will now tell you the reasons that moved Boaz's heart to let Ruth go among the sheaves. The master motive was *because he loved her.* He allowed her to go there because he had an affection for her, which later he displayed in grander ways. The Lord lets his people come and glean among the sheaves, because he loves them. Did you have a soul-enriching season among the sheaves the other Sabbath? Did you carry home your sack, filled like those of Joseph's brothers when they returned from Egypt? Did you have an abundance? Were you satisfied? If so, it was all because of the Master's goodness. It was because he loved you. Look on all your spiritual enjoyments as proof of his eternal love. Look on all heavenly blessings as tokens of heavenly grace. It will make your corn grind all the better and taste all the sweeter, if you will remember that it was given by eternal love. Your sweet seasons, your high enjoyments, your unspeakable joys, are all proofs of divine affection; therefore be doubly glad of them.

Boaz Was Ruth's Relative

There was another reason why Boaz allowed Ruth to glean among the sheaves; it was because he was her *relative*. This is why our Lord gives us choice favors at times, and takes us into his banqueting-house in so gracious a manner. He is our next of kin, bone of our bone, and flesh of our flesh. Our Redeemer, our kinsman, is the Lord Jesus, and he will never be a stranger to his own flesh. It is a high and charming mystery that our Lord Jesus is the Husband of his church; surely he may well let his spouse glean among the sheaves, for all that he possesses is hers already. Her interests and his interests are one, and so he may well say, "Beloved, take all you please; I am none the poorer because you partake of my fullness, for you are mine. You are my partner, and my choice, and all that I have is yours."

What, then, will I say to you who are my Lord's beloved? How will I speak with a tenderness and generosity equal to his desires, for he would have me speak right lovingly in his name. Enrich yourselves out of that which is your Lord's. Spiritually glean as often as ever you can. Never lose an opportunity to pick up a golden blessing. Glean at the mercy seat; glean in private meditation; glean in reading pious books; glean in associating with godly men and women; glean everywhere; and if you can get only a little handful, it will be better than none. You who are so busy and so distracted by cares, if you can only spend five minutes in the Lord's field gleaning a little, be sure to do so. If you cannot bear away a sheaf, carry an ear; and if you cannot find an ear, pick up even a grain of wheat. Take care to get a little, if you cannot get much, but gather as much as you can.

Just one other remark. Child of God, never be afraid to glean. Have faith in God, and take the promises home to yourself. Jesus will rejoice to see you making use of his good things: "Eat, O friends; drink, yea, drink abundantly, O beloved" (Song of Solomon 5:1). If you find a rich promise, live upon it. Draw the honey out of the comb of Scripture, and live on its sweetness. If you meet with a most extraordinary sheaf, carry it away rejoicing. You cannot believe too much concerning your Lord; do not let Satan cheat you into contentment with a meager portion of grace when all the granaries of heaven are open to you. Glean on with humble industry and hopeful confidence, and know that he who owns both fields and sheaves is looking upon you with eyes of love, and will one day espouse you to himself in glory everlasting. Happy gleaners who find eternal love and eternal life in the fields in which they glean!

SIXTEEN

MEALTIME IN THE CORNFIELDS

And Boaz said unto her, At mealtime come thou hither,
and eat of the bread, and dip thy morsel in the vinegar.
And she sat beside the reapers: and he reached her
parched corn, and she did eat, and was sufficed, and left.

[RUTH 2:14]

We are going to the cornfields, not so much to glean but as to rest with the reapers and gleaners when, under some wide-spreading oak, they sit down to take refreshment. We hope some timid gleaner will accept our invitation to come and eat with us, and will have confidence enough to dip *her* morsel in the vinegar. May all of us have courage to feast to the full on our own account, and kindness enough to carry home a portion to our needy friends at home.

GOD'S REAPERS HAVE THEIR MEALTIMES

Those who work for God will find him a good Master. He cares for oxen, and he has commanded Israel, "Thou shalt not muzzle the ox when he treadeth out the corn" (Deuteronomy 25:4). Much more does he care for his servants who serve him: "He hath given meat unto them that fear him: he will ever be mindful of his covenant" (Psalm 111:5). The reapers in Jesus' fields will not only receive a blessed reward at the last, but they will have plenteous comforts by the way. He is pleased to pay his servants twice; first in the labor itself, and a second time in the labor's sweet results. He gives them such joy and consolation in the service of their Master that it is a sweet employ, and they cry, "I delight to do thy will, O my God" (Psalm 40:8). Heaven is made up of serving God day and night, and a foretaste of heaven is enjoyed when we serve God on earth with earnest perseverance.

God has ordained certain mealtimes for his harvesters, and he has appointed that one of these will be *when they come together to listen to the Word preached*. If God is with ministers, they act as the disciples did of old, for they received the loaves and the fishes from the Lord Jesus, and then they handed them out to the people. *We*, of ourselves, cannot feed one soul, much less thousands; but when the Lord is with us, we can keep as good a table as Solomon himself, with all his fine flour, and fat oxen, and roebucks, and fallow deer. When the Lord blesses the provisions of his House, no matter how many thousands there may be, all the poor will be filled with bread. I hope, beloved, you know what it is to sit under the shadow of the Word with great delight, and find the fruit sweet to your taste. Where the doctrines of grace are boldly and plainly delivered to you in connection with the other truths of revelation; where Jesus Christ upon his cross is always lifted up; where the work of the Spirit is not forgotten; where the glorious purpose of the Father is never despised, there is sure to be rich provision for the children of God.

Often, too, our gracious Lord appoints us mealtimes *in our private readings and meditations*. Here it is that his "paths drop fatness" (Psalm 65:11). Nothing can be more fattening to the soul of the believer than feeding upon the Word and digesting it by frequent meditation. No wonder that people grow so slowly when they meditate so little.

Cattle must chew the cud; it is not what they bite with their teeth, but that which is masticated, and digested by rumination, that nourishes them. We must take the truth and turn it over and over again in the inward parts of our spirit; this is how we will extract suitable nourishment from it. Brothers and sisters, is not meditation the land of Goshen to you? If people once said, "There is corn in Egypt," may they not always say that the finest of the wheat is to be found in secret prayer? Private devotion is a land which flows with milk and honey, a paradise yielding all manner of fruits, a banqueting house of choice wines. Ahasuerus might make a great feast, but all his hundred and twenty provinces could not furnish such dainties as meditation offers to the spiritual mind.

Where can we feed and lie down in green pastures in so sweet a sense as we do in our musings on the Word? Meditation distills the quintessence of joy from the Scriptures and gladdens our mouth with a sweetness which excels the virgin honey. Your periods of rest and occasions of prayer should be to you refreshing seasons, in which, like the reapers at noonday, you sit with the Master and enjoy his generous provisions. The Shepherd of Salisbury Plain was wont to say that when he was lonely, and his wallet was empty, his Bible was to him meat and drink, and company too; he is not the only one who has found a fullness in the Word when all else has been empty. During the battle of Waterloo, a godly soldier, mortally wounded, was carried by his comrade into the rear. Placed with his back propped up against a tree, he requested that his friend open his knapsack and take out the Bible which he had carried in it. "Read to me," he said, "one verse before I close my eyes in death." His comrade read him that verse: "Peace I leave with you, my peace I give unto you: not as the world giveth, give I unto you" (John 14:27), and there, fresh from the whistling of the bullets and the roll of the drum and the tempest of human conflict, that believing spirit enjoyed such holy calm that he fell asleep in the arms of Jesus, saying, "Yes, I have a peace with God which passes all understanding, which keeps my heart and mind through Jesus Christ." Saints most surely enjoy delightful mealtimes when they are alone in meditation.

Let us not forget that there is one specially ordained mealtime which ought to occur at least once in the week—I mean *the Supper of the Lord*. There you have literally, as well as spiritually, a meal. The table is richly spread—it has upon it both bread and wine; and looking at what these symbolize, we have before us a table richer than that which kings could furnish. There we have the flesh and the blood of our Lord Jesus Christ; if we eat of it, we will never hunger and never thirst, for that bread will be to us everlasting life. Oh, the sweet seasons we have known at the Lord's Supper! If some of you knew the enjoyment of feeding upon Christ in that ordinance, you would chide yourselves for not having united with the church in fellowship. In keeping the Master's commandments there is "great reward," and consequently in neglecting them there is great loss of reward. Christ is not so tied to the sacramental table as to be always found among those who partake of it, but still, it is "in the way" that we may expect the Lord to meet with us. "If ye love me, keep my commandments" (John 14:15), is a verse of touching power. Sitting at this table, our soul has mounted up from the emblem to the reality; we have eaten bread in the kingdom of God, and have leaned our head upon Jesus' bosom. "He brought me to the banqueting house, and his banner over me was love" (Song of Solomon 2:4).

Besides these regular mealtimes, there are others which God gives us, *at seasons when, perhaps, we little expect them*. You have been walking down the street, and suddenly you have felt a holy flowing out of your soul toward God; or in the middle of business, your heart has been melted with love and made to dance for joy, even as the brooks, which have been bound with winter's ice, leap to feel the touch of spring. You have been groaning, dull and earthbound, but the sweet love of Jesus has enfolded your heart when you scarcely thought of it, and your spirit, all free and all on fire, has rejoiced before the Lord with timbrel and dance, like Miriam of old. I have had times occasionally in preaching when I have kept on far beyond the appointed hour, for my soul has been overflowing. Seasons, too, we have had on our sickbeds, when we would have been content to be sick always if we could have had our bed so well made by tender love, and our head so softly pillowed on loving grace.

Our blessed Redeemer comes to us in the morning and wakes us up by dropping sweet thoughts upon our souls; we know not how they came, but it is as if, when the dew was visiting the flowers, a few drops had taken pity upon us. In the cool eventide, too, as we have gone to bed, our meditation of him has been sweet; and in the night watches, when we tossed to and fro and could not sleep, he has been pleased to become our song in the night.

God's harvesters find it hard work to harvest; but they gain a blessed solace when in one way or another they sit down and eat of their Master's rich provisions; then, with renewed strength, they rise with sharpened sickle, to reap again in the noontide heat.

Let me observe that, while these mealtimes come we know not exactly when, there are *certain seasons when we may expect them*. Harvesters in the warmest parts of the world generally sit down in the shade to take refreshment during the heat of the day. I am certain that when trouble, affliction, persecution, and bereavement become the most painful to us, it is then that the Lord hands out to us the sweetest comforts. We must work until the hot sun forces the sweat from our faces, and then we may look for repose; we must bear the burden and heat of the day before we can expect to be invited to those choice meals the Lord prepares for true laborers. When your day of trouble is the hottest, then the love of Jesus will be the sweetest.

Again, these mealtimes frequently occur *before* a trial. Elijah must be entertained beneath a juniper tree, for he is to go on a forty days' journey on the strength of that meat. You may suspect some danger coming when your delights are overflowing. If you see a ship taking in great quantities of provision, it is probably bound for a distant port, and when God gives you extraordinary seasons of communion with

Jesus, you may look for long leagues of tempestuous sea. Sweet cordials prepare for stern conflicts.

Times of refreshing also occur *after* trouble or arduous service. Christ was tempted of the devil, and *afterward* angels came and ministered to him. Jacob wrestled with God, and afterward, at Mahanaim, hosts of angels met him. Abraham fought with the kings and returned from their slaughter, and then it was that Melchisedec refreshed him with bread and wine. After conflict, content; after battle, banquet. When you have waited on the Lord, then you will sit down, and your Master will prepare himself and wait upon you.

Let those who do not believe say what they will about the hardness of religion; we do not find it so. We admit that living for Christ has its difficulties and troubles; but still the bread which we eat is of heavenly sweetness, and the wine which we drink is crushed from celestial clusters:

> I would not change my blest estate
> For all the world calls good or great;
> And while my faith can keep her hold,
> I envy not the sinner's gold.[28]

To These Meals the Gleaner Is Affectionately Invited

That is to say, the poor, trembling stranger who has not strength enough to harvest, who has no right to be in the field except the right of charity—the poor, trembling sinner, conscious of his own demerit and feeling but little hope and little joy, is invited to the feast of love.

In the verse, *the gleaner is invited to come.* "At mealtime *come* thou hither." We trust none of you will be kept away from the place of holy feasting by any shame on account of your dress, or your personal character, or your poverty; nor even on account of your physical infirmities. "At mealtime come thou hither." I knew a deaf woman who could never hear a sound, and yet she was always in the house of God, and when asked why, her reply was that a friend found her the message, and then God was pleased to give her many a sweet thought upon it while she sat with his people. Besides, she felt that as a believer, she ought to honor God by her *presence* in his courts and by confessing her union with his people. Better still, she always liked to be in the best of company, and as the presence of God was there, and the holy angels, and the saints of the Most High, whether she could hear or not, she would go. If *such* people find pleasure in coming, we who *can* hear should never stay away. Though we feel our unworthiness, we ought to be desirous to be laid in the house of God, as the sick were at the pool of Bethesda, hoping that the waters may be stirred, and that we may step in and be healed. Trembling soul, never let the temptations of the devil keep you from the assembly of worshippers: "At mealtime come thou hither."

Moreover, *she was bidden not only to come but to eat.* Whatever there is sweet and comfortable in the Word of God, those who are of a broken and contrite spirit are invited to partake of it. "Christ Jesus came into the world to save *sinners* (1 Timothy1:15)—sinners such as you are. "In due time Christ died for the *ungodly*" (Romans 5:6)—such ungodly ones as you feel yourselves to be. You desire to be Christ's. You *may* be Christ's. You are saying in your heart, "Oh, that I could eat the children's bread!" You *may* eat it. You say, "I have no right." But the Lord gives you the invitation. Come without any other right than the right of his invitation.

> Let not conscience make you linger,
> Nor of fitness fondly dream.[29]

But since he bids you "come," take him at his word; and if there is a promise, believe it. If there is an encouraging word, accept it, and let the sweetness of it be yours.

Note further that she was not only invited to eat the bread but to *dip her morsel in the vinegar.* We must not look upon this as being some sour stuff. No doubt there are difficult souls in the church who always dip their morsel in the sourest imaginable vinegar and with a grim liberality invite others to share their misery with them, but the vinegar in our scripture is altogether another thing. This was either a compound of various juices expressed from fruits, or else it was that weak kind of wine mingled with water which is still commonly used in the harvest fields of Italy and the warmer parts of the world—a drink not exceedingly strong, but good enough to impart a relish to the food. It was, to use the only word which will give the meaning, *a sauce*, which some use with their bread. As we use butter, or as they on other occasions used oil, so in the harvest field they used what is here called "vinegar," as they believe it to have cooling properties. Beloved, the Lord's harvesters have sauce with their bread; they have not merely doctrines but the holy rite of healing which is the essence of doctrines; they have not merely truths, but a hallowed delight accompanies the truths. Take, for instance, the doctrine of election, which is like the bread; there is a sauce to dip it in. When I can say, "He loved *me* before the foundations of the world," the personal enjoyment of my interest in the truth becomes a sauce into which I dip my morsel. And you, poor gleaner, are invited to dip your morsel in it too. I used to hear people sing that hymn of Toplady's, which begins—

> A debtor to mercy alone,
> Of covenant mercy I sing;
> Nor fear, with your righteousness on,
> My person and off'ring to bring.

The hymn rises to its climax in the lines—

> Yes, I to the end shall endure,
> As sure as the earnest is giv'n;
> More happy, but not more secure,
> The glorified spirits in heav'n.[30]

I used to think I should never be able to sing that hymn. It was the sauce, you know. I might manage to eat some of the plain bread, but I could not dip it in that sauce. It was too high doctrine, too sweet, too consoling. But I thank God I have since ventured to dip my morsel in it, and now I hardly like my bread without it.

I would have every trembling sinner partake of the *comfortable* parts of God's Word, even those which some call "HIGH DOCTRINE." Let him believe the simpler truth first, and then dip it in the sweet doctrine and be happy in the Lord.

I think I see the gleaner half-prepared to come, for she is very hungry, and she has nothing with her; but she begins to say, "I have no right to come, for I am not a harvester; I do nothing for Christ; I am only a *selfish gleaner.*" Oh, but everyone is invited to come! No question about it. Boaz bids you; take his invitation and approach at once. "But," you say, "I am such a *poor* gleaner; though my labor is all for myself, yet it is little I win by it; I get a few thoughts while the sermon is being preached, but I lose them before I reach home." I know you do, poor weakhanded soul. But still, Jesus invites you. Come! Take the sweet promise as he gives it to you, and let no bashfulness of yours send you home hungry. "But," you say, "I am *a stranger*; you do not know my sins, my sinfulness, and the waywardness of my heart." But Jesus does, and he invites you. He knows you are but a Moabitess, a stranger from the commonwealth of Israel; but he bids you come. Is not that enough? "But," you say, "I owe so much to him already; it is so good of him to spare my forfeited life, and so tender of him to let me hear the gospel preached at all. I cannot have the presumption to be an intruder and sit with the harvesters." Oh! but he *bids* you. There is more presumption in your doubting than there could be in your believing. HE bids you.

Will you refuse Boaz? Shall Jesus' lips give the invitation, and will you tell him no? Come, now, come. Remember that the little which Ruth could eat did not make Boaz any the poorer, and all that you want will make Christ none the less glorious or full of grace. Are your needs great? His supplies are larger. Do you require great mercy? He is a great Savior. His mercy is no more to be exhausted than the sea is to be drained, so come at once. There is enough for you, and Boaz will not be impoverished by your feasting to the full. Moreover, let me tell you a secret—Jesus *loves* you and wants you to feast at his table. If you are a longing, trembling sinner, willing to be saved but conscious that you do not deserve it, Jesus loves you and will take more delight in seeing you eat than you will take in the eating.

Let the sweet love he feels in his soul toward you draw you to him. And what is more—but this is a great secret, and must only be whispered in your ear—*he intends to be married to you*; and when you are married to him, why, the fields will be yours; for, of course, if you are his spouse, you are joint proprietor with him. Is it not so? Does not the wife share with the husband? All those promises will be yours; indeed, they all *are* yours now, for "the man is near of kin unto [you]" (Ruth 2:20), and before long he will take you unto himself forever, espousing you in faithfulness, and truth, and righteousness. Will you not eat of your own? "But," you say, "how can it be? I am a stranger." Yes, a stranger; but Jesus Christ loves the stranger. "A publican, a sinner"—but he is "a friend of publicans and sinners" (Matthew 11:19). "An outcast"—but he "gathereth together the outcasts of Israel" (Psalm 147:2). "A stray sheep"—but the shepherd "leave[s] the ninety and nine" (Luke 15:4) to seek it. "A lost piece of money"—but he "sweep[s] the house" (Luke 15:8) to find you. "A prodigal son"—but he sets the bells a-ringing when he knows that you will return. Come, Ruth! Come, trembling gleaner! Jesus invites you; accept the invitation. "At mealtime come thou hither, and eat of the bread, and dip thy morsel in the vinegar."

Boaz Reached Ruth the Parched Corn

Here is a very sweet point in the narrative—Ruth did come and eat, yet where did she sit? Note well that she "sat beside the reapers." She did not feel that she was one of them, just like some of you do not come to the Lord's Supper but instead sit and look on. You are sitting "beside the reapers." You fear that you are not the people of God; still you love them, and therefore sit beside them. If there is a good thing to be had, and you cannot get it, you will sit as near as you can to those who *do* get it. "She sat beside the reapers."

And while she was sitting there, what happened? Did she stretch forth her hand and take the food herself? No, it is written, "He reached her parched corn." Nobody but the Lord of the harvest can hand out the choicest refreshments of spiritual minds. I give the invitation in my Master's name, and I hope I give it earnestly, affectionately, sincerely; but I know very well that at my poor bidding none will come until the Spirit draws them. No trembling heart will accept divine refreshing at my hand; unless the King himself comes near, and reaches the parched corn to each chosen guest, none will receive it. How does he do this? By his gracious Spirit, he first of all *inspires your faith*. You are afraid to think that it can be true that such a sinner as you are can ever be "accepted in the beloved" (Ephesians 1:6); he breathes upon you, and your faint hope becomes an expectancy, and that expectation buds and blossoms into an appropriating faith, which says, Yes, "I am *my* beloved's, and his desire is toward *me*" (Song of Solomon 7:10).

Having done this, the Savior does more; *he sheds abroad the love of God in your heart*. The love of Christ is like sweet perfume in a box. The person who put the perfume in the box is the only one who knows how to take off the lid. With their own skillful hand, they open the secret blessing and share the love of God with the soul.

But Jesus does more than this: he reaches the parched corn with his own hand when he *gives us close communion with himself*. Do not think that this is a dream; I tell you, there is such a thing as speaking with Christ today. As certainly as I can talk with my dearest friend or find solace in the company of my beloved wife, so surely may I speak with Jesus and find intense delight in his company. It is not a fiction. We do not worship a far-off Savior; he is a God close at hand. His word is in our mouth and in our heart, and we do today walk with him as the elect did of old, and commune with him as his apostles did on earth—not after the flesh, it is true, but after a real and spiritual fashion.

Yet once more let me add, the Lord Jesus is pleased to reach the parched corn, in the best sense, when *the Spirit gives us the infallible witness within, that we are "born of God."* We may know that we are Christians beyond all question. Philip de Mornay, who lived in the time of Prince Henry of Navarre, was wont to say that the Holy Spirit had made his own salvation to him as clear a point as a problem demonstrated in Euclid. You know with what mathematical precision the scholar of geometry solves a problem or proves a theorem, and with as absolute a precision, as certainly as twice two are four, we may "know that we have passed from death unto life" (1 John 3:14). The sun in the heavens is not clearer to the eye than his present salvation is to an assured believer; such a person could as soon doubt their own existence as suspect their possession of eternal life.

Now let the prayer be breathed by poor Ruth, who is trembling yonder. Lord, reach me the parched corn! "Show me a token for good" (Psalm 86:17). "Deal bountifully with thy servant" (Psalm 119:17). "Draw me, we will run after thee" (Song of Solomon 1:4). Lord, send your love into my heart!

> Come, Holy Spirit, Heav'nly Dove,
> With all thy quick'ning pow'rs,
> Come, shed abroad a Savior's love,
> And that shall kindle ours.[31]

There is no getting at Christ except by Christ revealing himself to us.

Ruth Ate, Was Sufficed, and Left

And now for the last point. After Boaz had reached the parched corn, we are told that "she did eat, and was sufficed, and left." So shall it be with every Ruth. Sooner or later every penitent shall become a believer, every mourner a singer. There may be a space of deep conviction, and a period of much hesitation, but there will come a season when the soul decides for the Lord and cries, "If I perish, I perish. I will go as I am to Jesus. I will not play the fool any longer with my *buts* and *ifs*, but since he bids me believe that he died for me, I *will* believe it, and will trust his cross for my salvation." Whenever you shall be privileged to do this, you shall be "*satisfied*." "She did eat, and was sufficed." Your *head* will be satisfied with the precious truth which Christ reveals; your *heart* will be content with Jesus, as the altogether lovely object of affection; your *hope* will be filled, for whom have you in heaven but Christ? Your *desire* will be satiated, for what can even your desire hunger for more than "to know Christ, and to be found in him." You will find Jesus charm your *conscience*, until it is at perfect peace; he will content your *judgment*, until you know the certainty of his teachings; he will supply your *memory* with recollections of what he did, and gratify your *imagination* with the prospects of what he is yet to do.

"She was sufficed, and left." Some of us have had deep drafts of love; we have thought that we could take in all of Christ, but when we have done our best, we have had to leave a vast remainder. We have sat down with a ravenous appetite at the table of the Lord's love, and said, "Nothing but the infinite can ever satisfy me," and that infinite has been granted us. I have felt that I am such a great sinner that nothing short of an infinite atonement could wash my sins away, and no doubt you have felt the same. But we have had our sin removed and found merit enough and to spare in Jesus; we have had our hunger relieved and found something remaining for others who are in a similar case. There are certain sweet things in the Word of God which you and I have not enjoyed yet, and which we cannot enjoy yet, and these we are obliged to leave for a while, until we are better prepared to receive them. Did not our Lord say, "I have yet many things to say unto you, but ye cannot bear them now" (John 16:12)? There is a special knowledge to which we have not attained, a place of intimate fellowship with Christ which we have not yet occupied. There are heights of communion which as yet our feet have not climbed—virgin snows of the mountain of God untrodden by the foot of man. There is yet a beyond, and there will be forever.

A verse or two further on we are told what Ruth did with her leavings. It is very wrong, I believe, at feasts to carry anything home with you; but *she* was not under any such regulation, for that which was left she took home and gave to Naomi (v. 18). It is the same for all who think they have no right to a morsel for themselves; they will be allowed to eat, and when they are quite sufficed, they will have courage to give a portion to others who are hungering at home. I am always pleased to find the young believer beginning to pocket something for others. When you hear a sermon you think, "My poor mother cannot get out today; how I wish she could have been here, for that sentence would have comforted *her.* If I forget everything else, I will tell her that." Cultivate an unselfish spirit. Seek to love as you have been loved. Remember that "the law and the prophets" are fulfilled in this, to love the Lord your God with all your heart, and your neighbor as yourself (Matthew 22:37–40). How can you love your neighbor as yourself if you do not love their soul? You *have* loved your own soul; through grace you have been led to lay hold on Jesus; love your neighbor's soul, and never be satisfied until you see them in the enjoyment of those things which are the charm of your life and the joy of your spirit. Take home your gleanings for those you love who cannot glean for themselves.

I do not know how to give you an invitation to Christ more pleasantly, but I would with my whole heart cry, "Come and welcome to Jesus." I pray my Lord and Master to reach a handful of parched corn of comfort to you if you are a trembling sinner, and I also beg him to make you eat until you are fully sufficed.

SEVENTEEN

THE LOADED WAGON

Behold, I am pressed under you, as a cart is pressed
that is full of sheaves.

(Amos 2:13)

We have been into the cornfields to glean with Boaz and Ruth, and I trust that the timid and fainthearted have been encouraged to partake of the handfuls which have fallen on purpose for them by the order of our generous Lord. We go today to the gate of the harvest field with another object—to see the wagon piled aloft with many sheaves come creaking forth, making ruts along the field. We come with gratitude to God, thanking him for the harvest, blessing him for favorable weather, and praying for him to continue the same until the last shock of corn shall be brought in, and the farmers everywhere shall shout the "Harvest Home."

A wagon loaded with corn is a picture of you and me, loaded with God's mercies. From our cradle up until now, every day has added a sheaf of blessing. What more could the Lord do for us than he has done? He has daily loaded us with benefits. Let us adore his goodness, and yield him our cheerful gratitude.

Yet such a sign is capable of another reading. While God loads us with mercy, we load him with sin. While he continually heaps on sheaf after sheaf of favor, we add iniquity upon iniquity, until the weight of our sin becomes intolerable to the Most High and he cries out, "I am pressed under you, as a cart is pressed that is full of sheaves."

Our verse begins with a *"Behold!"* and well it may. "Beholds" are put in the Bible as signs are hung from houses of business—to attract attention. There is something new, important, deeply impressive, or worthy of attention wherever we see a "Behold" in sacred Scripture. I see this "Behold!" standing, as it were, like a maiden upon the steps of the house of wisdom, crying, "Turn in hither, you who are wise-hearted, and listen to the voice of God." Let us open our eyes that we may "behold," and may the Spirit make a way through our eyes and ears to our hearts, that repentance and self-loathing may take hold of us because of our evil conduct toward our gracious God.

It is to be understood before we proceed farther, that our scripture is only a figure, since God cannot actually be oppressed by human-kind. All the sin that we may commit can never disturb the serenity of the divine perfection, nor cause so much as a wave upon his ever-lasting calm. He speaks to us after the manner of humankind, and brings down the sublimities and mysteries of heaven to the feebleness and ignorance of earth. He speaks to us as a great father may talk to his little child. Just as a cart has the axles bent, and as the wheels creak under the excessive load, so the Lord says that under the load of human guilt he is pressed down, until he cries out because he can bear no longer the iniquity of those who offend him. We will now turn to our first point; may the Holy Ghost make it pointed to our consciences!

Sin Is Very Grievous and Burdensome to God

Be astonished, O heavens, and be amazed, O earth, that God should speak of being pressed and weighed down! I do not read anywhere so much as half a suggestion that the whole burden of *creation* is any weight to the Most High. "He taketh up the isles as a very little thing" (Isaiah 40:15). Neither sun, nor moon, nor stars, nor all the celestial bodies which his omnipotence has created, cost him any labor in their sustenance. The heathen picture Atlas as stooping beneath the globe, but the eternal God, who bears up the pillars of the universe, "fainteth not, neither is weary" (Isaiah 40:28). Nor do I find even the most distant approach to a suggestion that *providence* fatigues its Lord. He watches both by night and day; his power goes forth every moment. It is he who brings forth Mazzaroth in his season and guides Arcturus with his sons. He bears up the foundations of the earth and holds the cornerstone thereof. He causes the dayspring to know its place and sets a boundary for darkness and the shadow of death. All things are supported by the power of his hand, and there is nothing without him. Just as a moment's foam subsides into the wave that bears it and is lost forever, so would the universe depart if the eternal God did not daily sustain it.

This incessant working has not diminished his strength, nor is there any failing or thought of failing with him. He works all things, and when they are wrought they are as nothing in his sight. But strange, most passing strange, miraculous among miracles, *sin* burdens God, though the world cannot; and iniquity presses the Most High, though the whole weight of providence is as the "small dust of the balance" (Isaiah 40:15). Oh, you careless sons and daughters of Adam, you think sin is a trifle; and as for you, you sons and daughters of Belial, you count it sport and say, "He regards not, he sees not—how does God know? And if he knows, he cares not for our sins." Learn from the Book of God that so far from this being the truth, your sins are a grief to him, a burden and a load to him until, like a cart that is overloaded with sheaves, God is weighed down with human guilt.

This will be very clear if we meditate for a moment upon what sin is, and what sin does. *Sin is the great spoiler of all God's works.* Sin turned an archangel into an archfiend, and angels of light into spirits of evil. Sin looked on Eden and withered all its flowers. Before sin had come, the Creator said of the new-made earth, "It is very good"; but when sin entered, it grieved God at his very heart that he had made such a creature as man. Nothing tarnishes beauty so much as sin, for it mars God's image and erases his superscription.

Moreover, *sin makes God's creatures unhappy*, and shall not the Lord, therefore, abhor it? God never designed that any creature of his hand should be miserable. He made the creatures on purpose that they should be glad; he gave the birds their song, the flowers their perfume, the air its balm; he gave to day the smiling sun and to night its coronet of stars; for he intended that smiles should be his perpetual worship, and joy the incense of his praise. But sin has made God's favorite creature a wretch and brought down God's offspring, made in his own image, to become naked, and poor, and miserable; and therefore God hates sin and is pressed down under it, because it makes the objects of his love unhappy at their heart.

Moreover, remember that *sin attacks God in all his attributes*, assails him on his throne, and stabs at his existence. What is sin? Is it not an insult to God's *wisdom*? Friend, God bids you to do his will; when you do the contrary, it is because you do as much as say, "I know what is good for me, and God does not know." You do in effect declare that infinite wisdom is in error, and that you are the best judge of happiness. Sin resists God's *goodness*, for by sin you declare that God has denied you that which would make you happy, and this is not the part of a good, tender, and loving Father. Sin cuts at the Lord's wisdom with one hand, and at his goodness with the other.

Sin also abuses the *mercy* of God. When you, as many of you have done, sin with the higher hand because of his long-suffering toward you; when, because you have no sickness, no losses, no crosses, and spend your time in revelry and obstinate rebellion—what is this but taking the mercy which was meant for your good and turning it into mischief? It is no small grief to the loving Father to see his creation engaging in sin; he cannot endure it that his child should be so degraded as to turn even the mercy which would woo him to repentance into a reason why he should sin the more against him. Besides, let me remind the careless and impenitent that every sin is a defiance of divine *power*. In effect, it is lifting your puny fists against the majesty of heaven and defying God to destroy you. Every time you sin, you defy the Lord to prove whether he can maintain his law or not. Is this a slight thing, that a worm, the creature of a day, should defy the Lord of ages, the God that fills and upholds all things by the word of his power? Well may he be weary, when he has to bear with such provocations and insults as those! Mention what attribute you will, and sin has blotted it; speak of God in any relationship you choose, and sin has cast a slur upon him. It is evil, only evil, and that continually—every view of it is offensive to the Most High.

Do you know that every act of disobedience to God's law is virtually an act of *high treason*? What do you do but seek to be God yourself, your own master, your own lord? Every time you swerve from his will, it is to put your own will into his place; it is to make yourself a god, and to undeify the Most High. And is this a little offense, to snatch from his brow the crown, and from his hand the scepter? I tell you, it is such an act that heaven itself could not stand unless it were resented; if this crime were to go unpunished, the wheels of heaven's commonwealth would be taken from their axles, and the whole frame of moral government would be unhinged. Such a treason against God shall certainly be visited with punishment.

To crown all, *sin is an attack against God himself*, for sin is atheism of heart. Let their religious profession be what it may, the sinner has said in their heart, "No, God." They wish that there were no law and no Supreme Ruler. Is this a small thing? To desire to put God out of his own world! Is this a situation to laugh about? Can the Most High hear it and not be pressed down beneath its weight? I pray you do not think that I would make a needless outcry against sin and disobedience. It is not in the power of human imagination to exaggerate the evil of sin, nor will it ever be possible for mortal lips, though they should be touched like those of Esaias with a live coal from off the altar, to thunder out the ten-thousandth part of the enormity of the least sin against God. Think, dear friends! We are his creatures, and yet we will not do his will. We are fed by him, the breath in our nostrils he gives us, and yet we spend that breath in murmuring and rebellion.

Once more, we are always in the sight of our omniscient God, and yet the presence of God is not enough to compel us to obedience. Surely if an individual should insult law in the very presence of the lawgiver, that would not be acceptable; but this is your case and mine. We must confess, "Against thee, thee only, have I sinned, and done this evil in thy sight" (Psalm 51:4). We must remember also that we offend, knowing that we are offending. We sin against extraordinary light and sevenfold knowledge, and is this a light thing? Can you expect that God will not notice our willful and deliberate offenses? Oh, that these lips had language, that this heart could burn for once! For if I could declare the horrible infamy of sin, it would make the blood chill in even haughty Pharaoh's veins, and proud Nebuchadnezzar would bow his head in fear. It is indeed a terrible thing to have rebelled against the Most High. The Lord have mercy upon his servants and forgive them.

This is our first point, but *I* cannot teach you it—God himself must teach it by his Spirit. Oh, that the Holy Ghost may make you feel that sin is exceedingly sinful, that it is grievous and burdensome to God!

SOME SINS ARE ESPECIALLY GRIEVOUS TO GOD

There is no such thing as a little sin, but still there are degrees of guilt, and it is foolish to say that a sinful thought has in it the same extent of evil as a sinful act. An ungodly imagination is sinful—wholly sinful and greatly sinful, but still an ungodly act has attained a higher degree of provocation. There are sins which especially provoke God. We read that *licentious behavior* does this. The Jewish people in the days of Amos seem to have gone to a very high degree of fornication and inappropriate behavior. This sin is not uncommon in our day; let our midnight streets and our divorce courts be the witness. I say no more.

Let each one keep their body pure; for want of chastity is a grievous evil before the Lord.

Oppression, too, according to the prophet, is another great provocation to God. The prophet speaks of selling the poor for a pair of shoes; and some would oppress the widow and the orphan, and make the laborer work for nothing at all. How many businessmen and women have no compassion? People form themselves into societies, and then charge an outrageous interest on loans from the unhappy individuals who fall into their hands. Cunning legal arguments and crafty evasions of just debts often amount to heavy oppression, and this is sure to bring down the anger of the Most High.

Also, it seems that *idolatry* and *blasphemy* are highly offensive to God, and have a high degree of heinousness. It is not good when people drink the wine of false gods. If anyone makes food and drink, or riches and wealth, their god, and if anyone lives to these instead of living to the Most High, they have offended by idolatry. Woe to such individuals, and equal woe to those who adore crosses, sacraments, or images.

Blasphemy is another God-provoking sin. For blasphemy there is no excuse. As George Herbert says, "Lust and wine plead a pleasure"; there is gain to be pleaded for avarice, "but the cheap swearer from his open sluice lets his soul run for nought." There is nothing gained by profane talk; there can be no pleasure in cursing; this is offending for offending's sake, and hence it is a high and crying sin, which makes the Lord grow weary of men and women. There may be some among you to whom these words may be personal accusations. Do I address the lecherous, or the oppressive, or the profane? Ah, soul, what a mercy God has borne with you for so long; the time will come, however, when he will say, "Ah, I will ease me of mine adversaries" (Isaiah 1:24), and how easily will he cast you off and appoint you an awful destruction.

Again, while some sins are grievous to God for their particular horribleness, many are especially obnoxious to God because of the *length* of their sin. That gray-headed man, how many times has he provoked the Most High! Why, those who are but lads have cause to count their years and apply their hearts to wisdom because of the length of time they have lived in rebellion; but what will I say of you who have been half a century in open war against God—and some of you sixty, seventy, what if I said near upon eighty years? Ah, you have had eighty years of mercies, and returned eighty years of neglect; for eighty years of patience, you have rendered eighty years of ingratitude. Well may God be wearied by the length and number of humankind's sins!

Furthermore, God takes special note of a particular weariness of sin that is mixed with *obstinacy*. Oh, how obstinate some men and women are! They *will* be damned; there is no helping them. They seem as if they would leap the Alps to reach eternal damnation, and swim through seas of fire that they may destroy their souls. I might tell you cases of people who have been terribly sick with fever, ague, and cholera, and they have only recovered their health to return to their sins. Some of them have had troubles in business: they were once in respectable circumstances, but they spent their living riotously, and they became poor; yet they still struggle on in sin. They are growing poorer every day; most of their clothes have gone to the pawnshop, but they will not turn from the tavern and the brothel. Another child is dead! The wife is sick, and starvation stares the family in the face; but they go on still with a high hand and an outstretched arm. This is obstinacy, indeed. God will let the sinner have their own way one of these days, and that way will be their everlasting ruin. God is weary of those who set themselves to do mischief, and, against warnings and invitations and entreaties, are determined to go on in sin.

Ingratitude also is intensely burdensome to God. He tells the people how he brought them out of Egypt; how he cast out the Amorites; how he raised up their sons for prophets, and their young men for Nazarites; and yet they rebelled against him! This was one of the things that pricked my heart when I first came to God as a guilty sinner, not so much the particular heinousness of my outward life, as the particular mercies that I had enjoyed. How generous God has been to some of us—some of us who never had a want! God has never cast us into poverty, nor left us to infamy, nor given us up to evil example, but he has kept us moral, and made us love his house even when we did not love *him*—all this he has done year after year, and what poor returns we have made! To us, his people, what joy he has given, what deliverances, what love, what comfort, what bliss—and yet we have sinned to his face! Well may he be as a cart that is pressed down, that is full of sheaves.

Let me observe, before I leave this point, that it seems from our verse that the Lord is so pressed, that *he even cries out*. Just as the cart when laden with the sheaves, groans under the weight, so the Lord cries out under the load of sin. Have you never heard those accents? "Hear, O heavens, and give ear, O earth: for the LORD hath spoken, I have nourished and brought up children, and they have rebelled against me" (Isaiah 1:2). Hear again: "Turn ye, turn ye from your evil ways; for why will ye die, O house of Israel?" (Ezekiel 33:11). Better still, hear the lament from the lip of Jesus, soft and gentle as the dew: "O Jerusalem, Jerusalem, thou that killest the prophets, and stonest them which are sent unto thee, how often would I have gathered thy children together, even as a hen gathereth her chickens under her wings, and ye would not!" (Matthew 23:37). Friend, God is cut to the heart by your sin; your Creator grieves over that which you laugh at; your Savior cries out in his spirit concerning that which you think to be a trifle—"Oh, do not this abominable thing that I hate" (Jeremiah 44:4). For God's sake do it not! We often say, "for God's sake," without knowing what we mean; but here see what it means, for the sake of God, that you do not grieve your Creator, that you do not cause the Eternal One himself to cry out by reason of weariness of you.

THE LORD BEARS THE LOAD OF SIN

While it is true that sin is grievous to the Lord, it magnifies his mercy when we see *that he bears the load*. As the cart is not said to break, but is pressed only, so is he pressed, and yet he bears. If you and I were in God's place, should we have borne it? No, within a week we should have burned the universe with fire, or trodden it to powder beneath our feet. If the law of heaven were as swift to punish as the law of man, what would happen? How easily could he avenge his honor! How many servants wait around him ready to do his bidding! As the Roman consul went out, attended by his lictors carrying the axe, so God is ever attended by his executioners, who are ready to fulfill his sentence. A stone, a tile from a roof, a thunderbolt, a puff of wind, a grain of dust, a whiff of gas, a broken blood vessel, and all is over, and you are dead, and in the hands of an angry God. Indeed, the Lord has to restrain the servants of his anger, for the heavens cry, "Why should we cover that wretch's head?" Earth asks, "Why should I yield at harvest to the sinner's plow?" The lightnings thunder, and say, "Let us smite the rebel," and the seas roar upon the sinner, desiring him as their prey. There is no greater proof of the omnipotence of God than his long-suffering, for it shows the greatest possible power for God to be able to control himself. Yet Jehovah bears with you. The angels have been astonished at it; they thought he would strike, but yet he bears with you. Have you ever seen a patient man insulted? He has been met in the street by a villain, who insults him before a mob of boys. He bears it. The fellow spits in his face. He bears it still. The offender strikes him. He endures it quietly. "Give him in charge," says one. "No," says he, "I forgive him all." The fellow knocks him down, but he bears it still; yes, and when he rises all covered with mud, he says, "If there is anything I can do to befriend you, I will do it now." Just at that moment the wretch is arrested by a sheriff's officer for debt; the man who has been insulted takes out his money, pays the debt, and says, "You may go free." And the wretch spits in his face after that! "Now," you say, "let the law have its way with him." Is there any room for patience now? So would it have been with us; it has not been so with God. Though like the cart he is pressed under the load of sheaves, yet like the cart the axle does not break. He bears the load. He bears with impenitent sinners still.

GOD, IN THE PERSON OF HIS SON, DID BEAR AND TAKE AWAY SIN

And this brings me to the fourth point, on which I would like your deepest attention. Some of you, I fear, have never seen sin in the light of grieving God, or else you would not wish to grieve him anymore. On the other hand, some of you feel how bitter a thing evil is, and you wish to be rid of it. This is our fourth point. Not only does God still bear with sin, but *God, in the person of his Son, did bear and take away sin.*

These words would have deep meaning if put into the lips of Jesus—"I am pressed under you, as a cart is pressed that is full of sheaves." Here stood the great problem. God must punish sin, and yet he desired to have mercy. How could it be? Jesus comes to be the substitute for all who trust him. The load of guilt is laid upon his shoulders. See how they pile on him the sheaves of human sin!

> My soul looks back to see
>> The burdens thou didst bear
> When hanging on the cursed tree,
>> And hopes her guilt was there.[32]

"The LORD hath laid on him the iniquity of us all" (Isaiah 53:6). There they lie, sheaf on sheaf, until he is pressed down like the wain that groans as it moves along. "He is despised and rejected of men; a man of sorrows, and acquainted with grief"(Isaiah 53:3). "And his sweat was as it were great drops of blood falling down to the ground" (Luke 22:44). Herod mocks him. Pilate jeers him. They have smitten the Prince of Judah upon the cheek. "I gave my back to the smiters, and my cheeks to them that plucked off the hair: I hid not my face from shame and spitting" (Isaiah 50:6). They have tied him to the pillar; they are beating him with rods, not this time forty stripes *save one*, for there is no "save one" with him. "The chastisement of our peace was upon him; and with his stripes we are healed" (Isaiah 53:5).

See him, like a cart pressed down with sheaves traversing the streets of Jerusalem. Well may you weep, daughters of Jerusalem, though he bids you dry your tears! Abjects hoot at him as he walks along bowed beneath the load of his own cross, which was the emblem of our sin. They bring him to Golgotha. They throw him on his back, they stretch out his hands and his feet. The accursed iron penetrates the tenderest part of his body, where most the nerves do congregate. They lift up the cross. O bleeding Savior, your time of woe has come! They dash it into the socket with cruel force, the nails are tearing through his hands and feet. He hangs in extremity, for God has forsaken him; his enemies persecute and take him, for there is none to deliver him. They mock his nakedness; they point at his agonies. They look and stare upon him. With ribald jests they insult his griefs. They make puns upon his prayers. He is now indeed a worm, and no man, crushed until you can scarcely think that divinity dwells within him. Fever parches him; his tongue is dried up like a potsherd, and he cries, "I thirst!" Vinegar is all they yield him. The sun refuses to shine, and the dense midnight of that awful midday is a fitting emblem of the tenfold darkness of his soul. Out of that all-encompassing horror, he cries, "My God, my God, why hast thou forsaken me?" (Matthew 27:46). Then, indeed, was he pressed down! There was never sorrow like his sorrow. All mortal griefs found a reservoir in his heart, and the punishment of human guilt spent itself upon his body and his soul.

Shall sin ever be a trifle to me? Shall I laugh at that which made my Savior groan? Shall I toy and dally with that which stabbed him to the heart? Sinner, will you not give up your sins for the sake of him who suffered for sin? "Yes," you say, "yes, if I could believe that he suffered for my sake." Will you trust your soul in his hands at once? Do you do so? He died *for you* and took *your* guilt, and carried all *your* sorrows, and you may go free, for God is satisfied and you are absolved. Christ was burdened that you might be lightened; he was pressed that you might be free. I wish I could talk of my precious Master as John would speak, who saw him and bore witness, for he could tell in plaintive tones of the sorrows of Calvary. Such as I have I give you; oh, that God would give you with it the power, the grace, to believe on Jesus at once.

WITHOUT CHRIST, THE LOAD OF SIN WILL CRUSH US FOREVER

Here is our last point: God will only bear the load of our provocation for a little while; and if we are not in Christ when the end shall come, *that same load will crush us forever.*

This scripture is translated by many learned individuals in a different way from the version before us. According to them it should be read, "I will press you as a cart that is full of sheaves presses your place." That is, just as a heavy, loaded wagon pressed into the soft roads and left deep furrows, so will I crush you, says God, beneath the load of your sin. This is to be your doom, my hearer, if you are out of Christ: your own deeds are to press upon you. Need we enlarge upon this terror? I think not. It only needs that you should make a personal application of the threatening! Divide yourselves now. Divide yourselves, I say! Answer each one for yourself: Do you believe on the Lord Jesus Christ? Then the threatening is not yours. But if you do not believe, I ask you to listen to me now as if you were the only person here. A Christless soul will before long be a castaway; those who do not believe in Christ are condemned already, because they do not believe. How will you escape if you choose to neglect so great a salvation? The Lord says to you, "Consider your ways" (Haggai 1:7). By time, by eternity, by life, by death, by heaven, by hell, I encourage you to believe in him who is able to save unto the uttermost those who come to him; but if you do not believe in Christ, you will die in your sins.

After death, the judgment! Oh, the judgment—the thundering trumpet, the multitude, the books, the great white throne, the "Come, ye blessed," the "Depart, ye cursed!"

After judgment, to a soul that is out of Christ, hell! Who among us shall abide with the devouring flame? Who among us shall dwell with everlasting burnings? I pray that none of us may. But we *must* unless we fly to Christ. I beseech you, my dear hearer, fly to Jesus! I may never see your face again; your eyes may never look into mine again; but I shake my skirts of your blood if you do not believe in Christ. My tears entreat you; let his long-suffering lead you to repentance. He wills not the death of any, but that they should turn to him and live, and this turning lies mainly in trusting Jesus with your soul. Will you believe in Christ? I know you will not unless the Spirit of God will constrain you; but if you will not, it shall not be for want of pleading and entreating. Come, 'tis mercy's welcome hour. I pray you, come. Jesus with pierced hands invites you, though you have long rejected him. He knocks again. His unconquerable love defies your wickedness. He begs you to be saved. Sinner, will you have him or no? "Whosoever will, let him take the water of life freely" (Revelation 22:17). God help you to come, for the glorious Redeemer's sake. Amen.

EIGHTEEN

THRESHING

For the fitches are not threshed with a threshing instrument, neither is a cart wheel turned about upon the cummin; but the fitches are beaten out with a staff, and the cummin with a rod. Bread corn is bruised; because he will not ever be threshing it, nor break it with the wheel of his cart, nor bruise it with his horsemen.

(ISAIAH 28:27–28)

The art of agriculture was taught to humankind by God. Men and women would have starved while they were discovering it, and so the Lord, when he sent them out of the garden of Eden, gave them a measure of elementary instruction in agriculture, even as the prophet puts it: "His God doth instruct him to discretion, and doth teach him" (Isaiah 28:26). God has taught us to plow, to break the clods, to sow the different kinds of grain, and to thresh out the different sorts of seeds.

Some farmers in the world could not thresh by machinery as we do, but still they were ingenious and discreet in that operation. Sometimes a heavy instrument was dragged over the corn to tear out the grain. This is what is intended in the first clause by the "threshing instrument," as also in that passage, "I will make thee a new sharp threshing instrument having teeth" (Isaiah 41:15). When the corn-drag was not used, they often turned the heavy, solid wheel of a country cart over the straw. This is alluded to in the next sentence: "Neither is a cart wheel turned about upon the cummin." They had also flails not very unlike our own, and then for still smaller seeds, such as dill and cumin, they used a simple staff, or a slender switch. "The fitches are beaten out with a staff, and the cummin with a rod."

This is not the time or place to give a dissertation on threshing. We can find information on that subject in proper books, but the meaning of the illustration is this—that as God has taught farmers to distinguish between different kinds of grain in the threshing, so does he in his infinite wisdom deal discreetly with different sorts of men and women. He does not try us all alike, seeing we are differently constituted. He does not pass us all through the same agony of conviction; we are not all to the same extent threshed with terrors. He does not give us all to endure the same family or bodily affliction— one escapes with only being beaten with a rod, while another feels, as it were, the feet of horses in his heavy tribulations.

Our subject is just this: *Threshing*. All kinds of seeds need it, and *all sorts of men and women need it*. Secondly, *the threshing is done with discretion*, and, thirdly, *the threshing will not last forever*; for so the second verse of the text says: "Bread corn is bruised; because he will not ever be threshing it, nor break it with the wheel of his cart, nor bruise it with his horsemen."

WE ALL NEED THRESHING

Some have a foolish conceit of themselves that they have no sin, but they deceive themselves, and the truth is not in them. The best of us are men and women at the best; and being human, we are not perfect, but are still compassed about with infirmity. What is the object of threshing the grain? Is it not to separate it from the straw and the chaff?

In even the best of men and women, there is still a measure of chaff. All is not grain that lies upon the threshing floor. All is not grain even in those golden sheaves which have been brought into our garner so joyfully. Even the wheat is joined to the straw, which was necessary to it at one time. About the kernel of the wheat the husk is wrapped, and this still clings to it even when it lies upon the threshing floor. About the holiest of men there is something superfluous, something which must be removed. We either sin by omission or by trespass. Either in spirit, or motive, or lack of zeal, or want of discretion, we are faulty. If we escape one error, we usually glide into its opposite. If before an action we are right, we err in the doing of it, or, if not, we become proud after it is over. If sin is shut out at the front door, it tries the back gate, or climbs in at the window, or comes down the chimney. Those who cannot perceive it in themselves are frequently blinded by its smoke. They are so thoroughly in the water that they do not know that it rains. So far as my own observation goes, I have found out no individual whom the old divines would have called perfectly perfect; the absolutely all-round individual is a being whom I expect to see in heaven, but not in this poor fallen world. We all need such cleansing and purging as the threshing floor is intended to work for us.

Now, *threshing is useful in loosening the connection between the good corn and the husk.* Of course, if it would slip out easily from its husk, the corn would only need to be shaken. There would be no necessity for a staff or a rod, much less for the feet of horses or the wheel of a cart to separate it. But there's the rub: our soul not only lies in the dust, but "cleaves" to it. There is a fearful intimacy between fallen human nature and the evil which is in the world, and this compact is not soon broken. In our hearts we hate every false way, and yet we sorrowfully confess, "When I would do good, evil is present with me." Sometimes when our spirit cries out most ardently after God, a holy will is present with us, but we do not understand how to perform that which is good. Flesh and blood have tendencies and weaknesses which, if not sinful in themselves, tend in that direction. Appetites need but slight excitement to germinate into lusts. It is not easy for us to forget our own kindred and our father's house even when the king does most greatly desire our beauty. Our alien nature remembers the luxuries of Egypt while the manna is still in our mouths. We were all born in the house of evil, and some of us were nursed upon the lap of iniquity, so that our first companionships were among the heirs of wrath. That which was bred in the bone is hard to get out of the flesh. Threshing is used to loosen our hold of earthly things and break us away from evil. This needs a divine hand, and nothing but the grace of God can make the threshing effective.

Something is done by threshing when the soul ceases to be bound up with its sin, and sin is no longer pleasurable or satisfactory. Still, as the work of threshing is never done until the corn is separated altogether from the husk, so chastening and discipline have never accomplished their design until God's people give up every form of evil and abhor all iniquity. When we shake right out of the straw, and have nothing further to do with sin, then the flail will lie quiet. It has taken a good deal of threshing to bring some of us anywhere near that mark, and I am afraid many more heavy blows will be struck before we will reach the total separation. From certain sorts of sins we are very easily separated by the grace of God early in our spiritual life, but when those are gone, another layer of evils comes into sight and the work has to be repeated. The complete removal of our connection with sin is a work demanding the divine skill and power of the Holy Ghost, and by him only will it be accomplished.

Threshing becomes needful for the sake of our usefulness, for the wheat must come out of the husk to be of service. We can only honor God and bless others by being holy, harmless, undefiled, and separate from sinners. The corn of the Lord's threshing floor must be beaten and bruised, or perish as a worthless heap! Eminent usefulness usually necessitates eminent affliction.

Unless we are thus severed from sin, we cannot be gathered into the garner. God's pure wheat must not be defiled by a mixture of chaff. Nothing that defiles can enter into heaven; every sort of imperfection must come away from us by some means or other before we can enter into the state of eternal blessedness and perfection. Even here we cannot have true fellowship with the Father unless we are delivered daily from sin.

Possibly some of us today are lying on the threshing floor, suffering from the blows of chastisement. What then? Why, let us rejoice, for *this testifies to our value in the sight of God.* If the wheat were to cry out and say, "The great drag has gone over me; therefore the gardener has no care for me," we should instantly reply—"The gardener does not pass the corn-drag over the darnel or the nettles; it is only over the precious wheat that he turns the wheel of his cart or the feet of his oxen." Because he esteems the wheat, he deals sternly with it and spares it not. Friend, do not assume that God hates you because he afflicts you, but interpret truly and see that he honors you by every stroke which he lays upon you. The Lord says, "You only have I known of all the families of the earth: therefore I will punish you for all your iniquities" (Amos 3:2). Because a full atonement has been made by the Lord Jesus for all his people's sins, he will not punish us as a judge; but because we are his dear children, he will chastise us as a father. In love he corrects his own children, that he may perfect them in his own image and make them partakers of his holiness. Is it not written, "I will cause you to pass under the rod, and I will bring you into the bond of the covenant" (Ezekiel 20:37)? Has he not said, "I have refined thee, but not with silver; I have chosen thee in the furnace of affliction" (Isaiah 48:10)? Therefore do not judge according to the sight of the eyes or the feeling of the flesh, but judge according to faith, and understand that, as threshing is a testimony to the value of the wheat, so affliction is a token of God's delight in his people.

Remember, however, that as threshing is a sign of the impurity of the wheat, so is *affliction an indication of the present imperfection of the Christian.* If you were no more connected with evil, you would be no more corrected with sorrow. The sound of a flail is never heard in heaven, for it is not the threshing floor of the imperfect but the garner of the completely sanctified. The threshing instrument is therefore a humbling token, and so long as we feel it, we should humble ourselves under the hand of God, for it is clear that we are not yet free from the straw and the chaff of fallen nature.

On the other hand, the instrument is *a prophecy of our future perfection*. We are undergoing from the hand of God a discipline which will not fail: we shall by his prudence and wisdom be delivered from the husk of sin. We are feeling the blows of the staff, but we are being effectively separated from the evil which has so long surrounded us, and for certain we shall one day be pure and perfect. Every tendency to sin shall be beaten off. "Foolishness is bound in the heart of a child; but the rod of correction shall drive it far from him" (Proverbs 22:15). If we are evil, yet we succeed with our children by our poor, imperfect chastening, how much more shall the Father cause us to live unto himself by his holy discipline? If the corn could know the necessary uses of the flail, it would invite the thresher to his work; and since we know where tribulation tends, let us glory in it and yield ourselves with cheerfulness to its processes. We need threshing—the threshing proves our value in God's sight, and while it marks our imperfection, it secures our ultimate cleansing.

God's Threshing Is Done with Great Discretion

"For the fitches are not threshed with a threshing instrument." The poor little fitches, a kind of small seed used for flavoring cakes, were not crushed out with a heavy drag, for by such rough usage they would have been broken up and spoiled. "Neither is a cart wheel turned about upon the cummin." This little seed, perhaps the caraway, would have been ground by so great a weight; it would have been preposterous to treat it in that rough manner. The fitches were soon removed from the stalks by being "beaten out with a staff," and the cumin needed nothing but a touch of a rod. For tender seeds the farmer uses gentle means, and for the hardier grains he reserves the sterner processes. Let us think of this, as it conveys a valuable spiritual lesson.

Reflect, my brother and sister, that your threshing and mine *are in God's hands.* Our chastening is not left to servants, much less to enemies: "We are chastened of the Lord" (1 Corinthians 11:32). The great Gardener himself personally bids the laborers do this and that, for they know not the time or the way except as divine wisdom shall direct; they would turn the wheel upon the cumin, or attempt to thresh wheat with a staff. I have seen God's servants trying both these follies; they have crushed the weak and tender, and they have dealt with partiality and softness with those who needed to be sternly rebuked. How roughly some ministers, some elders, some good men and women, will go to work with timid, tender souls; yet we need not fear that they will destroy the truehearted, for, however much they may vex them, the Lord will not leave his chosen in their hands, but will overrule their mistaken severity and preserve his own from being destroyed. How glad I am of this; for there are many nowadays who would grind the tender ones to powder if they could!

As the Lord has not left us in the power of humankind, so also he has not left us in the power of the devil. Satan may sift us as wheat, but he shall not thresh us as fitches. He may blow away the chaff from us even with his foul breath, but he shall not have the management of the Lord's corn: "the Lord preserveth the righteous." Not a stroke in providence is left to chance; the Lord ordains it, and arranges the time, the force, and the place of it. The divine decree leaves nothing uncertain; the jurisdiction of supreme love occupies itself with the smallest events of our daily lives. Whether we bear the teeth of the corn-drag, or men do ride over our heads, or we endure the gentler touches of the divine hand, everything is by appointment, and the appointment is fixed by infallible wisdom. Let this be a mine of comfort to the afflicted.

Next, let us note that *the instruments used for our threshing are chosen also by the great Gardener.* The farmer has several instruments at his disposal, and so has our God. No form of thresh-ing is pleasant to the seed which bears it; indeed, each one seems to the sufferer to be particularly objectionable. We say, "I think I could bear anything but this sad trouble." We cry, "It was not an enemy—then I could have borne it," and so on. Perhaps the ten-der cumin foolishly fancies that the horse hooves would be a less terrible ordeal than the rod, and the fitches might even prefer the wheel to the staff, but happily the matter is left to the choice of One who judges unerringly. What do you know about it, poor sufferer? How can you judge what is good for you? "Ah!" cries a mother, "I would not mind poverty, but to lose my darling child is too terrible!" Another laments, "I could have parted with all my wealth, but to be slandered cuts me to the quick." There is no pleasing us in the matter of chastisement. When I was at school, with my uncle for master, it often happened that he would send me out to find a cane for him. It was not a very pleasant task, and I noticed that I never once succeeded in selecting a stick which was liked by the boy who had to feel it. It was either too thin or too stout, and in consequence I was threatened by the sufferers with appropriate punishment if I did not do better next time. I learned from that experience never to expect God's children to like the particular rod with which they are chastened. You smile at my simile, but you may smile at your-self when you find yourself crying, "Any trouble but this, Lord. Any affliction but this." How idle it is to expect a pleasant trial; for it would then be no trial at all. Almost every really useful medicine is unpleasant: almost all effectual surgery is painful! No trial for the present seems to be joyous, but grievous, yet it is the right trial, and none the less right because it is bitter.

Notice, too, that God not only selects the instruments, *but he chooses the place.* Some farmers have large threshing floors upon which they throw the sheaves of corn or barley, and upon these they turn horses and drags. Near the house door, in places like Italy, is a much smaller circle of hardened clay or cement, and here I have seen the peasants beating out their garden seeds in a more careful manner than would naturally be used toward the greater heaps upon the larger area. Some saints are not afflicted in the common affairs of life, but they have peculiar sorrow in their innermost spirits; they are beaten on the smaller and more private threshing floor, but the process is none the less effectual. How foolish are we when we rebel against our Lord's appointment, and speak as if we had a right to choose our own afflictions! "Should it be according to thy mind?" (Job 34:33). Should a child select the rod? Should the grain appoint its own thresher? Are not these things to be left to a higher wisdom? Some complain of the time of their trial; it is hard to be crippled in youth, or to be poor in age, or to be widowed when your children are young. Yet in all this there is wisdom. A part of the skill of the physician may lie not only in writing a prescription, but in arranging the hours at which the medicine shall be taken. One draft may be most useful in the morning, and another may be more beneficial in the evening, and so the Lord knows when it is best for us to drink of the cup which he has prepared for us. I know a dear child of God who is enduring a severe trial in his old age, and I would gladly screen him from it because of his feebleness, but our heavenly Father knows best, and there we must leave it. The instrument of the threshing, the place, the measure, the time, the end, are all appointed by infallible love.

It is interesting to notice in the passage the limit of this threshing. The farmer is zealous to beat out the seed, but he is careful not to break it in pieces by too severe a process. His wheel is not to grind, but to thresh; the horses' feet are not to break, but to separate. He intends to get the cumin out of its husk, but he will not turn a heavy drag upon it utterly to smash it up and destroy it. In the same way, the Lord has a measure in all his chastening. Courage, friend—you shall be afflicted as you need, but not as you deserve; tribulation shall come as you are able to bear it. As is the strength, such shall the affliction be; the wheat may feel the wheel, but the fitches shall bear nothing heavier than a staff. No saint shall be tempted beyond the proper measure, and the limit is fixed by a tenderness which never deals a needless stroke.

It is very easy to talk like this when times are easy, and quite another thing to remember it when the flail is hammering you. Yet I have personally realized this truth upon the bed of pain and in the furnace of mental distress. I thank God at every remembrance of my afflictions; I did not doubt his wisdom then, nor have I had any reason to question it since. Our great Gardener understands how to divide us from the husk, and he goes about his work in a way for which he deserves to be adored forever.

It is a pleasant thought that God's limit is one beyond which trials never go—

> If trials six be fix'd for men
>> They shall not suffer seven.
> If God appoint afflictions ten
>> They ne'er can be eleven.

The old law ordained forty stripes save one, and in all our affliction there always comes in that "save one." When the Lord multiplies our sorrows up to a hundred, it is because ninety-and-nine failed to accomplish his purpose; but all the powers of earth and hell cannot give us one blow above the settled number. We shall never endure an excess of threshing. The Lord never sports with the feelings of his saints. "He doth not afflict willingly" (Lamentations 3:33), and so we may be sure he never gives an unnecessary blow.

The wisdom of the farmer in limiting his threshing is far exceeded in the wisdom of God by which he sets a limit to our griefs. Some escape with little trouble, and perhaps it is because they are frail and sensitive. The little garden seeds must not be beaten too heavily lest they be injured; those saints who live life with a delicate body must not be roughly handled, nor shall they be. Possibly they have a feeble mind also, and that which others would laugh at would be death to them; they shall be kept as the apple of the eye.

If you are free from tribulation, never ask for it; that would be a great folly. I did meet with a brother a little while ago who said that he was much perplexed because he had no trouble. I said, "Do not worry about *that*; but be happy while you may." What child would beg to be flogged? Certain sweet and shining saints are of such a gentle spirit that the Lord does not expose them to the same treatment as he metes out to others; they do not need it, and they could not bear it; why should they wish for it?

Others are very heavily pressed, but what of that if they are a superior grain, a seed of larger usefulness, intended for higher purposes? Let not regret that they have to endure a heavier threshing since their use is greater. It is the bread corn that must go under the feet of the horseman and must feel the wheel of the cart, and the most useful have to pass through the sternest processes. There is not one among us who would say, "I could wish that I were Martin Luther, or that I could play as noble a part as he did." Yes, but in addition to the outward perils of his life, the inward experiences of that remarkable man were such as none of us would wish to feel. He was frequently tormented with Satanic temptations and driven to the verge of despair. At one hour he rode the whirlwind and the storm, master of all the world, and then after days of fighting with the pope and the devil, he would go home to his bed and lie there broken-down and trembling. You see God's heroes only in the pulpit, or in other public places; you know not what they are before God in secret. You do not know their inner life; else you might discover that the bread corn is bruised and that those who are most useful in comforting others have to endure frequent sorrow themselves. Envy no man, for you do not know how he may have to be threshed to make him right and keep him so.

Friends, we see that our God uses discretion in the chastisement of his people; let us use loving prudence when we have to deal with others in that way. Be gentle as well as firm with your children, and if you have to rebuke your brother, do it very tenderly. Do not drive your horses over the tender seed. Recollect that the cumin is beaten out with a staff and not crushed out with a wheel. Take a very light rod. Perhaps it would be as well if you had no rod at all, but left that work to wiser hands. Go and sow and leave your elders to thresh.

Next, let us firmly believe in God's discretion and be sure that he is doing the right thing by us. Let us not be anxious to be protected from affliction. When we ask that the cup may pass from us, let it be with a "nevertheless not as I will" (Matthew 26:39). Most of all, let us freely part with our chaff. The likeliest way to escape the flail is to separate from the husk as quickly as possible. "Come out from among them" (2 Corinthians 6:17). Separate yourselves from sin and sinners, from the world and worldliness, and the process of threshing will all the sooner be completed. God make us wise in this matter!

THE THRESHING WILL NOT LAST FOREVER

The threshing will not last all our days even here: "Bread corn is bruised; because he will not ever be threshing it." Oh, no. "For a small moment have I forsaken thee; but with great mercies will I gather thee" (Isaiah 54:7). "He will not always chide: neither will he keep his anger for ever" (Psalm 103:9). "Weeping may endure for a night, but joy cometh in the morning" (Psalm 30:5). Rejoice, daughters of sorrow! Be comforted, sons of grief! Have hope in God, for you shall yet praise him who is the health of your countenance. The rain does not always fall, nor will the clouds always return. Sorrow and sighing shall flee away. Threshing is not an operation which the corn requires all the year round; for the most part the flail is idle. Bless the Lord, O my soul! The Lord will yet bring home his banished ones.

Above all, tribulation will not last forever, for we shall soon be gone to another and better world. We shall soon be carried to the land where there are neither threshing floors nor corn-drags. I sometimes think I hear the herald calling me. His trumpet sounds: "Up and away!

Boot and saddle! Up and away! Leave the camp and the battle, and return in triumph." The night is far spent with you, but the morning comes. The daylight breaks above the hills. The day is coming. Come, eat your bread with joy, and march onward with a merry heart; for the land which flows with milk and honey is but a little way before you. Until the day breaks and the shadows flee away, abide the great Gardener's will, and may the Lord glorify himself in you. Amen.

NINETEEN

WHEAT IN THE BARN

But gather the wheat into my barn.

(Matthew 13:30)

"But gather the wheat into my barn." Then the purpose of the Son of man will be accomplished. He sowed good seed, and he will have his barn filled with it at the last. Be not dispirited, Christ will not be disappointed. "He shall see of the travail of his soul, and shall be satisfied" (Isaiah 53:11). He went forth weeping, bearing precious seed, but he shall come again rejoicing, bringing his sheaves with him.

"Gather the wheat into my barn": then Satan's policy will be unsuccessful. The Enemy came and sowed tares among the wheat, hopeful that the false wheat would destroy or materially injure the true, but he failed in the end, for the wheat ripened and was ready to be gathered. Christ's garner shall be filled; the tares shall not choke the wheat. The Evil One will be put to shame.

In gathering in the wheat, good angels will be employed: "the reapers are the angels" (Matthew 13:39). This casts special scorn upon the great evil angel. He sows the tares and tries to destroy the harvest, and the good angels are brought in to celebrate his defeat and to rejoice together with their Lord in the success of the divine Gardener.

Satan will make a poor profit out of his meddling; he shall be stopped short in all his efforts, and so the threat shall be fulfilled: "Upon thy belly shalt thou go, and dust shalt thou eat" (Genesis 3:14).

By giving the angels work to do, all intelligent creatures—of whose existence we have information—are made to take an interest in the work of grace; whether for malice or for adoration, redemption excites them all. To all, the wonderful works of God are made manifest, for these things were not done in a corner.

We too often forget the angels. Let us not overlook their tender sympathy with us; they behold the Lord rejoicing over our repentance, and they rejoice with him. They are our watchers and the Lord's messengers of mercy; they bear us up in their hands lest we dash our foot against a stone, and when we come to die, they carry us to the bosom of our Lord. It is one of our joys that we have come to an innumerable company of angels; let us think of them with affection.

A WORD OF SEPARATION

At this time, I will keep to the passage, and preach from it almost word by word. It begins with "but," and that is *a word of separation.*

Here note that the tares and the wheat will grow together until the time of harvest shall come. It is a great sorrow of heart to some of the wheat to be growing side by side with the tares. The ungodly are as thorns and briers to those who fear the Lord. How frequently is the sigh forced forth from the godly heart: "Woe is me, that I sojourn in Mesech, that I dwell in the tents of Kedar!" (Psalm 120:5). Our foes are often found within our own household; those who should have been our best helpers are often our worst hinderers; their conversation vexes and torments us. It is of little use to try to escape from them, for the tares are permitted in God's providence to grow with the wheat, and they will do so until the end. Good men and women have emigrated to distant lands to found communities in which there should be none but saints, and sadly, sinners have sprung up in their own families. The attempt to weed the ungodly and heretical out of the settlement has led to persecution and other evils, and the whole plan has proved a failure. Others have shut themselves away in hermitages to avoid the temptations of the world, and so have hoped to win the victory by running away; this is not the way of wisdom. The word for this present is, "Let both grow together" (Matthew 13:30), *but* there will come a time when a final separation will be made. Then, dear Christian woman, your husband will never persecute you again. Godly sister, your brother will heap no more ridicule upon you. Pious workman, there will be no more jesting and taunting from the ungodly. That "but" will be an iron gate between the god-fearing and the godless; then will the tares be cast into the fire, *but* the Lord of the harvest will say, "Gather the wheat into my barn."

This separation must be made, for the growing of the wheat and the tares together on earth has caused much pain and injury, and therefore it will not be continued in a happier world. We can very well suppose that godly men and women might be willing that their unconverted children should dwell with them in heaven; but it cannot be, for God will not have his cleansed ones defiled nor his glorified ones tried by the presence of the unbelieving. The tares must be taken away in order for the wheat to be perfect and useful. Would you have the tares and the wheat heaped up together in the granary in one mass? That would not work. Neither of them can be put to appropriate use until they are thoroughly separated. Even so, mark you, the saved and the unsaved may live together here, but they must not live together in another world. The command is absolute: "Gather ye together first the tares, and bind them in bundles to burn them: *but* gather the wheat into my barn" (Matthew 13:30). Sinner, can you hope to enter heaven? You never loved your mother's God, and is he to endure you in his heavenly courts? You never trusted your father's Savior, and yet are you to behold his glory forever? Are you to go swaggering down the streets of heaven, letting fall an oath, or singing an ungodly song? You get tired of the worship of God on the Lord's day;

do you think that the Lord will endure unwilling worshippers in the temple above? The Sabbath is a wearisome day to you; how can you hope to enter into the Sabbath of God? You have no taste for heavenly pursuits, and these things would be profaned if you were permitted to partake in them; therefore, that word "but" must come in, and you must part from the Lord's people never to meet again. Can you bear to think of being divided from godly friends forever and ever?

That separation involves an awful difference of destiny. "Gather ye together first the tares, and bind them in bundles to burn them." I do not dare to draw the picture, but when the bundle is bound up there is no place for it except the fire. God grant that you may never know all the anguish which burning must mean, but may you escape from it at once. It is no trifle which the Lord of love compares to being consumed with fire. I am quite certain that no words of mine can ever set forth its terror. They say that we speak dreadful things about the wrath to come, but I am sure that we understate the case. What must the tender, loving, gracious Jesus have meant by the words, "Gather ye together first the tares, and bind them in bundles to burn them"? See what a wide distinction exists between the lot of the Lord's people and Satan's people. Burn the wheat? Oh, no—"Gather the wheat into my barn." There let them be happily, safely housed forever. Oh, the infinite distance between heaven and hell!—the harps and the angels, and the wailing and gnashing of teeth! Who can ever measure the width of that gulf which divides the glorified saint, white-robed and crowned with immortality, from the soul which is driven forever away from the presence of God and from the glory of his power? It is a dreadful "but"—that "but" of separation. I pray you, remember that it will interpose between brother and brother—between mother and child—between husband and wife. "One shall be taken, and the other left" (Matthew 24:40). And when that sword descends to divide, there will never be any after union. The separation is eternal. There is no hope or possibility of change in the world to come.

But, says one, "that dreadful '*but*'! Why must there be such a difference?" The answer is, because there always was a difference. The wheat was sown by the Son of man; the false wheat was sown by the Enemy. There was always a difference in character—the wheat was good; the tares were evil. This difference did not appear at first, but it became more and more apparent as the wheat ripened, and as the tares ripened too. They were totally different plants, as a saved person and an unsaved person are altogether different beings. I have heard an unsaved man say that he is quite as good as the godly man, but in so boasting he betrayed his pride. Surely there is as great a difference in God's sight between the unsaved and the believer as between darkness and light, or between the dead and the living. There is in the one a life which there is not in the other, and the difference is vital and radical. Oh, that you may never trifle with this essential matter, but be really the wheat of the Lord! It is vain to have the name of wheat, we must have the nature of wheat. God will not be mocked; he will not be pleased by our calling ourselves Christians while we are not so. Do not be satisfied with church membership, but seek after membership with Christ. Do not talk about faith, but exercise it. Do not boast of experience, but possess it. Be not *like* the wheat, but be the wheat. No shams and imitations will stand in the last great day; that terrible "but" will roll as a sea of fire between the true and the false. Oh, Holy Spirit! Let each of us be found transformed by your power.

A Word of Congregation

The second word of our passage is "gather"—that is *a word of congregation*. What a blessed thing this gathering is! I feel it a great pleasure to gather multitudes together to hear the gospel; and is it not a joy to see a house full of people, on weekdays and Sabbath days, who are willing to leave their homes and to come considerable distances to listen to the gospel? It is a great thing to gather people together for that, but the gathering of the wheat into the barn is a far more wonderful business. Gathering is in itself better than scattering, and I pray that the Lord Jesus may ever exercise his attracting power in this place—for he is no divider, but "unto him shall the gathering of the people be" (Genesis 49:10). Has he not said, "I, if I be lifted up from the earth, will draw all men unto me" (John 12:32)?

Observe that the congregation mentioned in our passage is selected and assembled by skilled gatherers: "The reapers are the angels" (Matthew 13:39). Ministers could not do it, for they do not know all the Lord's wheat, and they are apt to make mistakes—some by too great leniency, and others by excessive severity. Our poor judgments occasionally shut out saints, and often shut in sinners. The angels will know their Master's property. They know each saint, for they were present at his birthday. Angels know when sinners repent, and they never forget the people of the penitents. They have witnessed the lives of those who have believed, and have helped them in their spiritual battles, and so they know them. Yes, angels by a holy instinct discern the Father's children and are not to be deceived. They will not fail to gather all the wheat and to leave out every tare.

But they are gathered under a very stringent regulation; for first of all, according to the parable, the tares—the false wheat—have been taken out, and then the angelic reapers gather nothing but the wheat. The seed of the serpent, fathered by Satan, is thus separated from the seed of the kingdom, owned by Jesus, the promised deliverer. This is the one distinction, and no other is taken into consideration. If the most amiable unconverted people could stand in the ranks with the saints, the angels would not bear them to heaven, for the mandate is, "Gather the wheat." Could the most honest man be found standing in the center of the church, with all the members around him and with all the ministers entreating that he might be spared, yet if he were not a believer, he could not be carried into the divine garner. There is no help for it. The angels have no choice in the matter; the urgent command is, "Gather *the wheat*," and they must gather nothing else.

It will be a gathering from very great distances. Some of the wheat ripens in the South Sea Islands, in China, and in Japan. Some flourishes in France, broad acres grow in the United States; there is scarcely a land without a portion of the good grain. Where all God's wheat grows, I cannot tell. There is a remnant, according to the election of grace, among every nation and people, but the angels will gather all the good grain to the same garner.

"Gather the wheat." The saints will be found in all ranks of society. The angels will bring in a few ears from palaces, and great armfuls from cottages! Many will be collected from the lowly cottages of our villages and hamlets, and others will be raised up from the back slums of our great cities to the metropolis of God. From the darkest places, angels will bring those children of sweetness and light who seldom beheld the sun and yet were pure in heart and saw their God. The hidden and obscure shall be brought into the light, for the Lord knows those who are his, and his harvesters will not miss them.

To me it is a charming thought that they will come from all the ages. Let us hope that our first father Adam will be there, and mother Eve, following in the footsteps of their dear son Abel, and trusting in the same sacrifice. We shall meet Abraham, and Isaac, and Jacob, and Moses, and David, and Daniel, and all the saints made perfect. What a joy to see the apostles, martyrs, and reformers! I long to see Luther, and Calvin, and Bunyan, and Whitefield. I like the rhyme of good old father Ryland:

> They all shall be there, the great and the small,
> Poor I shall shake hands with the blessed St. Paul.

I do not know how that will be, but I have not much doubt that we shall have fellowship with all the saints of every age in the general assembly and church of the firstborn, whose names are written in heaven.

No matter when or where the wheat grew, it shall be gathered into the one barn; gathered never to be scattered; gathered out of all divisions of the visible church, never to be divided again. They grew in different fields. Some flourished on the hillside where Episcopalians grow in all their glory, and others in the lowlier soil, where Baptists multiply and Methodists flourish; but once the wheat is in the barn none can tell in which field the ears grew. Then, indeed, shall the Master's prayer have a glorious answer—"That they all may be one" (John 17:21). All our errors removed and our mistakes corrected and forgiven, the one Lord, the one faith, and the one baptism will be known of us all, and there will be no more vexing and envying. What a blessed gathering it will be! What a meeting! The elect of God, the *elite* of all the centuries, of whom the world was not worthy. I should not like to be away. If there were no hell, it would be hell enough to me to be shut out of such heavenly society. If there were no weeping and wailing and gnashing of teeth, it would be dreadful enough to miss the presence of the Lord, and the joy of praising him forever, and the bliss of meeting with all the noblest beings that ever lived. Amid the needful controversies of the age, I, who have been doomed to seem a man of strife, sigh for the blessed rest in which all spiritual minds will blend in eternal accord before the throne of God and of the Lamb. Oh, that we were all right, that we might be all happily united in one spirit!

A Word of Designation

In the passage there is next *a word of designation*: "Gather *the wheat.*" Nothing but "the wheat" must be placed in the Lord's homestead. Lend me your hearts while I urge you to a searching examination for a minute or two. The wheat was sown of the Lord. Are you sown of the Lord? Friend, if you have any religion, how did you get it? Was it self-sown? If so, it is good for nothing. The true wheat was sown by the Son of man. Are you sown of the Lord? Did the Spirit of God drop eternal life into your bosom? Did it come from that dear hand which was nailed to the cross? Is Jesus your life? Does your life begin and end with him? If so, it is well.

The wheat sown of the Lord is also the object of the Lord's care. Wheat needs a great deal of attention. The farmer would get nothing from it if he did not watch it carefully. Are you under the Lord's care? Does he keep you? Is that word true to your soul, "I the LORD do keep it; I will water it every moment: lest any hurt it, I will keep it night and day" (Isaiah 27:3)? Do you experience such keeping? Make an honest answer, as you love your soul.

Next, wheat is a useful thing—a gift from God for the life of men and women. The false wheat was of no good to anybody; it could only be eaten of swine, and then it made them stagger like drunk people. Are you one of those who is wholesome in society—who is like bread to the world, so that if others receive you and your example and your teaching, they will be blessed thereby? Judge whether you are good or evil in life and influence.

"Gather the wheat." You know that God must put the goodness, the grace, the solidity, and the usefulness into you, or else you will never be wheat fit for angelic gathering. One thing is true of the wheat—that it is the most dependent of all plants. I have never heard of a field of wheat which sprang up, and grew, and ripened without a farmer's care. Some ears may appear after a harvest, but I have never heard of plains in America or elsewhere covered with unsown wheat. There is no wheat where there are no people, and there is no grace where there is no Christ. We owe our very existence to the Father, who is the great Gardener.

Yet, dependent as it is, wheat stands in the front rank of honor and esteem, and so do the godly in the judgment of all who are of understanding heart. We are nothing without Christ, but with him we are full of honor. Oh, to be among those by whom the world is preserved, the excellent of the earth in whom the saints delight; God forbid we should be among the base and worthless tares!

A Word of Destination

Our last point, upon which also I will speak briefly, is *a word of destination*. "Gather the wheat *into my barn*." The process of gathering in the wheat will be completed at the day of judgment, but it is going on every day. From hour to hour saints are gathered; they are going heavenward even now. I am so glad to hear as a regular thing that the departed ones from my own dear church have such joy in being harvested. Glory be to God, our people die well. The best thing is to live well, but we are greatly gladdened to hear that our brothers and sisters in Christ die well, for often that is the most telling witness for vital godliness. Men and women of the world feel the power of triumphant deaths.

Every hour the saints are being gathered into the barn. That is where they want to be. We feel no pain at the news of ingathering, for we wish to be safely stored up by our Lord. If the wheat that is in the field could speak, every ear would say, "The ultimatum for which we are living and growing is the barn, the granary." For this the frosty night; for this the sunny day; for this the dew and the rain; and for this everything. Every process with the wheat is tending toward the granary. So is it with us; everything is working toward heaven—toward the gathering place—toward the congregation of the righteous—toward the vision of our Redeemer's face. Our death will cause no break in our life-music; it will involve no pause or even discord; it is part of a program, the crowning of our whole history.

To the wheat, the barn is the place of security. It dreads no mildew there; it fears no frost, no heat, no drought, no wet, when once in the barn. All its perils are past. It has reached perfection. It has rewarded the labor of the farmer, and it is housed. Oh, long-expected day, begin! Oh, friends, what a blessing it will be when you and I come to our maturity, and Christ sees in us the travail of his soul.

I delight to think of heaven as *his* barn; *his* barn, what must that be? It is but the poverty of language that such an expression has to be used at all concerning the home of our Father, the dwelling of Jesus. Heaven is the palace of the King, but to us it is a barn because it is the place of security, the place of rest forever. It is the homestead of Christ to which we shall be carried, and for this we are ripening. It is to be thought of with ecstatic joy, for the gathering into the barn involves a harvest home, and I have never heard of men and women sitting down to cry over an earthly harvest home, nor of their following the sheaves with tears. No, they clap their hands, they dance for joy, and shout right lustily. Let us do something like that concerning those who are already housed. With grave, sweet melodies, let us sing around their tombs. Let us feel that, surely, the bitterness of death is passed. When we remember their glory, we may rejoice like the laboring woman when her child is born, who "remembereth no more the anguish, for joy that a man is born into the world" (John 16:21). Another soul begins to sing in heaven; why do you weep, you heirs of immortality? Is the eternal happiness of the righteous the birth which comes of their death pangs? Then happy are they who die. Is glory the end and outcome of that which fills our home with mourning? If so, thank God for bereavements. He has promoted our dear ones to the skies! He has blessed them beyond all that we could ask or even think; he has taken them out of this weary world to lie in his own bosom forever. Blessed be his name if it were for nothing else but this. Would you keep your old father here, full of pain, and broken down with feebleness? Would you shut him out of glory? Would you detain your dear wife here with all her suffering? Would you hold back your husband from the crown immortal? Could you wish your child to descend to earth again from the bliss which now surrounds her? No, no. We wish to be going home ourselves to the heavenly Father's house and its many mansions, but concerning the departed we rejoice before the Lord as with the joy of harvest. "Wherefore comfort one another with these words" (1 Thessalonians 4:18).

NOTES

1. "Men of the Day, No. 16, The Rev. Charles Spurgeon," *Vanity Fair*, December 10, 1870, 237, http://www.romans45.org/spurgeon/fsl/vf.pdf.
2. Charles Spurgeon, *Lectures to My Students: Complete and Unabridged* (Grand Rapids, MI: Zondervan, 1954), 111.
3. Spurgeon, *Lectures to My Students*, 113.
4. Spurgeon, *Lectures to My Students*, 112.
5. Charles Spurgeon, *Sermons in Candles Being Two Lectures*, The Spurgeon Archive, accessed February 15, 2022, https://archive .spurgeon.org/misc/candles.php.
6. Charles Spurgeon, from the Preface to the original volume on which this edition is based, *Farm Sermons*, The Spurgeon Archive, accessed February 15, 2022, https://archive.spurgeon.org/misc/fspref.php.
7. Spurgeon slightly modifies a line spoken by the character of the Gardener in Shakespeare's history *The Life and Death of King Richard the Second* (commonly called *Richard II*), 3.4.40–42. References are to act, scene, and lines, Folger Shakespeare Library, accessed February 18, 2022, https://shakespeare.folger.edu/shakespeares-works/richard -ii/act-3-scene-4/.
8. Martin F. Tupper, "Of Trifles," *Proverbial Philosophy* (London: T. Hatchard, 1853), 123.
9. Isaac Watts, "Summer and Winter," Hymnary.org, accessed March 24, 2022, https://hymnary.org/hymn/DWIC1786/260.
10. John Milton, "Let Us with a Gladsome Mind," Hymnary.org, accessed March 24, 2022, https://hymnary.org/text/let_us_with_a_gladsome_mind.
11. Isaac Watts, "The Voice of My Beloved Sounds," Hymnary.org, accessed March 24, 2022, https://hymnary.org/text/the_voice_of_my_beloved _sounds_over_the.
12. Augustus Toplady, "How Happy Are We," Choral Public Domain

Library, accessed February 16, 2022, https://www.cpdl.org/wiki/index
.php/How_happy_are_we_(Benjamin_Milgrove).

13. Anne Steele, "Stern Winter Throws His Icy Chains," in *Songs of the Church*, ed. Rev. Charles S. Robinson (New York: Scribner and Company, 1879), 355.

14. Isaac Watts, "There Is a Land of Pure Delight," Hymnary.org, accessed February 16, 2022, https://hymnary.org/text/there_is_a_land_of_pure _delight_where_sa.

15. Isaac Watts, "Hymn 88," Hymnary.org, accessed February 16, 2022, https://hymnary.org/hymn/PHW/I.88.

16. Adapted from a line from Charles Wesley's hymn "Jesus! The Name High Over All," Hymnary.org, accessed February 16, 2022, https:// hymnary.org/text/jesus_the_name_high_over_all_in_hell_or.

17. Charles Wesley, "Shall I, for Fear of Feeble Man," Invubu.com, accessed February 16, 2022, https://www.invubu.com/music/show /song/Charles-Wesley/Shall-I%252C-For-Fear-Of-Feeble-Man.html.

18. Isaac Watts, "Lord, Help My Unbelief," Hymnary.org, accessed February 16, 2022, https://hymnary.org/text/how_sad_our_state_by _nature_is.

19. *Fitches* is thought to refer to the minute black seeds of *Nigella sativa*, a plant native to the Holy Land and still grown in Palestine. See also Spurgeon's discussion of fitches in chapter eighteen, "Threshing." *Encyclopedia of the Bible*, s.v. "fitch, fitches," BibleGateway.com, accessed March 18, 2022, https://www.biblegateway.com/resources /encyclopedia-of-the-bible/Fitch-Fitches.

20. John Fawcett, "Inward Religion," Hymnary.org, accessed February 17, 2022, https://hymnary.org/text/religion_is_the_chief_concern.

21. Mary Masters, "Let Us Walk in the Light," Hymnary.org, accessed February 17, 2022, https://hymnary.org/text/tis_religion_that_can _give_sweetest_plea.

22. Isaac Watts, "Hymn 74 (The Church the Garden of Christ)," Choral Public Domain Library, accessed February 17, 2022, https://www.cpdl .org/wiki/index.php/We_are_a_garden_walled_around.

23. Isaac Watts, "Christ's Dying Love," Hymnary.org, accessed February 17, 2022, https://hymnary.org/text/how_condescending_and_how_kind.

24. James Thomson, *The Seasons: A Poem* (New York: Clark and Maynard, 1869), 50.

25. Richard Chenevix Trench, "What, Many Times I Musing Asked," *Poems* (London: MacMillan and Company, 1865), 356.

26. Elizabeth H. Codner, "Even Me," Hymntime.com, accessed February 17, 2022, http://www.hymntime.com/tch/htm/e/v/e/n /evenme.htm.

27. Attributed either to George Keith or Robert Keen, "How Firm a Foundation," Hymnary.org, accessed February 17, 2022, https:// hymnary.org/text/how_firm_a_foundation_ye_saints_of.

28. Isaac Watts, "Hymn 43 Part 2," Hymnary.org, accessed February 18, 2022, https://hymnary.org/hymn/PHW/I.43.2.

29. Joseph Hart, "Come, Ye Sinners, Poor and Needy," Hymntime.com, accessed February 18, 2022, http://www.hymntime.com/tch/htm/c/o /m/e/y/comeyspn.htm.

30. Augustus Toplady, "Faith Triumphing," Hymnary.org, accessed February 18, 2022, https://hymnary.org/text/a_debtor_to_mercy_alone.

31. Isaac Watts, "Come, Holy Spirit, Heavenly Dove," Hymnary.org, accessed February 18, 2022, https://hymnary.org/text/come_holy _spirit_heavenly_dove_with_all.

32. Isaac Watts, "Hymn 142," Hymnary.org, accessed February 18, 2022, https://hymnary.org/hymn/PHW/II.142.

ABOUT THE AUTHOR

Charles Haddon Spurgeon (1834–1892) was an English preacher whose powerful sermons continue to captivate believers to this day. Known as the "Prince of Preachers," Spurgeon was pastor of the congregation of the New Park Street Chapel (later the Metropolitan Tabernacle) in London for thirty-eight years. Among many accomplishments there, he built an almshouse and an orphanage while strongly encouraging his parishioners to engage compassionately with the poor and destitute of Victorian London. A prodigious writer, Spurgeon authored countless sermons, many of which were transcribed as he spoke and later published in multiple collections. His private library comprised 5,103 volumes. His body of work also includes numerous commentaries, books on prayer, devotionals, faith-based magazines, poetry, and hymns.

 Grace is the gift of God, and is not to be created by man. It is also *needed* grace. What would the ground do without showers? You may break the clods, you may sow your seeds, but what can you do without the rain? As absolutely needful is the divine blessing. In vain you labor, until God the plenteous shower bestows, and sends salvation down.

—FROM SPURGEON'S *MORNING BY MORNING*